Crossing Segregated Boundaries

New Directions in the History of Education

Series editor, Benjamin Justice

The New Directions in the History of Education series seeks to publish innovative books that push the traditional boundaries of the history of education. Topics may include social movements in education; the history of cultural representations of schools and schooling; the role of public schools in the social production of space; and the perspectives and experiences of African Americans, Latinx Americans, women, queer folk, and others. The series will take a broad, inclusive look at American education in formal settings, from prekindergarten to higher education, as well as in out-of-school and informal settings. We also invite historical scholarship that informs and challenges popular conceptions of educational policy and policy making and that addresses questions of social justice, equality, democracy, and the formation of popular knowledge.

Diana D'Amico Pawlewicz, *Blaming Teachers: Professionalization Policies and the Failure of Reform in American History*
Dionne Danns, *Crossing Segregated Boundaries: Remembering Chicago School Desegregation*
Kyle P. Steele, *Making a Mass Institution: Indianapolis and the American High School*

Crossing Segregated Boundaries

Remembering Chicago School Desegregation

DIONNE DANNS

Rutgers University Press

New Brunswick, Camden, and Newark, New Jersey, and London

Library of Congress Cataloging-in-Publication Data

Names: Danns, Dionne, author.
Title: Crossing segregated boundaries : remembering Chicago school desegregation / Dionne Danns.
Description: New Brunswick, New Jersey : Rutgers University Press, 2020. | Series: New directions in the history of education | Includes bibliographical references and index.
Identifiers: LCCN 2020004916 | ISBN 9781978810051 (paperback) | ISBN 9781978810068 (hardcover) | ISBN 9781978810075 (epub) | ISBN 9781978810082 (mobi) | ISBN 9781978810099 (pdf)
Subjects: LCSH: School integration—Illinois—Chicago—History. | Public schools—Illinois—Chicago—History. | African American children—Education—Illinois—Chicago—History. | High school graduates—Illinois—Chicago. | Chicago (Ill.)—Race relations. | Chicago (Ill.)—Ethnic relations.
Classification: LCC LC214.23.C54 D359 2020 | DDC 379.2/630977311—dc23
LC record available at https://lccn.loc.gov/2020004916

A British Cataloging-in-Publication record for this book is available from the British Library.

Maps created by Jordan Blekking

∞ The paper used in this publication meets the requirements of the American National Standard for Information Sciences—Permanence of Paper for Printed Library Materials, ANSI Z39.48-1992.

www.rutgersuniversitypress.org

Manufactured in the United States of America

For my grandmothers, Deborah and Molly
And those who shared their stories

Contents

Crossing Segregated Boundaries

Introduction

Anthony grew up in a household with fourteen children on the segregated West Side of Chicago. He excelled in grammar school, finishing first in his class. When it was time to go to high school in 1984, Anthony was fortunate that Chicago Public Schools had implemented desegregation as part of the federal government's enforcement of the 1964 Civil Rights Act. Chicago's desegregation plan created a variety of school choice initiatives. A recruiter from Von Steuben High School came to Anthony's grammar school specifically to recruit him and another student, the valedictorian and salutatorian of their eighth-grade class, respectively. Anthony's opportunity to leave his segregated neighborhood and attend a desegregated school increased the likelihood that he would leave the poverty of his childhood, interact with a variety of racial and ethnic groups, and graduate.

Anthony's experience at Von Steuben led him to make friends with students from a variety of racial and ethnic backgrounds. In many ways, Anthony stood as an ambassador for integration, which only occurred as a result of school desegregation. He sat with diverse students in Von Steuben's cafeteria, participated in an integrated choir, and was called on by school administrators to squash a racial disturbance. He serves as an example of how students who attended desegregated schools made integration possible and the benefits they gained as a result. But his story also highlights the limitations of desegregation. Since he lived far away from Von Steuben and on the segregated West Side of the city, he had limited opportunities to interact with friends of different racial and ethnic backgrounds outside of school. He and his classmates were also among the few students in Chicago Public Schools to experience desegregation, and for Black students like Anthony, this meant traveling long distances to get to school and leaving behind friends and family who were relegated to underperforming, segregated schools.

Crossing Segregated Boundaries examines the experiences of sixty-eight graduates (mostly of the class of 1988) from three desegregated Chicago public high schools—Von Steuben, Bogan, and Whitney Young (map I.1). The primary purpose of this book is to detail the institutional role schools play in providing socialization and shared learning experiences that counter entrenched segregated boundaries. American schools have always been used to reinforce societal norms, Americanize immigrants, and served as a panacea for solving all the nation's problems.[1] It is little surprise that when the United States was forced to advance a more equitable society because of the national pressure from the civil rights movement and international pressure from ideological competition with the Soviet Union, schools were one of the core institutions chosen for this endeavor. In addition to providing socialization, schools can also play an important role in social mobility. Though they often reproduce society's inequities, many people have used them to advance socially and economically. However, despite schools' potential for socialization and mobility, race and ethnicity have continued to be a primary boundary to equitable treatment for Blacks and Latinos, and racial segregation has served as a key factor in maintaining racial stratification. Segregation has been an important boundary for Whites to ensure power and privilege and to hoard opportunities.[2]

School desegregation, which I am defining as the purposeful policy action by school officials to bring students of different races together, became an important way for students to cross segregated boundaries. Advocates of desegregation recognized that the important resources and opportunities that existed at White segregated schools were often limited at underfunded Black and Latino segregated schools. Though some segregated Black schools in Chicago thrived, many suffered from overcrowding, high teacher turnover rates, poor facilities, lower expectations, and high dropout rates.[3] Attendance at desegregated Chicago high schools could mean enriched academic opportunities, access to more resources, and the opportunity to cross racial boundaries. While some might have imagined that school desegregation would minimize racial segregation, the resistance to desegregation meant that it was often carried out in ways that privileged Whites. Many schools failed to determine how they would accommodate racialized groups, and students suffered from mistreatment and a curriculum that normalized whiteness.

In traditional histories of school desegregation, a lot of attention is paid to the difficulties of policy formation and implementation. Few investigate school-level desegregation policy implementation. This book focuses on policy initiatives to reduce racial segregation and social inequalities in the North. It is a case study of the struggles that students, schools, and communities undergo to integrate. It examines Chicago Public Schools' efforts to implement school

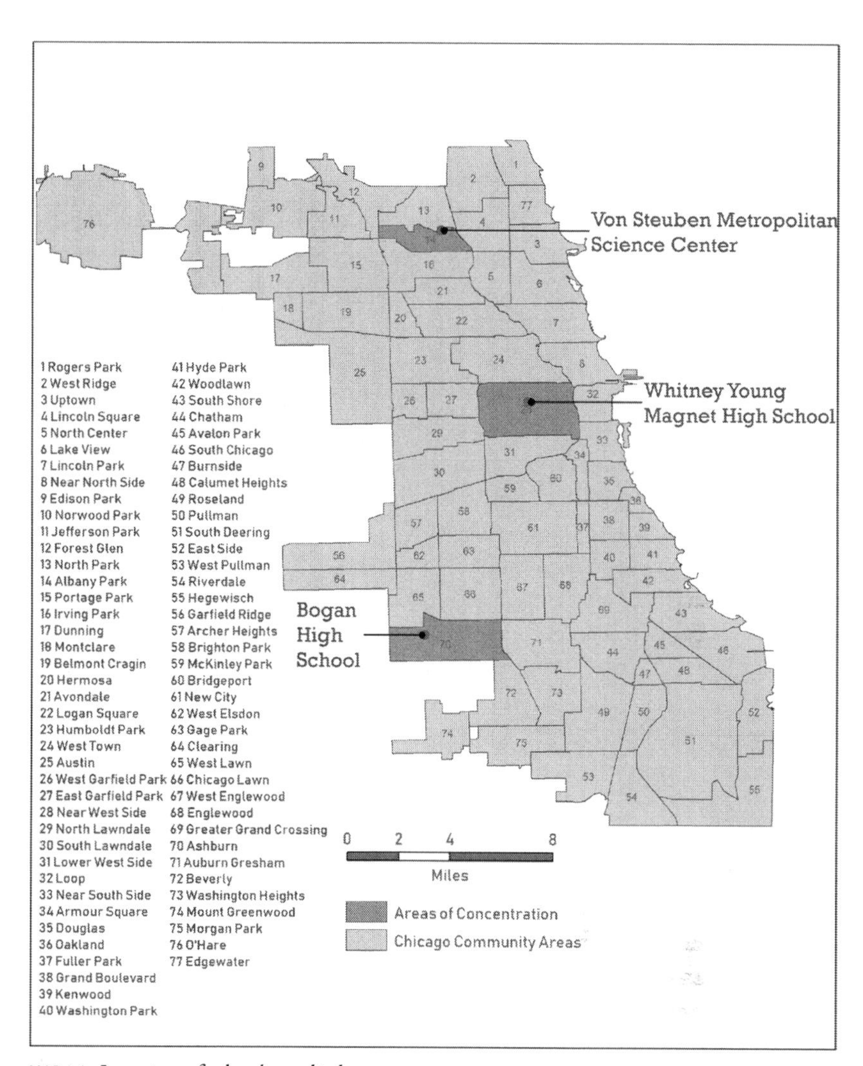

MAP I.1 Location of schools studied

desegregation policy through school choice initiatives, boundary changes, and the recruitment of students. It highlights how traditional forms of busing led to protests and how the use of public transportation averted protests. Finally, it describes integration as a process of school desegregation and determines the dynamics of crossing segregated boundaries to attend school, maintain friendships, and defy community norms.

Integration can happen when people of different races are together in the same place. At a basic level, integration occurs when students live in the same neighborhood and are zoned to attend the same school or attend a desegregated school. Racially diverse groups of students in the same schools have an opportunity to interact in classes, extracurricular activities, and the cafeteria. A by-product of integration is that students exchange, merge, or adapt each other's cultures; gain tolerance, appreciation, or respect for each other; and may even become friends or date one another. Erica Frankenberg and Elizabeth DeBray argue, "While school integration has been among the most successful educational reforms in terms of equalizing access to opportunity and improving the life chances for poor and minority students as well as helping to improve racial attitudes and interracial comfort by creating opportunities for students of all racial backgrounds to get to know one another, schools cannot sustain integration without addressing inequality and segregation in other parts of society."[4] In the present study, integration played out at the basic level, and participants at the very least learned tolerance of different racial and ethnic groups, some formed friendships, and many improved their life chances. At a deeper level, advocates of integration see it as a "cure to segregation." Elizabeth Anderson declares, "If segregation is a fundamental cause of social inequality and undemocratic practices, then integration promotes greater equality and democracy. Hence, it is an imperative of justice."[5] As Frankenberg and DeBray indicate, this deeper level of integration is well beyond what schools alone can offer.

Desegregation alone did not produce integration in schools. I argue that students had to actively engage to make integration work while navigating segregated boundaries. Racial segregation of Chicago's neighborhoods was often a prohibitive factor affecting students' abilities to integrate. School desegregation competed with established and engrained housing segregation without having an impact on the latter, and it certainly did not eliminate Whites' negative views of racialized groups.[6] As a result, students could not fully escape the influences of their parents and communities, and at times they lived in divided worlds where integration was accepted at school but not in their communities. Some study participants had to endure students who brought racially discriminatory practices or racially divisive norms into the schools. Along with student attitudes and community influence, housing segregation meant that some students had to cross racial boundaries, making it difficult to maintain friendships outside of school. Politically, participants remembered the negative reactions to the racially divisive mayoral race, election, and death of Harold Washington, which affected them as students. Despite their best efforts, segregation remained the proverbial elephant in the room, stunting the potentially transformative possibilities of integration beyond the school doors.

Chicago's schools were desegregated largely through school choice, a precursor to the contemporary school choice policies today. The very act of choosing schools exposed the inequality among them. Students chose between schools that could lead to college and those designated as dropout factories, which often served racialized groups and low-income students. Whitney Young, Von Steuben, and Bogan all reduced students' chances of dropping out. Yet even among the three schools, Bogan's curricular focus on technology meant that while students were more likely to graduate, they were less likely to attend four-year colleges and universities. The school one attended determined the privilege or disadvantage one received. Desegregation, with the use of school choice, gave options to some Black and Latino students. This meant they could take advantage of the opportunities that previously benefited mostly middle- and upper-class Whites. While participants in this study made use of school desegregation policy to leverage an academic advantage and their movement from their neighborhood schools benefited them, it further disadvantaged those left in segregated schools.

Boundary Crossing

Culture and identity are important elements in defining ethnicity, yet ethnicity is constantly evolving based on internal and external forces. Ethnic identity can be voluntary, as individuals can opt in based on social and political needs, or involuntary, if individuals are forced into an ethnic group based on society's structure. Likewise, ethnic groups can create internal boundaries to determine who is in and who is out (boundaries of acceptability). In the United States, race has been treated as a form of ethnicity, and though history has played a powerful role in determining racial boundaries, the boundaries have also been reconstructed over time. For example, the Great Migration of Blacks to the North reconstructed ethnic boundaries for both Blacks and Whites. The urban North was reconstructed with intensified racial segregation, racial stratification, and conflicts between ethnic groups that led to the creation of a Black underclass.[7]

Ethnic formation is a key ingredient in the creation of boundaries, and two important types of boundaries exist, symbolic and social. Symbolic boundaries are used to establish groups; group membership can promote a sense of likeness or pride and helps people gain status and hoard resources. Social boundaries are "objectified forms of social differences leading to the unequal distribution of resources," racial segregation, and other forms of exclusion, including class.[8] For the purpose of this study, I will interchangeably use segregated boundaries and racial boundaries as representations of social boundaries. In Chicago, segregation occurred by race and ethnicity as a result of the migration of Blacks and immigration and migration of Latinos. The segregated boundaries established were often physical or geographic, as housing policies and practices prevented Blacks and Latinos with darker complexions or Indian/mestizo phenotypes from living in and sometimes even passing through White neighborhoods.

Anthropologist Fredrik Barth makes clear that though individuals cross boundaries, achieve social mobility, and interact with others outside their ethnic group, ethnic boundaries persist. While boundaries exist, they can often be permeated. Research on immigration around the world highlights the ways boundaries can be negotiated. Richard Alba's research on boundaries captures the process of second-generation assimilation and the degree to which ethnic boundaries are bright (people understand where they fit and on which side of the boundary they belong) or blurred (boundaries are "less distinct" and more ambiguous).[9] Borrowing from Aristide Zolberg and Long Litt Woon, Alba identifies three different ways that ethnic groups assimilate into mainstream culture. First, boundary crossing is done by individuals without changing the boundaries that exist. It can be an individual form of assimilation. Those who cross boundaries risk distancing themselves from their culture and are at risk for being considered disloyal and feeling unaccepted. Accusations of acting white are an example of how individuals can negatively experience boundary crossing. Second, boundary blurring "implies that the social profile of a boundary has become less distinct: the clarity of the social distinction involved has become clouded, and individuals' location with respect to the boundary may appear indeterminate." Finally, boundary shifting occurs when ethnic groups are accepted, and they move from one side of the boundary to another (for example, Europeans becoming White in the American context).[10]

In this study, participants were able to cross segregated boundaries when they traveled to school, interacted with other racial or ethnic groups in school, and visited friends in other neighborhoods. Crossing boundaries was difficult for a select few, who were perceived as acting white. Often, community members saw Black participants as traitors either for leaving their neighborhoods to attend White schools or for talking white or proper. Some lighter-skinned Latinos were able to blur boundaries in White neighborhoods when they were viewed as insiders once Black students were bused into predominantly White schools. Whether Latinos crossed or blurred boundaries depended on where they lived and their phenotype.

As participants crossed and blurred boundaries, they experienced isolated integration. For the most part, segregated boundaries remained outside the school walls. But within schools, and as participants gathered in locations outside of schools, isolated integration occurred. The schools were tasked with making desegregation work, and even in instances in which racism was brought into schools, school leadership worked to alleviate racial disruptions to maintain the orderly function of the schools. The structure of schools still privileged Whites, though I lack evidence of tracking by race and disproportionality in disciplinary practices at these three schools. But Black and Latino participants still revealed that counselors often belittled their college choices and that they experienced microaggressions from teachers and other staff. Isolated integration meant that there were still boundaries to be crossed, even within the schools.

Desegregation and Oral History

School desegregation has been widely covered by scholars from different fields, including historians, journalists, lawyers, and sociologists. Most histories present case studies of cities, counties, or states, while others take a national or regional approach.[11] The history of school desegregation exemplifies the complexity of policy implementation, the role of the courts, massive resistance, and protest for and against desegregation. While some regions may have similar narratives, local context makes a difference in how, when, and to what extent desegregation occurred. Much of the focus has been on the southern context, largely because of Jim Crow and the legal nature of segregation.[12] Scholars have also closely examined northern areas and have essentially demystified the view of northern exceptionalism.[13] In the midst of the North-South divide, other scholars also draw our attention to desegregation in the border states.[14] These desegregation studies have largely told the stories of Black-White desegregation, but scholars in the Southwest have focused on Latino-White desegregation, demonstrating the complexity of ethnicity, language, and the construction of race.[15]

With an emphasis on Black and White or Latino and White school desegregation, few bring these groups together, and even fewer do so in spaces outside the Southwest. *Crossing Segregated Boundaries* adds to what we know about school desegregation in the North, moves beyond the Black-White binary, and showcases how Chicago's desegregation focused on school choice with magnet schools and other specialized programs. Scholars of school desegregation have also used oral history as an important source for their research, but few use oral history as the basis of their study, foregrounding the voices and collective experiences of students.

Oral history methodology has broadened interpretations of historical events. Barbara W. Sommer and Mary Kay Quinlan define oral history as a "primary-source material created in an interview setting with a witness to or participant in an event or a way of life for the purpose of preserving the process and the interview itself."[16] Likewise, Ken Howarth calls it "both a subject and methodology, a way of finding out more by careful thoughtful interviewing and listening."[17] Scholars have also used terms like *oral testimony*, *ethnographic interviews*, or *qualitative interviews* to describe the same process for uncovering history through interviewing. Jack Dougherty, in his early analysis of the state of educational history and its use of oral history, notes, "We intentionally label our field oral history (as opposed to oral interviewing) because we draw upon diverse analytical traditions to point out how the stories we hear are not merely anecdotes but rich sources with which we may better understand the significance of the past."[18]

Paul Thompson, one of the early advocates of oral history, saw the methodology as transformative and a way to centralize the makers of and participants in history. William W. Cutler III acknowledged oral history as a tool to fill the gap in traditional written archival records and provide perspective for understanding the past.[19] Oral history extends our understanding of the past through a collaboration with history makers and provides additional perspective for historians. It lends itself to discovering new and hidden information, as most people do not readily leave behind the written records of their lives. The perspective scholars gain from hearing people's stories is a key attribute of oral history. As Vanessa Siddle Walker discovered in the research process for *The Lost Education of Horace Tate*, as one builds trust with the people being interviewed, not only do they become co-creators of knowledge, but that trust opens doors to archival materials and additional participants who can further catapult a study and lead to an important reconstruction of history.[20]

Even as a highly effective tool, oral history is not without its shortcomings. To start, memories are sometimes unreliable. Richard White writes that history and memory are sometimes "enemies" and scholars need to serve as detectives in interrogating memories since memories "can mislead as well as lead."[21] For him, memory was a tool that guided his path to new discoveries, but at times, the discovery could be that certain memories were inaccurate. References to memories in popular culture also seem to provide caution for scholars. On an episode of *Star Trek: Voyager*, the stiff and unemotional Vulcan Tuvok quips, "Human memory is rarely perfect."[22]

Historians who have interviewed participants more than once have noticed the participant's story sometimes changes. As people reflect on their answers, or grow older, their perspectives on events can change as well.[23] Barbara Shircliffe noted the nostalgia in the romanticized memories of former students and teachers about southern Black segregated schools. She argues, "The study of nostalgia can enhance, rather than diminish, the use of oral history for understanding how we use historical consciousness to make sense of and comment on the present."[24] Hilton Kelly disagrees with the idea that these memories should be reduced to nostalgia and forthrightly states, "While I never accepted 'nostalgia' as the only way to understand the conflict in memory over legally segregated schools for Blacks, I did assume originally that it was simply a matter of color—Blacks remembering one way and Whites remembering another way." For Kelly, both individual and collective memories can be varied based on race, place, age, and other factors.[25]

Scholars have grappled with how to interpret people's perspectives and memories. Some prefer to give more credence to the meaning people ascribe to their memories. This does not mean that facts are dismissed, but rather how people perceive their role in events and their memories speaks to how they both view themselves and interpret the world. Caroline Eick, for example, argues that her book "foregrounds historical protagonists' meaning, beliefs, and perceptions as historical facts rather than anecdotal evidence to corroborate or challenge established historical facts."[26] Like Kelly, Eick acknowledges the ways in which people's identities can determine their perspectives.

How people make meaning of themselves and their stories should not be readily dismissed. But the role of the historian is to analyze and contextualize what is heard in the same way archival sources are analyzed and contextualized. This can seem at odds with a participant's perspective, but it broadens how we understand and interpret people's memories and perspectives within the context in which these experiences occurred. Historians are tasked with finding the balance between the amount of trust they place in people's memories and how they analyze that information when it conflicts with the memories of others and the information they find in other sources. "Trust but verify" is certainly the most appropriate approach when incorporating oral history into a study. But when studies rely on oral history, as this one does, the meaning people make of their memories is significant.

Regardless of the debates over oral history, it has served as a useful methodology in the history of African American and Mexican American education both pre- and post–*Brown v. Board of Education*. It has helped recover information about exceptional Black segregated schools from the existing historiography, which did not seem to contain evidence of any redeemable qualities of such schools.[27] As Sharon Gay Pierson surmises, such a view of these schools was necessary to build a case to end Jim Crow segregation.[28] Yet that meant that the history of thriving Black schools, their leaders, and the networks that existed was buried.[29] Historians have also used oral history to uncover the rich history of independent private schools in the North and South.[30] For Mexican American education, oral history furthered research on segregation, desegregation, and the meaning of whiteness. Rubén Donato has used oral histories in his studies on educational activism and school desegregation in California during the civil rights era. He has also used them to tell the history of Mexicans and Hispanos in Colorado communities. Oral history in Donato's research has uncovered the hidden educational history and struggles of groups that were invisible because of the racial binary in American history.[31] David G. García has used oral history to "recover some of the many perspectives missing from the official archives," and he believes that it deepened his "analysis of mundane racism as it evolved and was challenged in Oxnard [California]."[32] Because Mexican Americans were considered legally White but not treated like Whites, oral history is an important tool to recover their educational history. Mirelsie

Velázquez has also used history to uncover Puerto Rican educational struggles in Chicago, documenting student and community activism and the important role of women in creating a place for Puerto Ricans in the city.[33]

Research on school desegregation has certainly benefited from oral history as scholars have successfully utilized oral history in numerous desegregation studies. Most do so in ways that corroborate written history, bring depth to analyses, and expand our understanding of school desegregation. Oral history uncovers the challenges for and against school desegregation, provides vital information about teachers in the process, and gives us a broader sense of policy makers' decisions. It has helped us better understand how people experience desegregation.[34]

Along with studies that are infused with oral history, there are studies that further centralize oral history and use historical context as the support. Two important studies, one on Louisville, Kentucky, and the other on Jefferson County, Kentucky, give us a fuller picture of the impact and unraveling of desegregation. Tracy E. K'Meyer gives a "long" history and follows how desegregation evolved over time in Louisville. She allows the interviews to speak for themselves while providing context at the beginning and end of each chapter. Sarah Garland uncovers how Black students' desire to gain access to the desegregated and quota-enforced Central High School in Jefferson County eventually led to the 2007 *Meredith v. Jefferson County* Supreme Court case, which dismantled desegregation.[35] These are important studies foregrounding the voices of ordinary people and showcasing the variety of responses to desegregation.

A third way in which oral historians have utilized the method in desegregation studies is to foreground oral history while examining individual schools or a set of schools. This approach gives a better sense of group experiences within schools. Caroline Eick and Amy Stuart Wells and colleagues have produced important studies that push the limits of school desegregation literature. Eick focuses on one school in Baltimore County and chronicles the generational changes that happened when the school was divided, integrated, and redivided. Wells and colleagues look at the collective experiences of graduates of the class of 1988 at six different high schools in the North and South and argue that the students valued their experiences, but segregation in the larger society hampered changes beyond the schools.[36] Like the Wells and colleagues study, *Crossing Segregated Boundaries* draws from multiracial and multiethnic student desegregation experiences.

Methodology

As I was conceptualizing this project, I read Wells and colleagues' "How Desegregation Changed Us," which provided a road map for conducting this research.[37] In 2008, I received an Indiana University New Frontiers in the Arts and Humanities grant (funded by the Lilly Foundation), got institutional review board approval, searched for twentieth class reunions occurring in 2008, and hired and trained four graduate research assistants. I searched for Chicago high schools with a strong representation of Black, White, Latino, and Asian students, and ten such schools fit the profile. Next, I looked for which of those schools were having class reunions in the summer of 2008. Only five of the schools had reunions, and I only gained access to two schools, Von Steuben and Bogan. It was often easier to gain access to reunions planned by graduates than those planned by companies, which would often ignore emails. If the contact person was the reunion or website coordinator, he or she was more likely to respond to a request to attend a reunion. Once I gained access, the coordinators often posted study information on school or reunion websites, so reunion attendees could be made aware of the study.

In the summer of 2008, I paid for one or two graduate students and me to attend the reunions held in the Chicago area. We had clipboards and stood at the welcome tables or walked around to solicit names for the study, and we also sat with reuniongoers for dinner. The reunions were quite diverse, though there were fewer Asians in attendance. While graduates intermingled, some dinner tables were racially distinct, like the cafeteria tables participants would later describe in their interviews. After the reunions, we contacted the graduates who signed up, most of whom agreed to do the interviews, though others changed their minds. The research team traveled to Chicago to conduct interviews in people's homes or offices, at libraries, and wherever else they wanted to meet. For those who no longer lived in Chicago, we conducted phone interviews. We had semistructured interview questions and recorded the interviews. We met to discuss our findings after the Von Steuben interviews and tweaked the questions for the Bogan interviews.

Whitney Young had no reunion in 2008, but participants recommended their siblings, and I contacted two graduates I knew from Whitney Young. In 2009, I attempted to get access to the class of 1989 reunion. In the end, the reunion committee denied me access. I tried to get information about the study to Whitney Young's social media site to no avail. While there are other ways to gather participants, the reunions were the best way to ensure participants attended the schools and represented a critical mass of students. I had access to a few more graduates from personal contacts, but all had graduated after 1988. I only had four graduates from that school, and none were from the class of 1988. The four Whitney Young participants are in no way representative of the school or a particular class, but they provided information about Black socioeconomic class dynamics that was missing from my data on the other two schools. Moreover, the school is the only magnet school in the study and was the top school in the city at the time.[38]

Table I.1
Racial Data

School	Black	White	Latino	Mixed race	Total
Von Steuben	18	11	3	4	36
Bogan	9	6	11	2	28
Whitney Young	3	1	0	0	4
Total	30	18	14	6	68

Table I.2
Class Data

Class	Number interviewed
Class of 1986	1
Class of 1987	1
Class of 1988	60
Class of 1989	2
Class of 1990	3
Class of 1991	1

In all, sixty-eight graduates of desegregated schools were interviewed. Table I.1 highlights the racial data of the students interviewed from the three schools. The study examines a representative ethnic and racial mix of Black, White, and Latino students, as these groups were most of the attendees at the class reunions. There were sixty graduates from the class of 1988, but graduates referred other participants, usually siblings who were not part of their class. Other study participants graduated from 1986 to 1991. As indicated in table I.2, we interviewed one graduate each from 1986, 1987, and 1991; two 1989 graduates; and three 1990 graduates. Despite the inconsistency in the class year, the participants outside of the class of 1988 provided fascinating stories and perceptions of their schooling experiences that enriched the study.

The interviews were conducted between June and August 2008; most were transcribed between the summer of 2008 and spring of 2009, and four in the spring of 2012. I created themes based on interview questions and data, then used Atlas.ti software to code the interviews. The oral history interviews were used along with traditional archival research, newspaper articles, and secondary sources for this study. The Chicago Board of Education archives provided demographic data, school desegregation plans, records of board meetings, and other primary sources about school desegregation.

Though this is an oral history project, I decided to give participants the option of using their first name or a pseudonym, so that they could speak candidly about their experiences. I have also chosen to let participants tell their stories in their own words. As a result, the chapters with their stories include numerous quotes. Sometimes the participants were the best narrators of their experiences.

Book Layout

Chapter 1 provides national and local historical context concerning housing, politics, and school desegregation policy. It highlights the housing policies and practices that led to segregation and White defense of segregated boundaries. This chapter also details how national politicians both championed civil rights and school desegregation with the passage of the Civil Rights Act in 1964 and weakened the tools necessary for social change. Locally, racially divisive politics limited effective governing. Finally, the policy intent of school desegregation will be explored. Chicago's school desegregation plan led to a series of school choice initiatives that negated the typical negative reactions often associated with desegregation. Housing, politics, and school desegregation initiatives, along with economic and demographic changes, all led to the maintenance of segregation and provided an environment that made crossing boundaries more difficult.

Chapter 2 explores the impact of busing as participants attended elementary school. Latinos who moved into White neighborhoods and integrated schools and communities on the Southwest Side of the city faced difficulties and discrimination from their White peers and neighbors. Yet their presence in those neighborhoods and schools stood in stark contrast to that of Blacks, who would later be bused in to desegregate the same schools. With antibusing protests to keep Black students out of the schools, the boundaries Latinos once struggled to cross were suddenly blurred as they became the preferred racialized group. The racial hierarchy placed Latinos between Blacks and Whites while maintaining racial stratification.

Chapter 3 highlights the actual process of choosing a high school and the limited opportunities that were available. Desegregation provided choices that broadened educational opportunities for highly motivated students and parents. As participants and their parents made their choices about which school to attend, many purposely avoided neighborhood high schools that had high dropout rates, lacked the academic rigor they sought, or were in neighborhoods known for gang activity. Though participants made choices they believed were appropriate for their goals, they recalled community members who ridiculed, praised, or were curious about their choices. Crossing boundaries, for some, meant alienation or estrangement from their racial group. For many, their school choices resulted in a lengthy commute to school, as well as culturally enriching opportunities, as they passed through many of Chicago's neighborhoods. Because they were not the initial group of students who desegregated, and because they utilized school choice initiatives and public transportation instead of school buses, their crossing of segregated boundaries was far less threatening to White communities.

In chapter 4, the academic experiences of participants—such as incidents with teachers, professional staff, and the school curriculum—show whether their integrated experiences were helped or hampered while in school. Desegregation places students in the same buildings, but structural policies in schools—including curriculum design and interaction with teachers and school staff—are often obstacles to fully integrating students within a school. Several Black and Latino participants noted the subtle forms of racism or microaggressions they experienced in their interactions with teachers and counselors. Additionally, the curriculum failed to be fully inclusive of the multiethnic and multiracial school population and served to normalize whiteness.

Chapter 5 examines the interracial experiences of participants in school cafeterias and during extracurricular activities and explores interracial friendships and dating in and out of school. Classroom interaction and extracurricular activities increased the opportunities for interracial friendships, as well as the likelihood that students would sit together in the cafeteria. Though most participants noted that their closest friends were of the same race or ethnicity, many crossed segregated boundaries to visit friends' homes and met up at locations outside of school when parental opposition or spatial distance in a segregated city made maintaining friendships difficult. As friendships formed, some participants also ventured to date outside their race, though this was not always readily accepted by their peers or parents.

Chapter 6 explores some of the difficulties students experienced in trying to fit in, sorting out their identities, and handling differences in social class. Though some participants believed they "all got along," there were times when racial differences caused problems. Additionally, some faced problems within their own groups as mixed-race and mixed-ethnicity students straddled the line between two worlds without always fitting into either, and Black students who had predominantly White friends faced ridicule. The process of discovering identity, common among this age group, was in some ways complicated even more as desegregation brought together students from different parts of the city while often simultaneously widening the differences among them. Further, as many poorer students encountered students of much higher socioeconomic statuses for the first time, class issues were highlighted and at times prohibited friendships. Students who effectively crossed racial boundaries were able to maintain a sense of self while interacting with people from different racial, ethnic, or class groups; for others, crossing boundaries led them to be less assured and to experience alienation.

Chapter 7 discusses the participants' experiences after high school. Their college choices indicated the quality of the high schools they attended, with students from Whitney Young and Von Steuben much more likely to attend flagship state universities, liberal arts colleges, and prestigious universities. Bogan graduates were more likely to attend community colleges, if they attended college at all. While in college, some participants were faced with racism that they had not anticipated after attending desegregated schools. It became clear that they had experienced isolated integration, despite the fact that most thought it was a highly beneficial experience.

The conclusion provides details about the end of the city's desegregation consent decree, fewer spots at top schools for Black students, and the new iteration of school choice in the current policy environment.

1

Segregation, Politics, and School Desegregation Policy

In a 1964 speech, Martin Luther King Jr. proclaimed that "the arc of the moral universe is long, but bends towards justice." Borrowing from Minister Theodore Parker's 1853 speech, King expressed the American optimism regarding the inevitability of progress to inspire his audience to action.[1] King was in no way naïve about the work and sacrifice needed to ensure progress, but his faith and actions required a dose of optimism to counter the intensity of the civil rights movement. Historians have long recognized that unrelenting faith in American racial progress is illusionary at best. As much as progress is inevitable, so too is regress. Speaking of the decline in residential integration since 1880, Richard Rothstein writes, "We like to think of American history as a continuous march of progress toward greater freedom, greater equality, and greater justice. But sometimes we move backward, dramatically so."[2]

While progress is desired and advocates of school desegregation see it as one strategy for getting there, the realities of residential segregation remain entrenched. As participants in this study came of age in the 1980s and embarked on racial integration in their desegregated schools, the historical and social context in which they functioned affected how they experienced school desegregation. Housing segregation, racially charged politics, deindustrialization, and demographic changes were intertwined in ways that maintained segregated boundaries and racial stratification. Racially segregated housing, which was created and maintained through local and national policies, stunted opportunities for those within the segregated Black and Latino areas. Discriminatory housing policies, along with labor market discrimination, underperforming schools, and mass incarceration, have meant that those within segregated Black and Latino neighborhoods were much more likely to experience the ills of urban decay, regardless of their socioeconomic class status.[3] Segregation made it easier for Whites to hoard resources and power while maintaining racial stratification.[4] The increase of Puerto Ricans and Mexicans in Chicago further complicated the Black-White binary. Though many Latinos were also segregated, some, depending on phenotype, could integrate into White neighborhoods. This integration was tenuous, as Latinos faced discrimination and were often treated as outsiders in integrated communities.

Before school desegregation, residential segregation, along with Chicago Public School (CPS) leaders' administrative decisions to maintain neighborhood schools and avoid desegregation, led to segregated schools. Many Black segregated schools were historically underresourced and overcrowded and had higher teacher turnover rates. Latino segregated schools also faced similar issues as their population in the city increased. As the federal government insisted on school desegregation nationally, Chicago school officials, like others across the country, resisted. When CPS finally created a plan, it was largely built on boundary changes and voluntary school choice initiatives. These efforts were then marketed as school choice, lessening resistance and privileging Whites. The focus on school choice led to a brain drain, as some of the best students from segregated Black and Latino schools chose to attend desegregated, high-quality schools. The national and local context in which students attended desegregated schools made their efforts at integration even more noteworthy. They had to, at times, cross literal segregated boundaries while attempting to blur the distinctions segregation produced.

Housing Segregation

In *The Color of Law*, Richard Rothstein argues that federal, state, and local housing policies created, maintained, and ensured the persistence of segregation throughout the twentieth century. Public housing, zoning laws, and government enforcement of private housing agreements solidified racial stratification. Numerous policies, particularly those enforced by the Federal Housing Authority (FHA), blocked Black homeowners from receiving mortgages, prevented builders from building integrated subdivisions, and enforced restrictive covenants even after the Supreme Court outlawed it. This intensified segregation in places where integration could have occurred. Government support of housing segregation led to Blacks often paying far more for properties bought or rented in transitioning neighborhoods.[5] White residents often failed to understand the costs Blacks paid for moving into White neighborhoods. Real estate agents were guilty of ramping up fear in White homeowners and overpricing housing stock for new Black residents. Enormous profiteering resulted from these deals, which often left Blacks unable to afford repairs on their homes.[6] Federal government policies also exacerbated these problems. Historian Kevin Kruse discusses how these very policies affected transitioning neighborhoods in Atlanta: "The resistance of these whites to the 'encroachment' of blacks resulted not solely from their personal racism but also from the larger manifestations of racism in real-estate practices." The Home Owners' Loan Corporation typically red-lined areas with old housing stock often lived in by Blacks and other minorities. Banks, in turn, would not approve loans for those neighborhoods. By accepting those standards, the FHA and Veterans Administration (VA) encouraged the barriers that kept Blacks out of White neighborhoods.[7] According to historians Leon Litwack and Hilary Moss, Black bodies in White neighborhoods have historically been perceived as a trigger for lower property values.[8]

National policies, local policies, and individual actions simultaneously maintained residential segregation and racial stratification and created boundaries. As Blacks and Latinos migrated to places like Chicago, they were segregated and had limited access to the job market. Although Chicago laws did not explicitly condone housing segregation, the housing industry and violence in the city effectively prevented Blacks, and in some cases Latinos, from integrating into White neighborhoods. As more Blacks and Latinos entered the city in large numbers throughout the twentieth century, segregation intensified and Whites slowly moved out of the city. From the mid-1910s to the late 1970s, southern Blacks participated in the Great Migration to the North. The migration began during World War I, as migrants were escaping the terrorism of the South and northern industries needed workers to replace the European immigrants and American soldiers who once held those spots.[9] As the second wave of the migration occurred in the post–World War II era, Chicago's Black population increased from 812,637 in 1960 to 1,087,711 in 1990 (from 22.8 to 39.0 percent of the city's population), though the Black population had peaked a decade earlier (maps 1.1 and 1.2).[10]

Mexican immigrants who were recruited to work in the steel and meatpacking industries slowly trickled into the city beginning in the 1910s. In 1942, the U.S. and Mexican governments created the Bracero Program (Mexican Farm Labor Program), which brought temporary contract workers from Mexico to the United States during a labor shortage. More than fifteen thousand braceros came to work on the railroads in Chicago. The program was highly exploitative, but it brought many workers who remained in the United States and Chicago even after the program ended. The Mexican population significantly increased after the 1960s because of the availability of jobs and the growing community of Mexicans in the city. Puerto Ricans entered the city

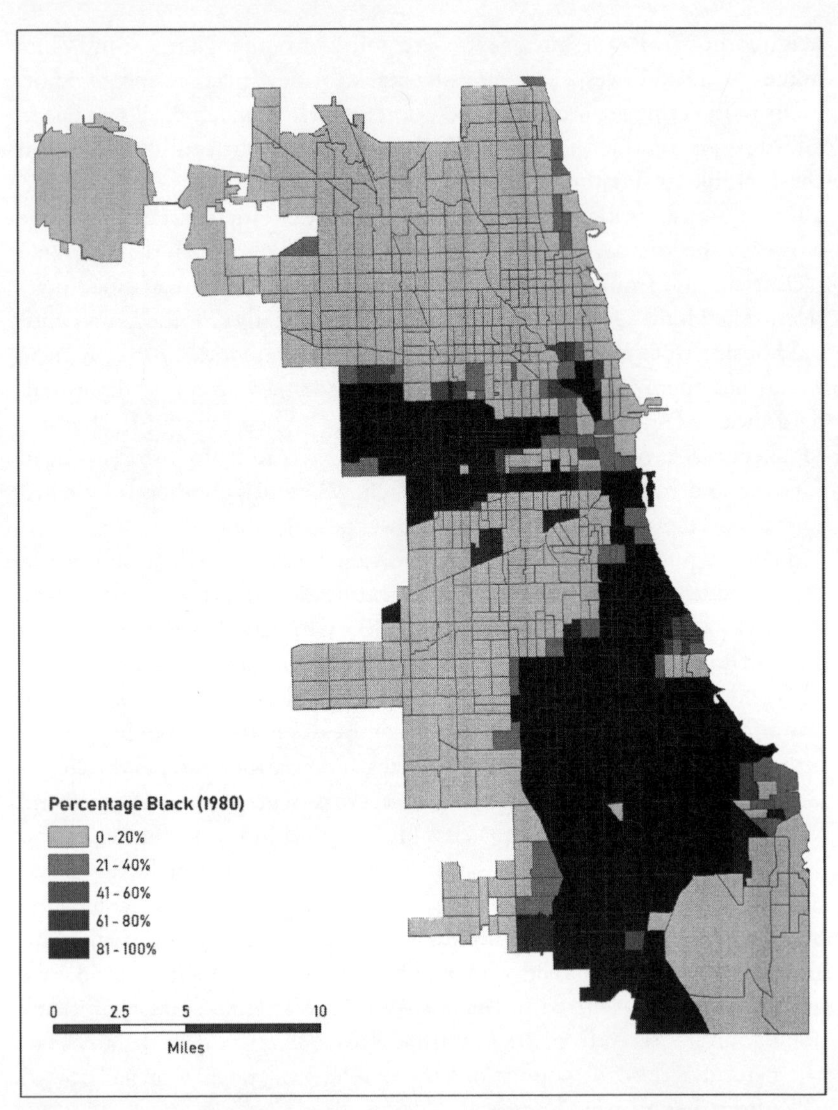

MAP 1.1 Racial demographics for Blacks, 1980

looking for work in the late 1940s as part of Operation Bootstrap, or Manos a la Obra, the federal government's plan to industrialize Puerto Rico's economy with outside investments. To solve the island's "overpopulation" and labor issues, Operation Bootstrap facilitated the migration of Puerto Ricans to the mainland while new business interests opened on the island. Chicago became one of the principal destinations for Puerto Rican migrants, second only to New York.

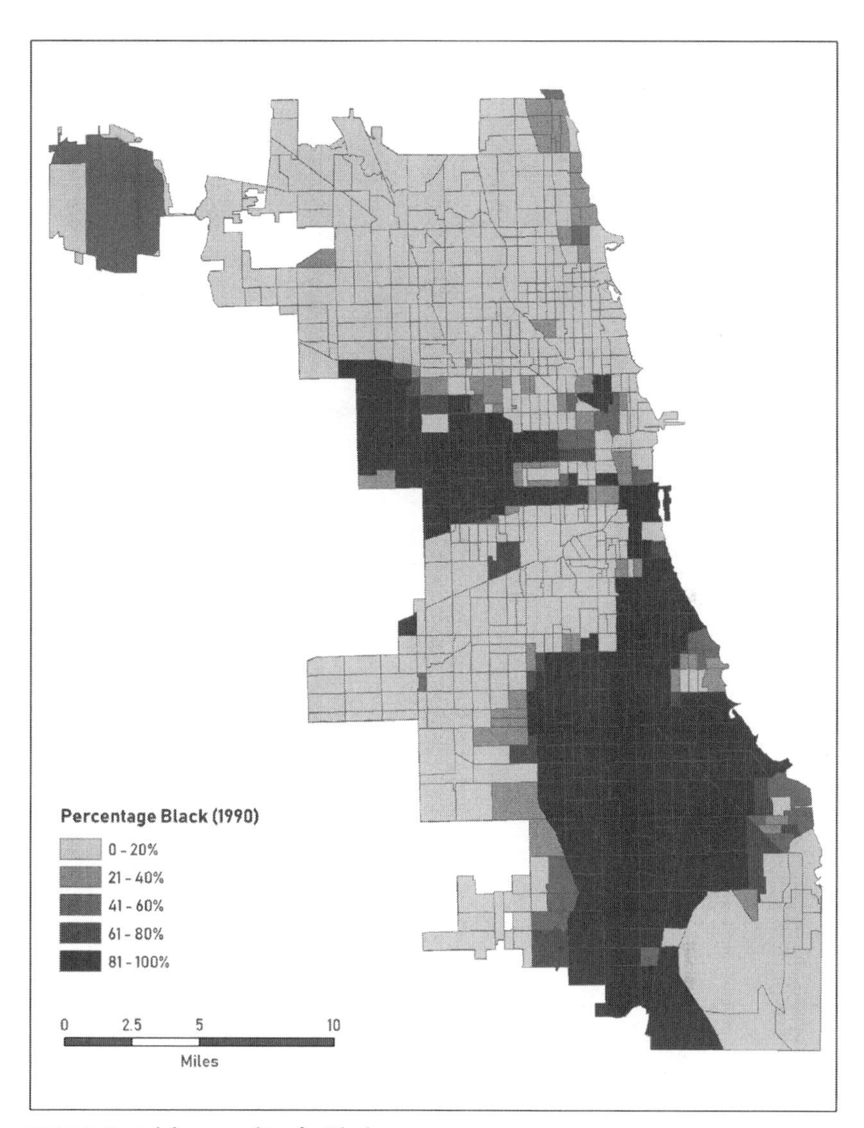

MAP 1.2 Racial demographics for Blacks, 1990

Cubans and other Latinos from Central America and the Caribbean would also migrate beyond the Southwest, Florida, and New York.[11] The Latino population in the city grew from approximately 110,000 in 1960 to 545,852 in 1990 (from 3.1 to 19.6 percent; maps 1.3 and 1.4). While the Black and Latino populations surged, Chicago's White population declined from 2,712,748 in 1960 to 1,263,524 in 1990 (from 76.4 to 43.3 percent). Despite the increases in Blacks and Latinos, Chicago lost 766,678 residents in that thirty-year span. CPS's

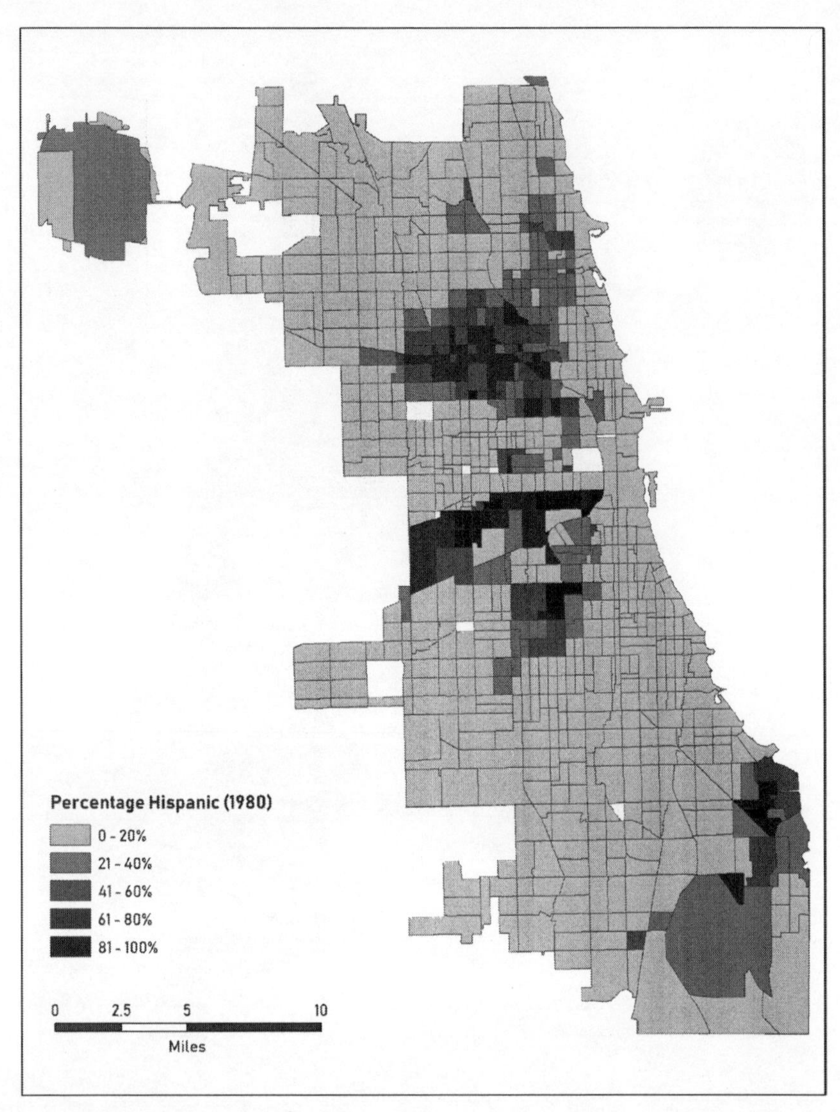

MAP 1.3 Racial demographics for Latinos, 1980

population also declined, from 580,207, its height in 1968, to 408,714 in 1990. These demographic shifts led to increased segregation both in neighborhoods and in schools as Blacks and Latinos were steered into segregated housing. Blacks were already highly segregated, but Latino segregation intensified as their population increased. When Latinos entered the city in greater numbers, they were also gradually contained in certain communities, including

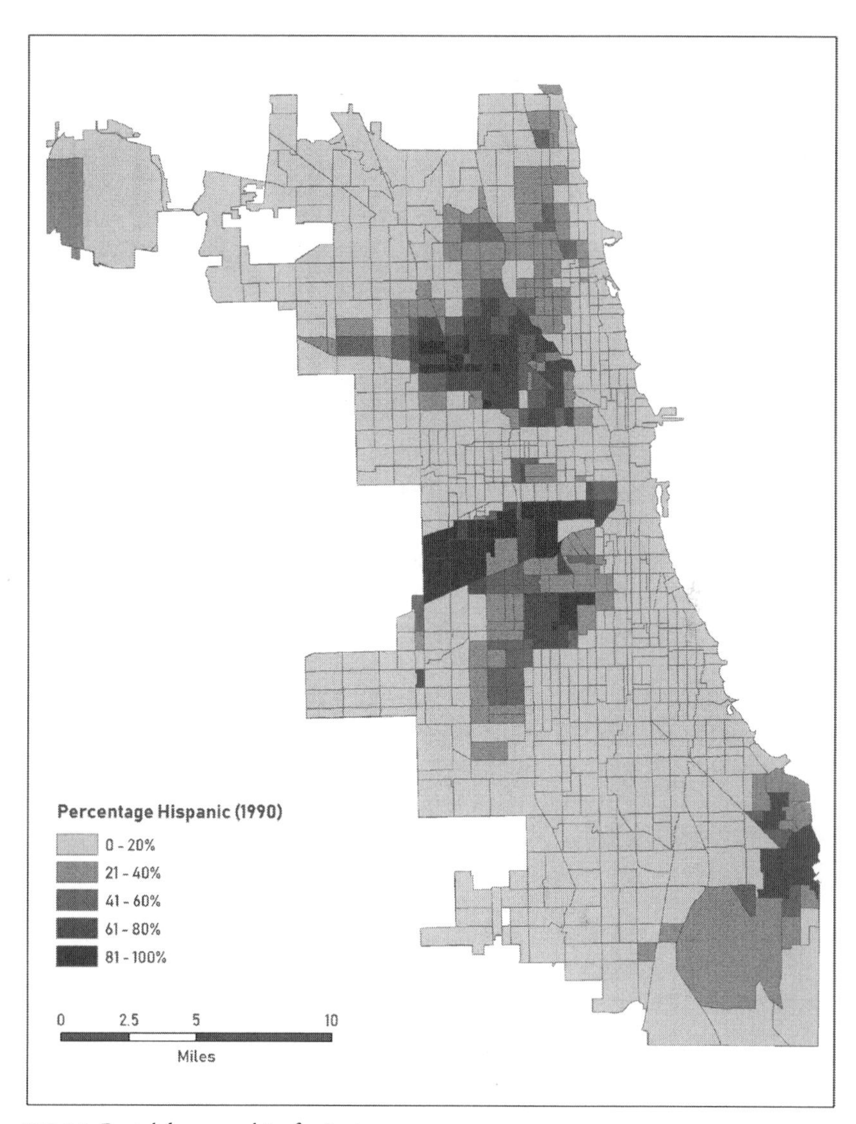

MAP 1.4 Racial demographics for Latinos, 1990

Humboldt Park, West Town, Lower West Side (Pilsen), and South Lawndale (Little Village).[12]

Chicago's discriminatory housing industry was quite sophisticated even after court cases and legislation outlawed restrictive covenants, blockbusting, and racial steering.[13] Chicago Lawn's Marquette Park neighborhood, near Bogan High School, is one community where discriminatory housing tactics occurred.

Some study participants lived in or near this community. The violence and economic tactics used to maintain this segregated White neighborhood typified the ways in which resources were guarded and how the hierarchy of Whites, Latinos, and Blacks developed to suit the needs of Whites. Latinos were accepted in the neighborhood in ways that Blacks were not, but they also experienced discrimination.

Journalists from United Press International investigated the housing practices and found that White real estate agents sold homes in the neighborhood only to Whites and Latinos. After Black real estate agents sold the first homes to Blacks, the real estate market opened for Black home buyers. Agents steered Blacks into FHA and VA mortgage programs. White sellers were persuaded to use these government programs to sell homes to Blacks, and Blacks were encouraged to buy homes with these loans. Brokers and mortgage bankers would sell the homes to people who barely or fraudulently met loan requirements, and the homes were foreclosed when the family missed one payment. The mortgage company would then receive full payment for the mortgage from the Department of Housing and Urban Development and new tenants would move in, beginning the process again. United Press International investigators found that most homes sold to Blacks (82 percent) were FHA or VA financed. Real estate brokers and mortgage companies profited from this unscrupulous practice, as many homeowners defaulted on their government mortgages. In the mid-1970s the government began to crack down on falsified applications and tightened its standards.[14] However, the damage had already been done.

These housing practices led to profiteering, violence, and neighborhood instability. The community of Chicago Lawn had historically fought to limit the settlement of Black residents in its neighborhoods. Despite hostile and vigorous protests against Black encroachment, Chicago Lawn's White residents were losing their hold on the community, as the city was bursting at the seams with Black and Latino migrants and immigrants in need of housing. The racial changes in this community were less drastic than in other areas of the city, where White residents abandoned communities wholesale.[15] The critical need for housing meant that White neighborhoods adjacent to Black communities opened to Black residents. This expansion was not taken lightly in Chicago Lawn's Marquette Park neighborhood. The neighborhood along Western Avenue saw an expansion of Black residents from West Englewood and other South Side communities. The *Chicago Sun-Times* reported, "In recent years the mixing of races in this area of Chicago had produced violence, and this violence now contributes to the tension felt by both Blacks and Whites over school desegregation."[16]

The Marquette Park neighborhood gained its infamous reputation in 1966 when Martin Luther King Jr. was hit in the head with a rock during one of the city's civil rights marches. The marches were part of the Chicago Freedom

Movement and protested the city's segregated housing market. Marchers were bombarded by hostile Whites who threw rocks and fireworks at them. King himself noted that his experiences in Chicago rivaled only the terror he had faced in Mississippi.[17] In 1967, the American Nazi Party held a rally in Marquette Park and their leader, George Lincoln Rockwell, spoke degradingly of Blacks to a crowd of cheering Whites. That same year, Frank Collin based the headquarters of the National Socialist Party of America (a Nazi group) close to the area's Western Avenue border. A large "Stop the Niggers" sign was hung from the building.[18]

Nazi groups' ability to openly operate in the area, as well as their hostility toward Black marchers, spoke to the level of disdain some Whites had for Blacks moving into the area. While not all White residents of these neighborhoods were comfortable with Nazis operating in their community, the physical and verbal hostility Blacks endured showed that resistance to Blacks moving into White communities and attending predominantly White schools went beyond just a few members of a hate group. The Urban League reported that the first Black family moved into Marquette Park in December 1974. By 1976, more than two hundred Black families had moved into the neighborhood. Their move was accompanied by over sixty reported acts of vandalism and violence, including windows broken, Molotov cocktails and other incendiary devices launched, shots fired, cars and garages set on fire, cars vandalized, and children attacked by fellow students. The violence intimidated many Black families, whose homes were repeatedly attacked.[19] Discrimination against Latinos was not tracked by the Urban League.

Marches continued in Marquette Park in 1976, and White mobs continued to hurl stones at Black marchers.[20] A group called the Martin Luther King Jr. Movement established its headquarters close to Marquette Park. The group formed from King-led marches in the 1960s and marched to continue King's legacy. According to one of its leaders, Rev. Edgar Jackson, the marches were also to "prove to the world that Black people had a right to walk through any area in America." The King Movement organized marches despite little support from Black residents in Marquette Park. In the two marches it held, the Ku Klux Klan and the Nazi Party organized countermarches of White residents, and dozens were arrested and injured.[21]

School protests soon became another means through which White residents in Chicago Lawn and Ashburn (the community where Bogan High School was located) expressed their discontent with racial changes in both the schools and the neighborhoods. Coupled with housing protests, these school protests illustrated White residents' deep-seated racial discrimination and provided public displays of hostility toward school desegregation and busing. These combined housing and school protests helped maintain segregation and discrimination. Though the protests had died down by the time the study participants attended high school, the reputation and racial attitudes of these communities lingered, making it especially difficult to cross racial boundaries to integrate Bogan.

While segregation kept working-class Whites in communities like Chicago Lawn in a better position than Blacks, the successes of the civil rights movement, coupled with deindustrialization, meant those on the lower end of the economic bracket battled for declining access to high-paying working-class positions. Working-class Whites were vilified as racists in the media and by middle- and upper-class Whites. Sociologist Maria Kefalas captures the socioeconomic class differences between Whites when it came to issues of race: "From the perspective of those living on the front lines of the battles over race, middle-class America had come by its progressive views on race on the cheap. Suburbanites watched Washington, Los Angeles, Boston, Philadelphia, and Chicago burn on the nightly news; middle-class urbanites were not being asked to live down the street from towering housing projects. While the true victims of race in America were, of course, African Americans, working-class Whites could legitimately claim that upper-class Whites could more easily avoid the costs of racial change."[22] Middle-class Whites had the power to integrate on their own terms or leave the city for the suburbs. But working-class Whites, many of whom were Chicago public employees (police, firefighters, municipal employees), had to live within city limits. To distinguish their neighborhoods from Black neighborhoods, they created a garden-like utopia, where lawns were meticulously cared for and neighbors pressured each other to make sure their homes had curb appeal and their holiday decorations were tastefully done. This was to contrast what they viewed as the decay that came from having Blacks in a neighborhood. They wanted to keep Blacks out at all costs but were willing to allow some Latinos who could meet their exacting standards.[23]

Latinos (typically Mexican American) were the one racialized group that gained tentative acceptance by White residents in communities like Chicago Lawn and Ashburn. Latinos in Chicago did not face the hypersegregation that Blacks faced, and Whites often saw them as preferable because Mexican Americans reminded them of White ethnic immigrants, such as Italians and Poles.[24] Stereotypes still existed about them, and they were not fully accepted, but they moved into every census tract in these predominantly White communities. Meanwhile, Blacks were relegated to census tracts adjacent to Black communities. Historian Lilia Fernandez eloquently captures how real estate brokers used Mexicans and Puerto Ricans in Chicago as a "'buffer' between Blacks and Whites." She explains, "Latinos/as in Chicago's neighborhoods tested the limits of residential integration. Because their 'race' could be negotiated, contested, and reevaluated in a variety of contexts, this sometimes gave them access that was denied African Americans, though not always. Race in the urban north was not so Black and White. Mexicans and Puerto Ricans complicated what was perceived as a rather linear and dualistic narrative of postwar racial succession."[25] In Chicago, housing needs and severe segregation meant lighter-skinned or White Latinos were more acceptable in White communities, though they also experienced discrimination. Black Puerto Ricans or those with an indigenous phenotype faced greater difficulty getting landlords to rent to them. Some landlords avoided renting to Spanish-speaking families altogether. Puerto Ricans in Chicago were charged higher prices for rent and faced difficulty as they tried to expand beyond the barrio on the North and Northwest Sides. They were also displaced as the city's urban renewal plans in the 1960s and 1970s demolished their neighborhoods.[26]

Racial boundaries were evident in Chicago as Blacks and Latinos experienced housing segregation, though at different rates. Even when both groups were able to move into White communities, they faced harassment, violence, and discrimination. In a time of severe housing crisis when Whites benefited from suburbanization, highway construction, and the GI Bill, most Blacks and Latinos were prevented from doing the same. This often diminished their quality of life and access to intergenerational wealth and increased the likelihood of their children attending segregated schools. Like housing, the job market was unfavorable to racialized groups.

As housing struggles endured, economic and social changes occurred in the city. Just as the numbers of Blacks and Latinos increased in the city, the economy shifted as deindustrialization occurred. Manufacturing jobs previously available to immigrants and migrants with limited educational backgrounds disappeared with the advent of automation, suburbanization, and globalization. Between 1960 and 1970, the suburban percentage of Chicago's metropolitan manufacturing jobs increased to 57.8 percent, while the city's percentage declined to 34.2 percent.[27] Chicago lost 60 percent of its manufacturing jobs, a total loss of 326,000 jobs, between 1967 and 1987.[28] This shift meant that educated workers benefited from technological changes, but those with less education were displaced, struggled to find jobs that provided a livable wage, and were far more likely to be unemployed and underemployed.

In the 1980s, the crack epidemic began, and it decimated some communities both through addiction and through the violence that came from drug trafficking. The loss of jobs, the underground economy created by drug trafficking, and the war on drugs ramped up mass incarceration.[29] These changes left some Chicago neighborhoods, which were already highly segregated, with a higher concentration of the poor. The combination of racial and socioeconomic segregation further constrained job opportunities, and adults in some neighborhoods were less likely to maintain full-time jobs, had fewer skills for white-collar work, lacked the social network (or social capital) to access jobs, and were increasingly seen as unemployable by the city's employers.[30] These changes were particularly devastating for Black men.

Housing segregation made crossing boundaries more difficult, but maintaining racial stratification easier. Poorer schools, fewer job opportunities, and police surveillance could contain Blacks and increasingly Latinos in certain geographic areas.[31] As study participants discussed their reasons for choosing desegregated schools, the negative reputations of certain schools and neighborhoods were an important factor that was largely a product of segregation and the conditions that resulted from it. The poor reputations of Black neighborhoods and schools, even when untrue, in turn produced inequality.[32] Along with housing segregation and the resulting racial boundaries, the national and city-level political changes promised hope but instead stood as waves that crashed on the shores of reality, as the passage of progressive laws and the election of a Black mayor failed to dismantle segregated boundaries.

Politics

National and local politics played an important role by providing the tools to end discrimination, on the one hand. But on the other hand, because of White political resistance, opportunities were provided for only certain people to cross segregated boundaries. No sooner than the Supreme Court decided *Brown v. Board of Education* in 1954 and *Brown II* in 1955, southern politicians organized massive resistance to school desegregation.[33] After years of civil rights protests throughout the country and political negotiations with two presidential administrations, Congress passed the 1964 Civil Rights Act under President Lyndon B. Johnson's leadership. The Civil Rights Act, while broadly denouncing discrimination, directly mentioned school desegregation and provided the executive branch with enforcement abilities. Federal agencies were empowered to implement desegregation. The Department of Health, Education, and Welfare (HEW) could withhold federal funds (Title VI), and the Justice Department could sue (Title IV) institutions or school districts that practiced discrimination. This act, along with court cases, was essential for school desegregation policy enforcement.

However, despite the hope that came with the Civil Rights Act, each changing presidential administration led to shifting desegregation enforcement. As public antibusing protests occurred throughout the country, emboldened politicians weakened the Civil Rights Act.[34] Consequently, whatever little political support there was for school desegregation quickly waned. As the nation lost interest in the civil rights movement and feared the Black Power movement, Congress chipped away at the desegregation enforcement of the Civil Rights Act just as southern desegregation was showing success. Southern politicians demanded that HEW investigate all regions of the nation, not just the South, but did not add additional personnel. President Richard Nixon ordered the Justice Department to file suits that restricted HEW's role in withholding federal funds. This slowed desegregation enforcement since suing districts was far more time consuming than threatening to withhold funds. An amendment to the Civil Rights Act, cosponsored by Joe Biden, also restricted the use of busing. These political tactics successfully slowed the enforcement of desegregation.[35] Along with federal political efforts, state and local officials across the country colluded to delay, limit, and reverse school desegregation efforts. With each political step forward, those against progress sought to reassert control leading to regression.

Ronald Reagan ushered in an anti–civil rights platform that effectively completed America's political right turn in the 1980s. In a backlash to civil rights, conservatives argued that civil rights had gone from individual rights to group rights, which unfairly gave preferential treatment to Blacks and undermined the rights of individual Whites. Reagan stood in stark opposition to gender- or race-based policies and worked to undermine affirmative action. Though his administration was against desegregation and other civil rights policies, several initiatives were already court ordered and under way and had to be implemented. But those in his administration championed a return to what they believed to be the promise of America. Reagan expressed his beliefs that America gave everyone opportunities, and the provision of special privileges to one group over another was a perversion of those rights.[36]

As the federal government's desegregation policy enforcement and the political right turn were under way, Chicago's politics were changing. The 1980s was the first post–Mayor Richard J. Daley decade. Daley controlled the city's politics for over two decades until his death in 1976. He commanded the city's Democratic machine responsible for delivering patronage jobs and favors for votes. Beginning in the late 1960s and early 1970s, his grip on Black and Latino populations lessened as those communities endured segregation and limited city resources in exchange for their loyalty, while White ethnics and business elites received the bulk of the political favor.[37] Just three years after Daley's death, Black and Latino voters helped elect Mayor Jane Byrne in 1979. Byrne removed Blacks from important city departments, including the Chicago Board of Education, and she mishandled the Chicago Transit Authority, teacher, and firefighter strikes, which disproportionally affected Black residents who depended on public transportation, were left with unsupervised children, and suffered more fire-related deaths. When Byrne failed to deliver on her promises of reform and inclusion, Black voters abandoned her.[38]

The political climate in Chicago was highly racialized as the city elected Harold Washington, its first Black mayor, in 1983. In the mayoral primary, Washington garnered the vast majority of the Black vote, leaving his Democratic rivals—incumbent Mayor Byrne and States Attorney Richard M. Daley, son of the legendary political machine boss Richard J. Daley—to split the White vote.[39] The general election took a nasty turn almost immediately as

White Democratic politicians and longtime Democratic voters traded party loyalty for racial loyalty and supported White Republican Bernard Epton. Epton was deemed Chicago's "Last White Hope." When Washington made a campaign stop at Saint Pascal's Church with Walter Mondale, the door bore the recently spray-painted words NIGGER DIE. Hordes of Washington's opponents jeered him and carried signs in support of Epton. One of Epton's campaign slogans read "Epton for Mayor—Before It's Too Late." While he and his campaign manager insisted that the slogan referred to Washington's financial missteps, very few people believed that to be the case. Although Whites on the Southwest Side and the Northwest Side overwhelmingly voted for Epton, Washington won because of record Black voter turnout, three-to-one support from Latinos (mostly Puerto Ricans), and 12.3 percent of the liberal White vote. The coalition of Blacks, Latinos, and liberal Whites was enough for Washington to eke out a 46,250-vote win.[40]

As an astute politician, Washington emphasized the shared concerns between Black and Latino communities. Despite his political savvy, governing the city proved difficult during his first term as Washington's rival, Edward Vrdolyak, and Vrdolyak's supporters in the city council (dubbed the Vrdolyak 29) blocked Washington's reforms at every turn, motivated by racism and hostility toward his agenda.[41] City hall was often a place of shouting matches between White aldermen and Mayor Washington. Special elections were held after a successful court case on redistricting, and Washington gained control of city hall after his re-election. However, he passed away in November 1987, not long after he had begun to make reforms that enhanced Black and Latino communities. Washington's election and death affected participants of this study as they witnessed the city's racial divisions in their desegregated schools.

The passage of the Civil Rights Act and the election of a Black mayor were challenged and resisted by White politicians and their constituents. Advances promising more equality and political representation created opportunities for some but remained merely symbolic gestures of hope. White politicians stood as guardians of racial stratification and segregation, readjusting the boundaries of acceptability. Overt racial discrimination was less endorsed and additional members of racialized groups were able to prosper, but racial boundaries continued. The federal government eroded the Civil Rights Act and delayed it enforcement. When Washington ran for office, he faced stiff opposition from White politicians willing to vote against their party to ensure the preservation of segregated boundaries.[42]

School Desegregation

School districts around the country desegregated after years of litigation and massive resistance to the 1954 *Brown v. Board of Education* Supreme Court decision. Desegregation was carried out in a myriad of ways across the country, with policies often favoring White students. Early on, southern districts resisted desegregation by not creating desegregation plans, financing White private academies, and using freedom-of-choice plans. Freedom of choice gave Whites the choice to remain in segregated White schools, and the few Blacks allowed to utilize the policy were isolated in hostile White schools while their parents faced economic reprisals.[43] In *Green v. County School Board* (1968), the Supreme Court decided that freedom-of-choice plans were inadequate unless they led to substantive desegregation. The Supreme Court pressed southern districts to end delays with the *Green* and *Alexander v. Holmes County Board of Education* (1969) cases, and the executive branch pressed for desegregation compliance. Districts around the country responded by busing (county-wide busing, one-way busing of Black students from cities to suburbs or to White schools in the same cities), desegregating Black students with Mexican American (legally White) students instead of privileged Whites, and using magnet schools, among other techniques.[44]

As schools desegregated, Black schools were closed or downgraded to junior highs or elementary schools, Black teachers were fired, and principals were demoted. School administrators devised ways to segregate students within schools with academic tracking, segregation of activities such as certain sports and proms, and the creation of disciplinary and academic structures that labeled Black children as problematic in terms of their behavior and their learning abilities.[45] Standardized testing also prevented students from gaining acceptance into certain schools, teachers from receiving equal pay, and students from accessing higher academic tracks.[46] Each of these tactics meant that Black students often had less access to the best education even when they were in school with White children.

Like northern Blacks, Latinos in the Southwest faced forms of segregation codified not in law but in policy. Mexican Americans were considered White because of the Treaty of Guadalupe Hidalgo, but they were not treated as such. In early Mexican American school desegregation cases in the Southwest, attorneys argued that Mexicans were White and should therefore be integrated. This led to mixed results. Superintendents often argued that language and culture were legitimate reasons for segregation, though other immigrants were integrated and a "Latinized" appearance was often the cause of segregation. In the *Mendez v. Westminster* (1946) case, closely followed and supported by the NAACP before *Brown v. Board of Education*, the California Supreme Court ruled that Mexican Americans could not be segregated for educational purposes because segregation limited their English language development. As the Chicano movement ensued, Mexican Americans began to argue that they were an identifiable minority, and they were recognized as such in *Cisneros v. Corpus Christi* (1970). Despite their legal White status, Mexican Americans were racialized and treated as "socially brown."[47] The dozens of school desegregation cases won or lost did little to change the increasing segregation Mexican Americans faced as their population increased. Their racialized status—due to language, culture, surname, and skin color—created segregated boundaries for them in ways that other ethnic groups did not encounter once those groups became White.

Like elsewhere in the country, Chicago's schooling inequality resulted from segregation. Residents had long fought for improvement in Black segregated schools. Before the 1960s, the fight was to build more schools, to reduce overcrowding, and to increase the quality of education. In the 1960s, interracial groups fought for school desegregation, while Blacks fought to improve the quality of segregated schools through community control, and Latinos advocated for bilingual education. Large protests for desegregation and, later, community control became the hallmark of the 1960s school reform efforts. While some schools succeeded despite racial isolation, many others suffered from high teacher turnover rates and high dropout rates.[48]

In Chicago, school desegregation occurred after two decades of federal involvement. Federal policy enforcement of the 1964 Civil Rights Act constantly shifted as a result of changing presidential administrations and agency leadership, congressional limits to the law, and protests from Chicago's politicians, school leaders, and residents.[49] In the early 1960s, local and prominent civil rights organizations led a series of protests for school desegregation. These efforts included failed court cases, school boycotts, and sit-ins during Superintendent Benjamin Willis's administration, all of which led to negligible school desegregation. Willis was seen by Chicagoans as the symbol of segregation as he gerrymandered school boundaries and used mobile classrooms (labeled Willis Wagons) to avoid desegregation. When pressed to desegregate, Willis responded with permissive transfer plans that allowed a limited number of students to transfer to other schools and resulted in minimal desegregation. In fact, early versions of permissive transfer plans hastened segregation, as White students used the transfers to leave the schools transitioning from predominantly White to predominantly Black.[50]

The federal government engaged in Chicago's school desegregation efforts beginning in 1965 when a leading civil rights group, the Coordinating Council of Community Organizations, filed a Civil Rights Act Title VI complaint to the U.S. Office of Education in HEW. As a result of the complaint, federal funds were temporarily withheld from CPS as punishment for little progress on desegregation; but politics interfered with policy enforcement, and the funds were released when Chicago's powerful Mayor Daley made a personal appeal to President Johnson in New York.[51] Superintendent James Redmond took the helm of CPS after Willis retired in 1967 and responded to a federal compromise with what became known as the Redmond Plan. The ambitious plan called for educational parks and magnet schools.[52] It also discussed two small desegregation plans in which Black students would transfer from the two schools in Austin to schools on the Northwest Side and Black students would transfer to White schools in the South Shore community. The Austin plan was implemented despite vicious responses from White Northwest Side residents. Five hundred mostly Black students were transferred to the Northwest Side annually. The South Shore plan was also protested, as Black middle-class residents already had good schools and did not want their children to bear the burden of desegregation, White liberals preferred managed integration, and both groups preferred high-quality magnet programs.[53]

As the fight for school desegregation was occurring, Black and Latino students called for the fundamental educational restructuring of their high schools. Their demands included the elimination of tracking, a college preparatory education, culturally relevant curriculum, and more homework, as well as more Black and Latino teachers, counselors, and school leadership.[54] These protests produced mixed results. The Woodlawn Experimental Schools Project was another form of community control that occurred at the same time students were protesting schools. This educationally decentralized experiment came from a partnership of three typically antagonistic groups, CPS, the University of Chicago, and the Woodlawn Organization, and was funded by the Elementary and Secondary Education Act. Like community control efforts in New York, the experiment failed to truly give the local community the control it sought, and CPS resisted the changes director Barbara Sizemore wanted.[55]

Community control efforts were largely unsuccessful, as the federal government began to focus on faculty desegregation, while the state tackled student desegregation. In 1969, the federal government mandated teacher desegregation in addition to student desegregation. As the Nixon administration looked for alternatives to student desegregation, teacher desegregation seemed like an easier route. Yet it took eight years of negotiations, and a threat to withhold federal funding, for Chicago's teachers and principals to finally be desegregated in 1977. The State of Illinois pressed CPS to desegregate its students beginning in 1971. But despite exerting consistent pressure and placing the city on probationary status for several years, the state failed to force meaningful desegregation. All that came from state pressure was the Access to Excellence school desegregation plan, which provided only voluntary and choice options that did little to desegregate. According to school board data, just over sixteen thousand out of well over five hundred thousand students were desegregated as a result of state pressure and the Access to Excellence plan.[56] In 1979, the Urban League conducted a study that critiqued CPS's 1978 Access to Excellence school desegregation plan for its continued systemic failure to provide quality education to most of the city's Black and Latino students. An analysis of Advanced Placement (AP) courses found that all predominantly White schools had at least one

AP course, while fifteen predominantly Black and Latino high schools had no AP courses.[57] The Chicago Board of Education was heavily criticized for not adequately preparing students attending predominantly Black and Latino schools for college.

Because the state was unsuccessful in attaining greater desegregation, the federal government took over student desegregation negotiations in 1979. HEW demanded desegregation, but because of additional congressional restrictions to busing, the agency could not withhold funds from school districts like Chicago, which would need busing to accomplish desegregation. Consequently, the Justice Department negotiated a court-supervised consent decree with the Chicago Board of Education, compelling the city to desegregate its schools. The consent decree acknowledged the disadvantages of the racial isolation of students and called for a plan to mitigate those effects. From the consent decree, the Chicago Board of Education created a plan in 1982 that would reduce the White population of any school to less than 70 percent of the student body, and the remaining segregated schools would receive compensatory funding. School desegregation occurred as the population of Whites in CPS declined, making them only the third-largest racial or ethnic group, behind Blacks and Latinos. These demographic shifts, the spatial separation of the city, and segregated neighborhoods made large-scale school desegregation impractical. Many remaining Whites would likely flee the system if they were forced to attend predominantly Black or Latino schools. Still, the board had to desegregate all groups to the greatest possible extent.[58] After a series of revisions to the Comprehensive Student Assignment Plan, the board eventually desegregated its White schools through boundary changes and a series of school choice initiatives. However, most Black and Latino schools in the district remained segregated. By 1985, all but two White schools had less than 70 percent Whites.

Because Blacks were over 60 percent of CPS students in the early 1980s and lived in mostly segregated neighborhoods, Black Chicago Board of Education members were acutely concerned about desegregation occurring with limited Black participation. CPS's desegregation plan recognized the necessity of Black participation, stating, "Among the circumstances which may be considered in determining what constitutes 'substantial participation' may be the historical and anticipated enrollment in a particular program or school, the anticipated stability of a school, the extent to which efforts have already been made to elicit and facilitate enrollment of Black students in a program or school, policies or administrative practices that might operate to deter enrollment of Black children, and geographical or administrative factors that may limit the practicability of increasing Black participation."[59] Along with CPS's racial demographics, geography remained a great obstacle to school desegregation. North Side schools with sizable proportions of Latino and Asian students were already considered stably integrated. Since Latinos and Asians lived closer to larger numbers of Whites, particularly on the North Side, they were more likely to attend desegregated or integrated schools. Residential segregation meant most Black students lived far from White schools, and CPS's racial demographics limited the number of Black students who could get access to desegregated schools.

School Choice

School choice became an important strategy for school desegregation in Chicago. Gaining popularity in the 1970s, magnet schools and other academically enhanced programs were a voluntary way for school officials in urban environments to entice Whites to participate in school desegregation.[60] In Chicago, Black middle-class parents and White liberals advocated for magnet schools and school choice as an effective strategy, though for different reasons. Black parents and activists saw school choice as a tool to dismantle the educational limitations that came with neighborhood schools. This was particularly important since Whites who were opposed to busing argued that the neighborhood school was essential to freedom and democracy, masking their desire to maintain segregation. Liberal Whites saw school choice as a way manage integration and slow the racial demographic shifts occurring in schools and neighborhoods. Even though both groups wanted school choice, these discussions initially emerged out of a desire for equity for Black students but shifted to a focus on keeping Whites anchored in the city.[61] Each successive school desegregation plan CPS created focused on eliminating White flight. School choice became an important feature to keep Whites in CPS and was a key technique in the 1978 Access to Excellence desegregation plan. Though business groups and other community organizations contributed ideas for Access to Excellence, the current market-driven ideas about choice were not the driving force. Magnet schools and broader choices beyond the neighborhood schools had been recommended in sociologist-led reports about Chicago since the 1960s. These reports focused on effective ways to desegregate while maintaining White students in the public schools.[62]

When Chicago created its consent-decree-ordered desegregation plan in the early 1980s, it brought a myriad of school choice initiatives, boundary changes, and other desegregation techniques. The Chicago Board of Education's Comprehensive Student Assignment Plan was designed to achieve maximum desegregation through an array of programs. The plan was marketed as school choice, rather than desegregation. Superintendent Ruth Love's *Chicago Sun-Times* announcement declared that Chicagoans could pick the school of their choice. The policy framing that promoted school choice abetted the political, racial, and ethnic hostilities that desegregation and busing embodied.[63]

School choice did not end segregation or racial stratification. Instead, it provided additional options for academically talented students with savvy parents or attentive staff members who made sure they took advantage of them. As students and parents vied for limited spots at schools like Von Steuben, Whitney Young, and Bogan, it became clear how segregation stunted the educational opportunities for Black and Latino students. Those who remained segregated were mainly in schools with exceptionally high dropout rates and the perception of increasing violence.

CPS initiated three opportunities for school choice in its desegregation plan: open enrollment (students could transfer to increase desegregation at a receiving school), permissive transfers (students could transfer from certain sending and receiving schools), and Options for Knowledge (students could transfer to magnet or specialty programs). Participation in these programs was voluntary, even in instances in which busing was used. The Chicago Board of Education created two academic categories for schools: Options for Knowledge and the Effective Schools Program. Options for Knowledge schools were magnet or magnet-like programs. Effective Schools Program schools, on the other hand, were segregated schools that received compensatory funding.[64] There were twenty-nine magnet schools in the Options for Knowledge program, twenty-six of which were established in predominantly Black and Latino schools to help desegregate those schools, as well as to provide enhanced educational options for schools that would remain segregated. Of those twenty-nine magnets, twenty-seven were elementary schools. Along with magnet schools, magnet programs were established in fourteen predominantly Black and Latino schools. There were also several other specialized school programs. Scholastic academies, for instance, were designed to attract students attending private or parochial schools. These academies had citywide admission but had no achievement-based entrance requirements like magnets. Scholastic academies asserted strict codes of conduct and dress codes for students, required active parental involvement, and were academically enhanced. Other Options for Knowledge programs included metropolitan high schools, specialty programs, team schools, and community academies.[65] Study participants attended several of these schools while in elementary, junior high, or grammar school.

Choice initiatives and academically enhanced programs certainly had their critics. The Chicago Urban League and Black Chicago Board of Education members, for example, recognized the limitations of such programs. These programs tended to benefit the middle class and academically talented and did little to desegregate or provide an improved education for the segregated schools without special programs. Those who benefited were certainly fortunate, but so many others were not. A number of predominantly Black and Latino schools received magnet programs, yet according to the study *Who Benefits from Desegregation?*, "students in desegregated schools received a double benefit. They benefited from desegregation as well as from enriched academic programs, while students in segregated and racially isolated schools received the same or often less money, for the 'compensatory' educational programs." The benefits of compensatory funding were often negated because the Chicago Board of Education provided the same services for desegregated schools from other parts of its budget.[66]

Segregated boundaries were in place, though not totally entrenched. School desegregation provided students with a way to cross these boundaries. The local and national context of politics, housing, economics, and demographic shifts determined how flexible the boundaries would become. The desegregation policy framing that ushered in school choice quelled protests, interrupted segregation, and led to isolated integration. The boundaries were tested early, as study participants either integrated White schools or were bused for the purpose of desegregation. Some participants witnessed the volatility that came with boundary crossing and the ways in which issues in the larger society played out in and around their schools.

2

Busing, Boycotts, and Elementary School Experiences

In 1977, the Chicago Urban League declared, "For the past two and a half years, the White residents have actively demonstrated their resistance to an integrated community. . . . The Board of Education's voluntary school transfer plan, however, has given the White community a public platform for articulating their irrational and racist sentiments."[1] Each time the Chicago Public Schools (CPS) produced a new voluntary school desegregation plan for students, teachers, or administrators targeting the Ashburn and Chicago Lawn communities, residents initiated school boycotts to express their discontent. Women dubbed Bogan Broads organized through PTAs and other groups to ensure successful antibusing boycotts. When the 1978 Access to Excellence school desegregation plan led to the busing of relatively few Black students to Bogan High School and other schools in the area, boycotts and protests were utilized as resistance.[2] The Urban League report correctly analyzed the sentiment in the community: "Bogan area [Ashburn] parents and Chicago Lawn residents have consistently expressed their opposition to the presence of Black people either in 'their' schools or 'their' community. Their statements indicate an assumed right to White schools, White neighborhoods, White parks, White public facilities. Such an assumed right is not only inconsistent with the present day realities, it is patently illegal."[3]

Although buses transported millions of students to schools, opposition to busing for desegregation became an effective issue for Whites to "compress legitimate concerns and irrational fears into a single word whose racial neutrality lent it public legitimacy." Gregory S. Jacobs argues that Whites "were able to mask profound racial fear, resentment, and disdain with exaggerated arguments about a mode of transportation never questioned when it was used to facilitate rather than eliminate segregation." Likewise, Matthew F. Delmont contends that "with 'busing' northerners found a palatable way to oppose desegregation without appealing to the explicitly racist sentiments they preferred to associate with southerners."[4] Antibusing boycotts symbolized the desire to maintain segregation and reaffirm racial boundaries. For Black students who were bused, it meant they had to literally cross segregated boundaries and pass through protesting Whites to enter school. White residents of the Ashburn and Chicago Lawn communities, who in the past had already organized housing protests and open-housing counterprotests, regarded busing as a symbolic affront to their desires to keep Blacks out of their neighborhoods. Like protesters in the South, Boston, and other areas around the country, White Chicagoans were openly hostile, expressed racial animus, and organized to defend segregation. However, unlike other areas that had antibusing and antidesegregation protests, Ashburn and Chicago Lawn also included Latino residents who had integrated the schools and neighborhoods before busing. Latinos experienced bullying and harassment in schools and housing, like Black residents, but their struggle was largely invisible, as the Chicago Urban League and Chicago newspapers failed to report their experiences. Once Black students were bused to schools in these communities, the racial boundaries that only Latinos had once been able to cross suddenly became blurred as Latinos became more acceptable because they lived in those communities and were no longer viewed as outsiders. As White residents fought to maintain neighborhood schools, Latinos were conveniently accepted. Latino study participants' stories complicate the history of busing.

Busing as a technique for desegregation was highly controversial and even recently brought up in a 2019 Democratic primary debate between Joe Biden and Kamala Harris. Harris told the story of how busing affected her as a child to distinguish herself from Biden, who introduced policies that weakened busing. That busing is still a lightning-rod issue long after the heightened protests in the 1960s, 1970s, and 1980s signifies the divide on the issue. In Chicago, busing was mostly voluntary. The schools in Chicago Lawn and Ashburn that participants attended (Carroll, Dawes, Stevenson, Eberhart, and Marquette; map 2.1) experienced busing with the Access to Excellence desegregation plan in 1978, as well as the Comprehensive Student Assignment Plan in 1982, and both were protested. The 1982 plan led to boundary adjustments, open enrollment, permissive transfers, and teaming for these five schools.[5]

CPS also utilized school choice initiatives, which allowed students once confined to segregated neighborhood schools to attend magnet and academically

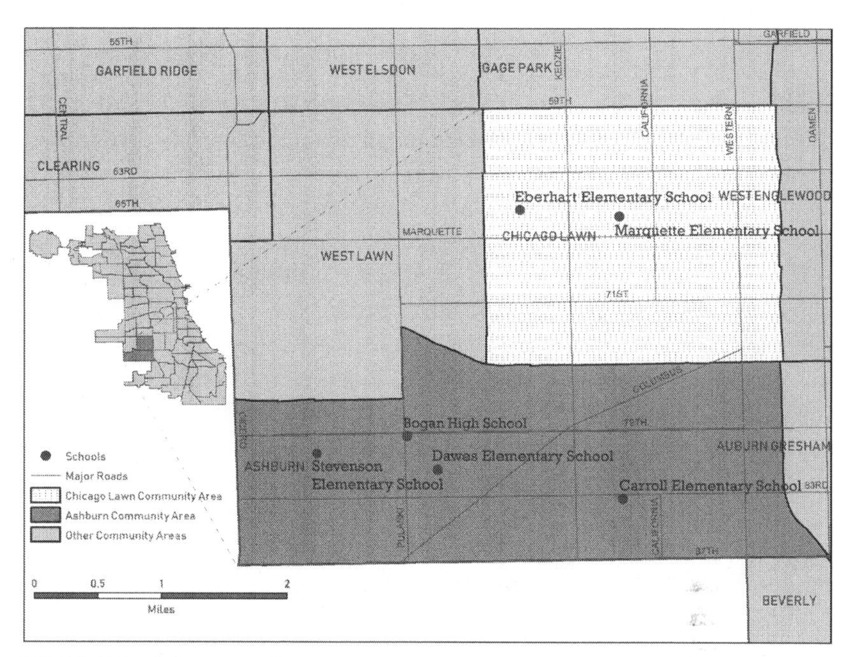

MAP 2.1 Schools in protested areas

enhanced schools through the Options for Knowledge program. This broadened the opportunities for academically talented youths. Most of the participants who attended desegregated elementary and grammar schools outside Chicago Lawn and Ashburn did not experience boycotts and busing protests. Even in instances in which community protests were absent, as Black and Latino participants crossed segregated boundaries, some became aware of the racially polarizing election of Chicago's first Black mayor, Harold Washington, and its impact on them and their classmates. School choice also revealed the effects of brain drain on neighborhood schools, as the best and brightest usually made use of choice, stripping neighborhood schools of talented students.

Study participants' experiences with integration, busing, and school choice reflect the diverse experiences of students in a variety of desegregated schools across the city. They faced challenges with crossing and blurring racial boundaries, navigating the city's racial and ethnic complexities, and combating the external political influences on their schooling. At a young age, they could not escape the world outside their schools; instead, they learned their place in the city's racial and ethnic spectrum. Even with a school desegregation plan, school segregation remained, the integration of White neighborhoods led to difficulties for racialized groups, and city politics and segregated boundaries affected students who attended desegregated schools.

Integration and Desegregation in Ashburn and Chicago Lawn

Ashburn and Chicago Lawn communities were among the most active antibusing communities in Chicago in the late 1970s and early 1980s. Other communities where desegregated schools were located had fewer racial incidents. The historical racial tensions in Chicago Lawn and Ashburn were a factor for study participants of all racial and ethnic groups who recalled witnessing or participating in antibusing school boycotts and protests. Both communities had almost equal percentages of Black and Latino (mostly Mexican American) residents in 1980—2.7 percent and 2.2 percent, respectively, in Ashburn and 10.3 percent and 10.6 percent, respectively, in Chicago Lawn. Yet while there were Latinos living in every census tract in both communities, Black residents could only move into one of five census tracts in Ashburn and three of ten census tracts in Chicago Lawn, each adjacent to Black communities.

Latino participants' experiences growing up in these communities and attending their schools highlight the ways in which segregation was preserved and challenged and boundaries were crossed and blurred. Two Latinas had memories of how discrimination played out in their communities. Lourdes attended a private Catholic school but recalled racist incidents in her neighborhood: "Where we lived in Marquette Park area, Blacks weren't allowed to come to our area. I didn't know this growing up; I had been living there since I was five, five and a half years old." According to Lourdes, the Klan marched through the neighborhood when she was a child, but her parents shielded her from those experiences. Even though Blacks had begun to make inroads into some blocks of the neighborhood, the presence of Nazi groups and the KKK dictated who was acceptable. Lourdes did not remember any personal experiences with discrimination, but Oralia did. Oralia and her family moved to Ashburn in 1977, and she recalled her early days in the neighborhood: "It was hard. It was hard. We had our windows broken." Like Blacks who moved into White neighborhoods, Latinos also endured property destruction. Oralia also had to avoid White bullies on her way to school. "I lived on Seventy-Eighth and I would walk all the way to Eighty-First Street. And, just going to school . . . it's like me and my brother would stick together. He was three years older than me." They often had to hurry to school because they knew "that certain kids would come through certain blocks" to harass them. Once they arrived at school, they "felt somewhat safe."

While fewer participants mentioned discrimination in the neighborhood, Latino participants who integrated the schools were discriminated against based on their ethnicity, language, and perceived intelligence. Julian began his Chicago public schooling experience at the segregated, Latino Gary Elementary School. Around third grade he moved to Ashburn and began attending Carroll Elementary. In the 1978–1979 school year, Carroll was 91.6 percent

White, 2.7 percent Latino, and less than 1 percent Black. Julian recalled "a little bit of tension with the students" when he first arrived at the majority-White school because he was one of few Latinos. He and his sister attended Carroll Elementary together, but Julian noted, "It was more myself that had problems with some of the kids at school. . . . They'd like chase me home [*laughter*] just 'cause they knew I was different than what they were. And you know, they would yell names at you—call you like taco and stuff like that." When the harassment continued, Julian involved his family. His aunt, who was a teacher at the time, went up to the school with his mother to speak with Julian's teacher and the principal about the problems he faced. His mother's advice was "that if they would call me taco to go ahead and turn around and call them Polish sausage. [*Laughter.*]" His mother and aunt helped the situation subside. Though he acknowledged that there was "still . . . some tension," Julian assumed that the teacher had probably spoken with other students and their families, eventually alleviating his problems.

As tension lessened for Julian, Blacks were bused to Carroll Elementary, prompting protests from the community. Julian's family helped him navigate the protests:

> I should mention . . . during my seventh and eighth grade, they forced our school to integrate. So they actually started busing African Americans into our school. . . . I didn't have a problem with it, but the neighborhood itself did. They actually sent out letters and stuff asking people to boycott the school and not to go. But my mother was big on how they treated us. . . . So she's like, "No, you're going." [*Laughter.*] 'Cause at first, the tension, it was a little bit tense. But then afterwards it seemed, parents you know, I don't want to say they were forced to get along.

Julian's mother thought it was important for her children to attend school during the boycott because she refused to contribute to other children's negative experiences. In January 1982, close to 50 percent of Carroll's students boycotted as Black students were bused to the school.[6]

Others had similar experiences as Julian. Nora attended Jungman Elementary in the Pilsen neighborhood and McCormick Elementary in Little Village in the mid-1970s, both predominantly Mexican schools and neighborhoods. Nora remembered that Jungman had more Latino teachers and offered bilingual education classes. She had done well at Jungman and McCormick, even receiving academic awards. She recalled that when her family moved into the predominantly White Ashburn community, three other Latino families were living in her neighborhood. Although she thrived at her predominantly Mexican schools, Nora faced difficulties in her new White school as one of the few Latinas. She acknowledged that there was a lot of racism at Dawes and that it took some time for her to be accepted. For example, the staff at Dawes wanted to send Nora to "the slow room," where she would have taken classes with students with Down syndrome, just because of her Spanish accent. Nora was both shocked and humiliated by the prospect of being in a special-needs class simply because she spoke Spanish. Her mom, who spoke limited English, went to Dawes to demand that her child be placed in regular classes. Nora remembered, "My mom has a really heavy accent but when she gets pissed, trust me, she learns English." Nora said, "I had always been like . . . in honors classes or receiving awards or, you know. . . . But I think that just shows the prejudice of how the school was." Tracking Mexican students into "slow classes" was not unusual. Scholars Gilbert Gonzalez and Rubén Donato discuss academic tracking as a technique used by teachers and school staff to limit school integration of Mexican American students at White schools in the Southwest. Language was often used as the reason for school segregation, and it was also used to segregate students within the same school.[7]

The federal government authorized CPS to provide bilingual education in the 1970s; however, it was mainly implemented at schools with large Spanish-speaking populations.[8] Guadalupe San Miguel argues that bilingual education is one of the most contested education policies, particularly when associated with Spanish speakers. Because bilingual education "raises questions about how one defines an American in general and the role of ethnicity in particular," it has had limited support in places where neighborhood and school integration is contested.[9] Insufficient desegregation and bilingual education plans led to CPS's repeated failure to acquire Emergency School Aid Act funds in the 1970s.[10] Dawes was among the schools that had too few non-English speakers to offer bilingual education. Nora's placement in a special education class illustrates the ways language was used to segregate her in an integrated school.

In addition to dealing with her academic misplacement in school, Nora faced harassment and bullying from students, as had Julian. Nora stated, "In grammar school there was a lot of bullying when we first got there. . . . One day they all like tried to beat me up—there was like boys and girls. . . . And yeah, so my dad found out and went up there. He just lost it, which just caused me more aggravation. But then, after awhile . . . they learned to accept [us]. It's grammar school. You're gonna get the bullying." Nora recognized the significance of her ethnicity in the bullying. "I know it was because of ethnicity. . . . It was the same crap that goes on in every grammar school. And yeah, 'cause there was always the bully who was picking on somebody." Like Julian, her parents' involvement was integral in minimizing the harassment, which teachers and school administrators ignored or were unaware of until parents brought it to their attention.

Nora acknowledged that the situation at school became "even worse because they would bus the Black kids in[to] school. So then they had this big thing at

Dawes where they were doing this boycott so people weren't sending their kids to school . . . because they didn't want [school officials] busing [Blacks] in." She noted that only Whites were boycotting and said, "It was kind of like weird because . . . I always went to segregated but primarily Latino [schools]. And then we were the minority at Dawes. But then you still had this other . . . minority."

The "other minority" attending Nora's elementary school led to the blurring of racial boundaries for Latinos. Once the target of discrimination when they crossed racial boundaries, they became more acceptable because it suited Whites who had an interest in maintaining segregation and racial stratification. Whites at Dawes wanted Nora to boycott school to keep Blacks out, but she was not allowed to do this. "Well, see it was difficult because since it took us a long time to kind of be accepted, so then all of a sudden the boycott starts and my parents are like, 'You're going to school.' So [we were] right in the middle! 'Cause then it's like . . . you were considered like a traitor if you went to school when they were boycotting." Nora's parents were unwilling to do to Black students what had been done to their child. They and other Latino parents were in solidarity with the arriving Black students, even though the racial boundary became blurred, and their children were in a more privileged position. Eighty-two percent of Nora's classmates participated in the boycott in 1982.[11]

Oralia also attended Dawes Elementary, was harassed by other children, and had to hide her native language. When she transferred to Dawes in second grade, there were fewer Latino children than there were at her previous school. She learned that she could not be herself at Dawes as she had been at her previous school. At Dawes, speaking Spanish was forbidden. Oralia recalled, "We learned real quick, we couldn't say a word of Spanish in school." On her first day of school, she went to say hi to her brother, but before she could finish saying his name, the teacher nearby told her, "'We will have none of that!' She thought I was going to say something in Spanish. . . . I was shut up before I could even say anything."

Oralia remembered the boycott at Dawes that the PTA organized. Though the discrimination she faced played a role, Oralia's aspirations for perfect attendance influenced her choice to attend school rather than participate in the boycott.

> Well I had perfect attendance from the day that I went into Dawes. . . . I'm like, I only missed two days in second grade and that was because of chicken pox, not because of me. And I was not gonna mess up my perfect attendance to boycott. They were boycotting the busing, the Black students coming. . . . And one of my friends [said], "Come on, we get a day off, we gotta boycott!" I'm like, "Do you realize what you're really saying when you're boycotting? Do you know what they're doing?" And these are our friends. They'd say, "Oh but they're just Blacks." Well I'm like, "Yeah, well I'm not like you." She was Polish.

> I said, "I'm not like you." If you're saying yes to that, you're saying the same thing to me. "But you live around here." "Still, you're saying that I'm not like you, that you don't want me here." "Oh," she thought about it. She still took the day off. But that was because of the parents. I remember being in the classroom, Mrs. [C's] classroom, room 206. And we, me and maybe three other kids being in class that day. Everybody else took the day off. They all went to Ford City, the mall.

Oralia's conversation with her Polish friend reveals how little White students thought about the impact of the boycotts on Black and Latino students, and how much their behavior mirrored their parents' and community leaders'. But it also reveals that because she lived in the neighborhood, she was suddenly acceptable.

Parents and other family members were important advocates for their children, assisting them with boundary crossing by going to the schools to demand that they be protected and treated with respect. As the racial boundaries were blurred, they rejected the new privilege their children received as a counterprotest to discrimination. The students who went to school symbolized resistance to segregation, and while many Latino students and their parents found the boycotts objectionable, many White study participants who attended predominantly White elementary schools in the Ashburn and Chicago Lawn communities participated in them. About 80 percent of students were out of school during the 1977 and 1982 boycotts. Some White study participants who attended those schools remembered that their mothers protested and kept them out of school or made them protest during boycotts.

Michelle, a White study participant, recalled participating in school desegregation protests at Dawes Elementary, the same school Oralia and Nora attended. Michelle remembered, "In the beginning, it was really difficult, because they weren't used to [desegregation]. My mom had me out marching with signs and stuff like that, protesting against it. I think the biggest thing was not knowing." Michelle's mother insisted that Michelle join the protests. As a child, Michelle was likely unaware of the racial issues, but protesting parents made it clear that the goal was to prevent Black students from being bused into their children's schools. Their protest strategy was intricately linked with neighborhood defense and residents' belief that Black residents would mean lower property values and limited freedom of association.[12] The *Chicago Tribune* reported that some parents sent a letter to President Jimmy Carter in August 1977 asking him "to honor our parental authority in recognizing our strong opposition to forced busing and race mixing programs."[13] In September 1977, the *Chicago Sun-Times* quoted a woman as saying, "I love this neighborhood, and I don't want it to change. If they force Blacks into our schools that will be the beginning of the end and we can't let it happen. We've tried to explain this in a peaceful way. I don't want anybody to get hurt, but why don't they listen." Another woman stated, "We know about Blacks. My relatives have had to move when neighborhoods changed. The kids were robbed and harassed on the streets. The houses started to deteriorate. We can't afford to move. We can't let this happen here."[14]

White Chicagoans agitated against busing and desegregation in order to maintain what they perceived as quality neighborhood (i.e., White) schools. Tracy, a White participant, grew up in Chicago Lawn and attended Eberhart Elementary School. She became aware of desegregation because of the antibusing protest activities of her mother and other neighbors. Her school was "desegregated to a certain point." Eberhart was 94.6 percent White in 1978, less than 1 percent Black, and 4 percent Latino. By 1983–1984, it was still more than 70 percent White (71.3 percent), but the percentage of Black students had grown to 15.2 percent and Latinos to 12.8 percent. Tracy acknowledged that her parents and their peers "fought very hard against desegregation in the late seventies, early eighties." She continued, "That was a big issue in Chicago, I remembered the time. No busing. That's what they were against—busing kids from school to school. They were more for neighborhood schools for neighborhood children. . . . My mom was actively involved in our schools. She even served, she had several different positions on the PTA, and she was even president for one or two terms." The defense of segregation was camouflaged as a defense of individual rights and, in this case, the rights of neighborhood schools.[15] Race was not named as the source of grievances, but most of the students being bused were Black.

Linda, another White student, attended Marquette Elementary, and she was aware of her neighborhood's history, stating, "Marquette Park was known for having their protests." She remembered her school being desegregated when she was in seventh grade. "That's when they started busing in African Americans, even though we always had [Black] teachers in class. I remember it being kind of a big deal, not to me, but [neighborhood] people picketing, the kind of stuff they did back then." Linda lived in a mixed neighborhood, and so she could not understand the commotion since she "wasn't raised that way." She also recalled a particular situation that caused protests: "I can't remember exact years. But I remember when we changed our principal. We had an African American principal, they protested then. And then they protested again when kids were going to be bused in." While she could not remember how pervasive the protests were, she remembered asking her mother why they protested a Black principal and her mom responding, "'I don't think this school should have a . . . Black principal,' which I didn't understand because we always had [Black] teachers in the school." The Black principal's presence at the White school was the result of the faculty desegregation that began in 1977, which also led to the desegregation of administrators.[16]

Linda, Michelle, and Tracy did not fully understand the reasons for the protests when they were younger. Instead, they believed that all of it was their parents' and the community's issues, not their own. Elementary students typically follow their parents' lead, even if they are unable to comprehend the larger issues at hand. Those who bullied Latino and eventually Black students were aware of those students' racialized status. How much their parents knowingly or unknowingly egged them on is difficult to know. But surely the race-based busing protests in the neighborhoods led some students to believe that they had a right to harass students from racialized groups.

Of all the Black study participants who attended desegregated elementary schools, only one recalled the agony he faced as a student. A school's location and the level of community protests determined the difficulty students faced. Stephen recalled trying times at Stevenson, the desegregated elementary school to which he was bused:

> I mean it was very different. . . . Do I think I got a better education? Yes. Racially it was terrible. . . . Second through sixth [grade] the racial [issue] was probably unbearable but you just had to deal with it. So, I mean, now that I look back, or, I probably would have preferred to stay with my own. . . . It's hard to go somewhere where people don't want you. . . . You're in and you're out. They didn't want us there. . . . They had no problem picketing. . . . They picketed the first couple weeks of every year for, like I said, the first four or five years I got bused over there. It was a[n] every-year routine. So, I mean, it was unbearable.

Stephen's experience captures some of the arguments that Black nationalists and Black Power advocates often made about school desegregation: Why would people want to go where they were unwanted, and what cost would children have to bear to desegregate schools?[17] Civil rights advocates believed the sacrifice was worth it because desegregated schools provided better resources than most segregated black schools.[18] Stephen, like others before him, was on the front line in desegregation efforts, facing difficulties in order to pave the way for other students. Stephen had to cross segregated boundaries through busing and cross protest lines to get to school. His presence, and that of other bused Black students, did not alter the racial boundaries. Instead he remained at the bottom of the expanded racial hierarchy.

Latino students' integration into White neighborhoods was initially contentious because of their racialized status. As they crossed racial boundaries, they were constantly harassed and bullied because of their ethnicity, but their difficulties only subsided when another racialized group became the target, at which point the racial boundary blurred to accept them. Consequently, when the three ethnic and racial groups attended the same schools on the Southwest

Side in the late 1970s and early 1980s, Latinos were preferred by Whites in comparison to Blacks. Though Blacks could cross the racial boundary, it was unlikely to become blurred for them as it had been for Latinos.

The fight against busing was often presented as an issue of maintaining the quality of neighborhood schools, but race and neighborhood racial change stood at the center of the fight. Whites feared that their segregated neighborhoods would become integrated once Blacks were bused into the neighborhood schools. This fear often manifested itself in violent forms of neighborhood protection, especially in Chicago Lawn's Marquette Park neighborhood, with the active presence of Nazi groups and the KKK severely increasing the difficulties for Blacks moving into the neighborhood. Groups selling and buying in transitioning neighborhoods were exploited, but Blacks were blamed for lower property values though they had no control over neighborhood disinvestment and property rates. The fears Whites had about racial transition were realized as some neighborhoods changed when more Blacks and Latinos eventually moved into those areas. The Chicago Lawn community, which was almost all White in 1970, became 77 percent White in 1980; but by 1990, only 43 percent of the community was still White. The Ashburn community did not experience as much racial transition in the ten-year period. In 1980, 94 percent of Ashburn residents were White. By 1990, it was still 83 percent White. The schools in Ashburn became more desegregated than the neighborhoods as a result of White students' withdrawal from the public schools, their attendance at magnet or specialty schools outside the community, and a reduction in the community's birthrate.[19]

Other Desegregation and School Choice Experiences

Black students who were bused to schools in Ashburn and Chicago Lawn utilized school choice through permissive transfers and open enrollment. As school choice became available with the Options for Knowledge portion of the school desegregation plan, participants of all racial and ethnic groups took advantage of it to gain access to better education. Many were bused to schools outside their communities to desegregate but did not encounter the antibusing protests. While utilizing Options for Knowledge, some Black and Latino students still ended up at predominantly Black and Latino schools, and their movement from one school to another symbolized the brain drain of top students from neighborhood schools. Additionally, the city's racial politics and racial and ethnic conflicts affected students as they crossed segregated boundaries to attend desegregated schools. Most study participants were in grammar school (K–8) or junior high (7–8) when Harold Washington became the first Black mayor of Chicago in 1983. Washington's election exacerbated the deep racial divisions in an already racially segregated city.

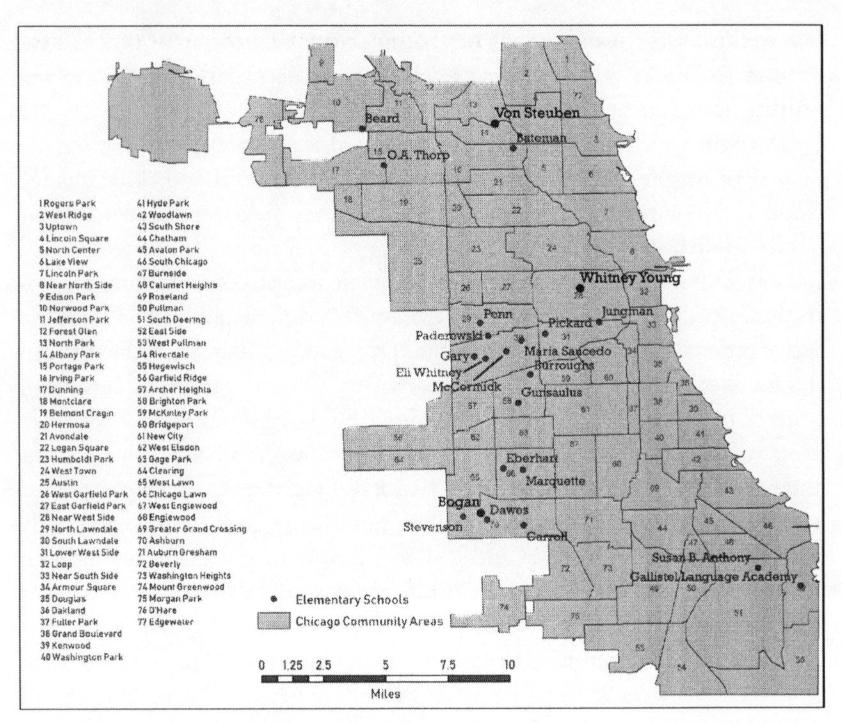

MAP 2.2 Elementary schools discussed

The racial tension from the election made its way to Chicago's schools. Study participants Eve and Keith both recalled incidents resulting from Washington's election. Eve, a Black participant, initially attended the 97 percent Black Susan B. Anthony Elementary School. In junior high, she attended the desegregated magnet school Gallistel Language Academy in the overwhelmingly White East Side community (map 2.2).[20] Her older sister attended the predominantly White Washington High School, also in that area. By 1983, Gallistel had become 48.6 percent White, 21.4 percent Black, and 29.2 percent Latino. Eve recalls that although the school was desegregated, "racism was really rampant there for me. I would see it. It was on a side of town that was predominantly White. There were always several racial incidents." Eve remembered her sister telling stories about constantly being chased when she went to catch the bus home. When Washington won the mayoral race, Eve recalled her interaction with a crossing guard: "At that point I'm not really all that into politics—I knew about it. I was like, 'Yeah, this is a big moment for us,' but the crossing guard was like, 'Yeah, you Negroes are happy now! You Negroes are happy now!' And I was like, 'O-kay.' And it just, you know, I'd hear it all the time."

Another student remembered Washington's election being an important racial moment for the city. Keith, who is half Mexican and half White, was bused with Black students to a White school. He noted how strange it was, first, to be bused with Black children and, second, to be racially unidentifiable to his peers:

> The school that they bused me to was all White kids and Black kids. Then it was very confusing when my brother and I came off the bus because we were the only non-Black kids on the bus. . . . When you were on the school bus, you left the classroom early so you would get on the bus. And so it was just kind of like, "Oh, you take the bus?" Because . . . 95 percent of the kids that came on the bus were Black. Again, because my brother and I . . . didn't have an accent, [and] we don't [have] Hispanic names . . . I think it was [confusing]. Kind of like, "Oh really, you come on the bus? Kids like you come on the bus?" And looking back on it, the only distinction that there would have been for the kids on the bus would have to be that they were Black and the other kids were not.

Keith also remembered when White neighborhood kids came to the playground to fight Black students. The fight left an indelible mark on him because it was the first time he had witnessed racial hatred.

> Some neighborhood kids that did not go to our school got in a fight with a bunch of the Black kids that did go to our school. And so we were on lockdown for like a week. And, I think, it had to be, it had to be right around time that Harold Washington was running for mayor. . . . That was totally the first time in my entire life that I kind of saw firsthand that White people and Black people did not necessarily get along.
>
> And it was really weird because it was the older neighborhood kids and the older grammar school kids. . . . And I don't remember exactly what day it was, but I clearly remember being on the playground and all of a sudden it just seemed, in my brain, it looked kind of like a game of football. Except they weren't playing football, they were beating each other up. So they called everybody off the playground, the police came and for the next week we had cops making sure that when like the kids were getting off the buses and stuff like that. I don't know how, if that was common or uncommon at that particular time in Chicago history.

Washington's election shifted White, Democratic Party machine control to a coalition of Blacks, Latinos, and liberal Whites. The White neighborhood youths who fought Black students at Keith's school represented a violent manifestation of the political and racial tensions that permeated the city. For Keith, witnessing the violence cemented his understanding that "White people and Black people did not personally get along," and showed him that he stood somewhere outside that experience. He was of mixed race/ethnicity and did not necessarily belong strictly to one category or the other, but he understood that the fight did not involve him.

Keith's older brother Kenneth did not mention the fight but recalled that they were "bused-in Latinos." The brothers spoke of attending Bateman Elementary, a more multiethnic elementary school, before being bused. Bateman was 48.3 percent White, 32.1 percent Latino, and 18.5 percent Asian in 1983 and was considered stably integrated. Although Bateman was less than 1 percent Black, a significant number of children of different ethnicities attended. Their mother wanted them to attend a better school, and so she signed them up to attend O. A. Thorp Elementary, a highly regarded, Options for Knowledge school that was 45.7 percent White, 46.1 percent Black, 5.4 percent Latino, and 2.2 percent Asian. Keith and Kenneth were bused there with Black students whose parents also wanted a better education for their children. O. A. Thorp, located in the Dunning community, was a scholastic academy, a school CPS designed to increase desegregation, as well as appeal to private school students.[21]

Karen was one of the few White participants bused to elementary school for desegregation. She lived on Chicago's North Side, and her experience was different from that of White students who grew up on the South Side in neighborhoods that protested desegregation and busing. Karen attended her neighborhood school, Bateman Elementary, until fourth grade, then transferred to Beard Elementary, another Options for Knowledge school. As it was for many other students who participated in school desegregation in Chicago, the opportunity to get a better education was Karen's driving force. Several desegregated schools offered enhanced or magnet curriculum to draw students from around the city. Karen recalled that teachers from her school opposed the transfer of the brightest students. She stated, "They would like pluck the smart kids out and then pop them in this school. . . . I remember my home school teachers being like very against it because they didn't want the one or two kids that were getting As to leave the school." The educational opportunities these academically enhanced schools provided did as Karen's teacher predicted—drained some of the best from neighborhood schools. Beard Elementary, though it was in a White middle-class neighborhood, attracted students from all over the city. Beard was 70 percent White until it became a magnet school in 1978.[22] In 1983, it was 47 percent White, 28.4 percent Black, 14.4 percent Latino, and 9.8 percent Asian.

Beard only educated students through the sixth grade, so Karen had the option to attend what Chicago called an upper grade center (junior high), which were in prestigious high schools on the South Side. However, the commute to Beard was too much for her. Karen recalled,

> But I was kind of tired. I mean I was only twelve years old and I was just kind of tired of it. Like, I got up for school an hour earlier than my brother and sister

> and I got home an hour later. 'Cause you know, I didn't get home 'til four o'clock whereas my brother and sister were home at like five after three. I didn't want to go even farther for seventh and eighth grade, so I went back to like my home school. But by that time, I guess . . . the landscape of my home school had changed a little. Like the neighborhood got a lot more Hispanic. And there were always Asians in the neighborhood but there was a mix of Puerto Rican and Mexican kids.

Karen remembered the long commute and other sacrifices that she and other students made to attend desegregated schools. Indeed, Black and Latino students were far more likely than Whites to make sacrifices in order to attend desegregated schools. Yet she could easily choose to go back to her original school and still be in an integrated space.

Jennifer, another White student, remembered her school Gunsaulus being desegregated when she was in sixth grade. Gunsaulus was a scholastic academy that was 85 percent White in 1978, and the rest of the population was Latino. In 1983, the school was 49.3 percent White, 21.9 percent Black, and 27.7 percent Latino. Unlike the other students in Ashburn and Chicago Lawn, Jennifer never witnessed protests. Her biggest concern was practical: losing the privilege of going home for lunch. "My mom never said anything bad. There was no PTA meetings or anything. . . . But I don't remember anybody at home saying anything bad." In the 1980s, desegregation was a peaceful process in many areas of the city. Yet Black and Latino students still experienced discrimination, even in areas where there were no community protests.

Three Latinos who grew up outside Ashburn and Chicago Lawn (Sirena, Maria, and Paul) integrated White neighborhoods or were bused to other schools for enhanced academic programs. Sirena, for example, transferred from one predominantly White elementary school to another when her family moved. She spent her early years in the Brighton Park neighborhood and attended Burroughs Elementary School. Brighton Park was 91.7 percent White in 1980 and 0.1 percent Black.[23] Sirena enjoyed her time in elementary school. Although her school was predominantly White and she was Latina, she said, "I remember there was a time where . . . they were going to start busing in [African American and Hispanic] students from other schools." A change in Burroughs' attendance area and Burroughs' teaming up with Paderewski Elementary School (99.6 percent Black) brought more Black students to desegregate Burroughs.[24] Burroughs went from 75.3 percent White and 23.8 percent Latino in 1978 to 48 percent White, 17.8 percent Black, and 33.7 percent Latino in 1983.

Sirena recalled the reactions of the community to busing students to her school. "What I can remember was it was a big shock, because, I think a lot of people just naturally assumed that you start bringing other people in, you know what, property values goes down or just that typical thinking of people. . . .

I remember it being kind of a big deal." Sirena's parents were open and did not object to busing, but "it was going to be a shock to a lot of people. But the teachers didn't treat us any differently. There was like no favoritism or anything like that." As far Sirena was concerned, it was exciting to have new students enter her small school, and she believed they got along well. Unlike in Ashburn and Chicago Lawn, even if parents objected to busing, they did not openly organize against it, making the boundary crossing less difficult for bused Black students.

Maria was the only study participant bused to a predominantly Black school. She was from Little Village, a predominantly Mexican American neighborhood, where she attended the segregated Eli Whitney Elementary School. Whitney was close to 87 percent Latino in 1978 but was 94 percent Latino by 1983. In the sixth grade, recruiters came to Whitney and announced that Penn had a new program. Penn was in the North Lawndale community, was one of the first schools to have a magnet computer program, and was interested in diversifying its student body.[25] In 1978, Penn was 95.4 percent Black, 3 percent Latino, and 1.6 percent White. In 1983, the school was 90 percent Black but recruited enough Latino students to increase that population to 8.8 percent. Maria saw attending Penn as a great opportunity. "If you took these computer classes and were accepted to the school, then it gives you a leg up when you go to high school because not that many schools had computers." Recognizing her opportunity to attend a school with innovative programming, Maria consulted her teachers when making her decision. Her teachers assured her that if she attended Penn and disliked the experience, she could always return to Whitney. Maria knew that computers would become an important aspect of society and wanted to be on the cutting edge of this developing technology.

The program itself was attractive, but Maria did not foresee the discrimination and harassment she would face from Black students. She thought maybe they were harassed because they were the first Latinos to attend the school, but there were some Latino students at the school before her arrival. As an adult she rationalized what occurred.

> We had it rough. . . . They didn't like the fact that we would go to their school. And, who knows, maybe because they've had it bad in the past, they kind of wanted to bring the bad to us so we could understand how they felt. We don't know. . . . We would get on the bus, they'd take us there, and then at first, they would just let us off. You had to wait [outside] until the doors opened like all the schools. And at that point they start throwing rocks at you, they were fighting with you. And you're just standing there like, "What is going on?"

According to Maria, the number of Latino students who transferred to Penn shrank because of the continued harassment. "Little by little people started not wanting to deal with it and not wanting to go anymore. But the computers was actually a good part of it. . . . I wasn't going to see a computer at my house at all. . . . The only bad effect was that the kids were roughing you before you went and after. . . . Soon as you get out the [school] door you were running to that bus because you were afraid." Teachers failed to act when they were informed of the harassment, or they assumed students would stop the harassment on their own. However, Latino students got fed up and returned to their neighborhood schools. Only when school leaders noticed the drop in Latino students did they finally respond. A teacher was then assigned to walk the students from the bus into the school.

Maria's story shows an instance of one racialized group harassing and bullying another and demonstrates how segregation made it less likely that students would automatically adjust to students from different racial and ethnic groups who were bused in. Though Latinos and Blacks were harassed by Whites in many schools, there were some schools in which Black and Latino students harassed each other. Students bullied those whom they considered ethnically or racially different. The difference between these communities and the Ashburn and Chicago Lawn communities was that in the latter, White parents and other adults rallied against busing in ways that Black adults did not when Maria attended Penn.

Like Maria, Paul changed schools because of a pilot program involving computers. Paul is half Puerto Rican and half White. He initially attended Pickard Elementary, which was overwhelmingly Latino (83.8 percent in 1978 and 91.8 in 1983). While at Pickard, he was in accelerated reading and math classes. He eventually attended Maria Saucedo Magnet School; both schools were in Little Village. Paul stated, "Maria Saucedo was a novelty at the time because it was the pilot program. Plus . . . most of the kids were like high honor kids from all the other areas where they were coming, or advanced or excelled in a certain area . . . and they were one of the first public schools to have computers." Paul did not face the harassment Maria experienced because he moved from a school with 91.8 percent Latinos to one with 91.7 percent Latinos. Both he and Maria used the Options for Knowledge program to move from one segregated school to another. The difference was that their new schools had enhanced academic programs.

A few other participants attended either Von Steuben or Whitney Young for seventh and eighth grade. Those schools had upper grade centers (junior high schools) in the same buildings. Early in their schooling, many students attended elementary schools that were predominantly one race; however, as Access to Excellence was introduced in 1978, and the consent decree and subsequent Comprehensive Student Assignment Plan further desegregated schools after 1980, many students were able to take advantage of school choices available to them, such as magnets, scholastic academies, team schools, and other special programs. Participants attended mostly desegregated grammar schools.

Despite desegregation efforts, most Chicago students remained in segregated schools and many Black and Latino participants still attended segregated schools at some point in their academic careers. According to CPS standards, stably desegregated schools (by policy) and stably integrated schools (by housing) were schools with fewer than 70 percent of one race. Out of the forty-seven public elementary schools that participants mentioned attending, thirty-five schools were segregated in 1978, but only twenty elementary schools remained segregated in 1983. Only one school remained over 70 percent White, down from seventeen in 1978. The number of racially identifiable Black schools (eleven) remained the same, and the racially identifiable Latino schools increased by one school (seven schools to eight) because of increased numbers of Latinos in the city.[26] By 1985, approximately 52 percent of CPS's 596 schools were still segregated (250 Black, 64 Latino).[27]

Chicago's school desegregation policy became an important disruption to segregation, though heavily contested when busing was used as the method to achieve it. Chicago Lawn and Ashburn were not unique in terms of the resistance to busing. That was a national phenomenon. What distinguishes those communities are the multiethnic demographics, which resulted in a racial hierarchy. Latinos integrated White neighborhoods, but Blacks were bused to desegregate. Both groups experienced racial boundaries, but those boundaries were blurred for Latinos when Blacks were bused in. The very fact that Latinos were already allowed to move into highly contested White neighborhoods meant that their skin color gave them an advantage over Blacks. Yet racial boundaries still existed for them, as they were harassed and bullied in both their schools and neighborhoods. The blurring of the boundary was allowed so Whites could continue to have an advantage over both groups.

Even in communities where busing was not protested, segregated boundaries remained. Harold Washington's election and the racial and ethnic conflicts were still reminders of the difficulties of disrupting segregation. In the end, whether communities supported desegregation was irrelevant. Busing desegregated schools in segregated communities by providing a way for students to participate in boundary crossing. These disruptions of various communities across the city were only momentary, as communities and a significant number of schools remained largely segregated. Nonetheless, school desegregation and policies like school choice led to more students choosing to attend schools outside their segregated communities.

3

"The World Is Bigger Than Just My Local Community"

Choosing and Traveling to High Schools

In her recent autobiography *Becoming*, Michelle Obama recalls her and her family's good fortune that her test scores gave her access to Whitney Young High School, the first magnet high school in the city. Because of their belief in the power of education, her parents had paid for her older brother, Craig, to attend Mount Carmel, a Catholic school; but her attendance at Whitney Young was a financial relief for the family. The options for good public high schools were limited, and while her family's financial burden was reduced, her personal sacrifice was still great. Obama describes her long commute in the late 1970s and early 1980s: "Chicago, I was learning, was a much bigger city than I'd ever imagined it to be. There was a revelation formed in part over the three hours I now logged daily on the bus, boarding at Seventy-Fifth Street and chuffing through a maze of local shops, often forced to stand because it was too crowded to find a seat." After a while, she and her friend devised a plan to take a bus fifteen minutes earlier in the wrong direction so they could catch their regular bus at an earlier stop, find a seat, and spend the ride studying or chatting. Like participants of this study, Obama found that her trip to school on multiple buses from the South Side to the West Side gave her a broader view of the city's neighborhoods, the differences between wealth and poverty, and the hustle and bustle of the professionals' world. As she traveled through multiple neighborhoods, it opened the world beyond her working-class neighborhood. However, she also arrived home late from school in the evenings and she spent far less time with her parents.[1]

Whitney Young High School, located in the Near West Side community, opened its doors in 1975 with the intention of being integrated. The superintendent at the time, James Redmond, wanted the school to bring "together students from a wide range of racial and ethnic backgrounds who have diverse academic abilities, interests and talents." The school was designed with three buildings to accommodate academics, physical education, and a performing arts center, as well as to have magnet programs in "physical sciences, medical sciences, and performing arts in addition to the innovative and extensive program for the hearing impaired."[2] It was named for the Black National Urban League executive director Whitney Young, who served as an adviser to Presidents John F. Kennedy, Lyndon B. Johnson, and Richard Nixon and was a 1968 recipient of the Medal of Freedom.[3] There were initial concerns about whether the school would be elitist or whether it would admit students from the West Side communities that surrounded the school. Early in its history, Whitney Young accepted students with various levels of ability, giving some preference to students from the surrounding community.[4] Beginning in 1980, the criteria for acceptance were based on high academic ability, and the school maintained a college prep curriculum for its students, moving from its modest beginnings to becoming one of the city's top schools. In addition to a high school, Whitney Young had an academic center for seventh- and eighth-grade students.[5] Though predominantly Black from its inception, Whitney Young also had a sizable number of White, Latino, and Asian students (table 3.1).

Unlike Whitney Young, which was a relatively new school, Von Steuben High School opened its doors as a junior high school in 1930 and was named after a Prussian officer, Baron Frederick Wilhelm Von Steuben, who trained American troops for the Revolutionary War.[6] Built in the Albany Park community on Chicago's North Side and located less than two miles south of the city's northern border, the school was called Von Steuben Senior High from 1933 to 1982, with part of the school reserved for elementary students. The school was remodeled twice, first in the early 1960s with funds from the 1958 National Defense Education Act, which provided an additional science lab. The act focused on science—along with math and foreign languages—to make the United States more competitive with the Soviet Union, which had launched the rocket Sputnik in 1957. The second major renovation included improvements to the physical plant, as well as new lockers, lights, and flooring.[7] The school changed its name to Von Steuben Metropolitan Science Center in 1982

Table 3.1
Whitney Young School Demographics (%)

	1977–1978	1980–1981	1985–1986	1986–1987	1987–1988	1988–1989	1989–1990	1990–1991
White	27.4	24.2	16.2	14.6	15.0	15.2	12.9	11.8
Black	53.5	57.2	62.6	64.1	63.9	64.1	65.1	67.2
Hispanic	13.6	13.1	13.7	13.0	13.4	12.9	13.8	13.2
Asian	—	—	7.0	—	—	7.6	8.1	7.6
Other[a]	5.4	5.4	0.6	8.4	7.8	—	—	—

SOURCES: Data for tables 3.1, 3.2, and 3.3 come from Chicago Public Schools, "Racial/Ethnic Survey: Students as of October 1977"; Chicago Public Schools, "Racial/Ethnic Survey: Students as of October 31, 1980"; Chicago Public Schools, "Racial/Ethnic Survey: Students as of October 31, 1985"; Chicago Public Schools, "Racial/Ethnic Survey: Students as of October 31, 1986"; Chicago Public Schools, "Racial/Ethnic Survey: Students as of October 31, 1987"; Chicago Public Schools, "Racial/Ethnic Survey: Students as of October 31, 1988"; Chicago Public Schools, "Racial/Ethnic Survey: Students as of October 31, 1989"; and Chicago Public Schools, "Racial/Ethnic Survey: Students as of October 31, 1990, Chicago Board of Education Archives.
[a]Asians and American Indians were considered *other* before 1988.

Table 3.2
Von Steuben School Demographics (%)

	1977–1978	1980–1981	1985–1986	1986–1987	1987–1988	1988–1989	1989–1990	1990–1991
White	58.9	48.6	37.0	34.2	33.3	31.5	32.0	32.4
Black	11.1	12.4	29.1	31.3	32.2	29.0	27.7	24.8
Hispanic	18.0	22.0	15.0	16.1	18.2	20.9	20.8	21.4
Asian	—	—	18.8	—	—	18.5	19.3	21.1
Other[a]	12.0	17.0	0.1	18.4	16.4	—	—	—

[a]Asians and American Indians were considered *other* before 1988.

as part of the desegregation plan created from the consent decree. It was an Options for Knowledge school, which meant it drew students from around the city and had an academically enhanced curriculum. Typically, 350 freshmen interested in math and science were admitted each year from over one hundred elementary schools. A 1990 self-study noted, "The freshman class is determined by lottery to ensure integration,"[8] though the school had been integrated since the 1960s and became increasingly desegregated as a result of Access to Excellence in 1978 and the consent decree in 1980 (table 3.2).

Bogan High School is on the South Side of Chicago in the Ashburn community. Named for former Chicago superintendent William J. Bogan, the school opened in 1959. When desegregation through permissive transfer plans was proposed in the mid-1960s, protests emerged, leading to Bogan's being

Table 3.3
Bogan School Demographics (%)

	1977–1978	1980–1981	1985–1986	1986–1987	1987–1988	1988–1989	1989–1990	1990–1991
White	98.2	95.0	43.9	41.9	42.1	39.1	38.1	35.2
Black	0.0	0.8	29.1	27.4	28.7	31.1	29.1	27.8
Hispanic	1.2	3.7	21.1	22.7	19.0	20.5	23.2	26.2
Asian	—	—	5.9	—	—	9.2	9.5	10.6
Other[a]	0.6	0.5	0.1	8.1	10.1	—	—	—

[a]Asians and American Indians were considered *other* before 1988.

taken off the list of potential schools to which Blacks could transfer. Additional attempts to desegregate Bogan occurred with a second permissive transfer plan in 1977 and the Access to Excellence plan in 1978, but very little desegregation occurred until after the consent decree in 1980. Beginning in the 1981 school year, Bogan was clearly desegregated (table 3.3). It was the only school of the three that had protests and boycotts against busing of students and the desegregation of teachers. Hundreds of students boycotted several times in the 1970s and 1980s.[9] The Ashburn community was among the most resistant to desegregation in the city. Unlike the other two schools, Bogan had a diverse curricular focus, as it included a variety of vocational options. Part of the school's purpose was to prepare its students for the work world. Students received career training in business classes and were given on-the-job training in office work, computer classes, and industrial arts classes like drafting, woodshop, architectural design, and television broadcasting.[10] Despite its vocational focus, the school still offered college prep courses.

In the mid-1980s, Von Steuben, Whitney Young, and Bogan were among the best schools in the city and had curricular advantages over many neighborhood high schools. Chicago school desegregation broadened the educational opportunities available to students fortunate enough to be chosen for academically enhanced high schools. While some study participants made use of school choice in elementary school, the rest waited until high school to branch out beyond their neighborhood schools. In many cases, predominantly Black and Latino high schools and schools for South Side Whites had over 40 percent dropout rates.[11] Participants avoided these schools because they were dropout factories and were viewed as unsafe because of fighting and gang activity. These educational choices exposed the limited opportunities that existed for thousands of students seeking high-quality education in Chicago Public Schools (CPS). The high dropout rates at the neighborhood schools reflected the difficulties of racial isolation, which were caused by segregation and the festering inequalities that existed between Black and White schools and Latino and

White schools, and between schools for the working class and those that catered to the middle class. Despite the noble fights to improve the quality of Chicago's Black and Latino schooling throughout the twentieth century, many of the schools remained spaces that perpetuated inequality.[12]

By the time study participants entered high school, much of the controversy around busing had dissipated. High school students were not bused to schools like elementary students. Instead, they used the Chicago Transit Authority (CTA) public transportation. Their selection of a high school was seen more as a result of school choice than of desegregation, and since they were not bused, the symbol often targeted for resistance was removed. The spatial separation of the city and the broad options students had for high school made traditional busing expensive and ineffective. It was also easier to justify high school students using the CTA than young elementary students using it.

Attending desegregated schools still came at a cost. The distance between these students' homes and the desegregated schools meant that some participants, like Michelle Obama before them, spent many hours on CTA buses and "L" (elevated) trains daily. Much of the literature on the impact of school desegregation notes the sacrifices Black students made in order to attend desegregated schools; namely, they traveled farther, they were bused to White schools. Additionally, Black schools were closed, downgraded, or reshaped to make Whites feel comfortable.[13] Opponents and critics of desegregation point to these sacrifices largely because White students and families often avoided making these same sacrifices, as they maintained much of their privilege when desegregation was implemented.

Joyce Hughes, a Black member of the Chicago Board of Education, best articulated concerns with the city's desegregation plan as it related to the sacrifices Black and Latino students would have to make. First, she worried that the burden of desegregation was placed primarily on Black and Latino students, as few plans were made for Whites to desegregate Black and Latino schools.[14] Second, she was concerned that there would be a brain drain from Black schools, as the best and brightest would leave neighborhood high schools to attend more selective schools. Finally, higher-income parents would also be better prepared than others to navigate the process for procuring spots at top schools.[15] These fears were substantiated, as the Black and Latino study participants often traveled the farthest and were among the highest performing at the grammar schools they departed. Their movement to better schools further eroded the reputations of their neighborhood schools. As an additional sacrifice, some participants were estranged from neighborhood peers, as some neighbors viewed their attendance at desegregated schools as "acting white." Boundary crossing meant both leaving one's segregated neighborhood to attend school in another neighborhood and having to navigate the perceptions of being a traitor while doing so.

Choosing Schools

Chicago's Comprehensive Student Assignment Plan gave students the choice to either apply to schools to increase desegregation or participate in Options for Knowledge—a program that included schools with enhanced academic programs like magnet schools. School choice became available through Options for Knowledge programs, open enrollment, and permissive transfers. Desegregation was rarely mentioned as the reason study participants chose Von Steuben, Bogan, or Whitney Young. The major factors for why participants chose the schools they attended were negative perceptions of neighborhood school environments, recruitment efforts from individual schools and the district, family influence, and school curriculum. Other reasons included attendance at the school's junior high (academic center or upper grade center), limited financial burden compared with private schools, and convenience of the school in terms of location and size. Black and Latino students were more likely to be recruited to Von Steuben and Bogan, while White North Side students who attended Von Steuben were more likely to discuss convenience as the reason for their school choices. North Side Whites experienced the most privilege in making their school selections; they never mentioned safety issues as a concern when making a school choice in the ways that Blacks, Latinos, and South Side Whites did. In the end, regardless of the available school choices, the schools still chose students based on standardized test scores, racial or ethnic quotas, or space availability.[16] Though schools made the ultimate choice of who could attend, students, with the assistance of their families or school staff, had to apply in order to be considered.

School Selectivity and Demographic Data

Participants' school choices were primarily based on their perceptions of individual schools. Most Black and Latino participants who attended the three schools, as well as White Bogan participants, had negative perceptions of their neighborhood schools and believed that those schools would have severely limited their educational opportunities had they attended. However, White students who attended Von Steuben or came from the North Side of the city were less pessimistic about their schooling options. Safety concerns related to gangs and fighting, low expectations of the teachers, poor reputations, nonacademic focus of students, and high dropout rates were cited as reasons that participants wanted to avoid their neighborhood schools. These are considered the push factors, as students would only consider leaving a neighborhood school and crossing segregated boundaries if their neighborhood schools failed to provide quality education. The pull factors were better-quality schools based on curriculum, graduation rates, and Options for Knowledge eligibility.

CPS recorded test scores and dropout rates as two important indicators of school quality. In a report on the dropout profile, CPS detailed students' Iowa Test of Basic Skills eighth-grade reading test scores and dropout rates for the class of 1988. Regardless of testing critiques, test scores, at the very least, demonstrate school selectivity. Schools that accepted students with higher test scores were more selective than schools that accepted students with lower test scores. CPS grouped students by scores into stanine 1 (lowest) through stanine 6+ (highest).[17] Stanine 6+ represents each school's level of selectivity. The district average for stanine 6+ was 25.6 percent. The stanine 6+ for the schools that participants attended are as follows: Bogan, 39.2 percent; Von Steuben, 64.2 percent; and Whitney Young, 66 percent. Only two other schools in CPS had a stanine 6+ over 60 percent (Lane Technical, 69.5 percent; and Lindblom, 64.8 percent). Based on the test scores, Von Steuben and Whitney Young were far more selective schools than Bogan, but Bogan was well above the city average.

Dropout rates were just as important a factor for assessing school quality. Dropout rates were calculated for the class of 1988 based on the number of students who entered schools in 1984 and dropped out before graduation in 1988, not including those who transferred out of the district or were still attending school. The cohort dropout rate was 40.1 percent, and CPS's overall dropout rate was 40 percent.[18] Over the course of the study, participants mentioned thirty schools as potential options for high school (table 3.4). Of those, nearly half (fourteen) had over 40 percent dropout rates, six more had dropout rates over 30 percent, and an additional four had dropout rates over 20 percent. Of the schools that participants attended, Bogan's dropout rate was 19.6 percent, Von Steuben's was 11.5 percent, and Whitney Young had the lowest with 8 percent. The dropout rates, combined with school selectivity as determined by test scores, provide some evidence for why participants discussed their neighborhood schools negatively.[19]

Schools were organized in a way that allowed only a few students to benefit from a college preparatory education. Middle- and upper-class students of all races had more access to high-quality schools, and when they were not chosen for those schools, they could more likely afford private schools. Working-class families like Michelle Obama's also made sacrifices for their children's education when they could afford it. Racialized students and those of poorer backgrounds were largely left out of the school choice opportunities that desegregation brought. Schools like Whitney Young and Von Steuben clearly fulfilled their academic missions by choosing from among the best students in the city and producing a high number of college-ready graduates. Most other schools were far less likely to prepare students for college, thus restricting social mobility and reproducing inequality.

Table 3.4
High School Demographics and Selectivity

School	1988 dropout rate (%)	1984 stanine 6+ (%)	1984 number of students	White students (%)	Black students (%)	Latino students (%)	Asian students (%)
Austin	69.5	9.0	1,584	0.0	99.7	0.2	0.0
Bogan	**19.6**	**39.2**	**2,165**	**44.8**	**29.6**	**22.2**	**3.1**
Calumet	48.5	13.7	1,428	0.1	99.9	0.0	0.0
Chicago Vocational	34.1	29.5	4,095	0.0	99.9	0.0	0.0
Clemente	58.3	12.9	3,189	4.8	15.4	76.7	2.1
Curie	23.7	32.4	3,248	38.4	25.2	32.8	3.5
Farragut	58.5	14.8	2,181	0.7	50.8	48.4	0.0
Gage Park	45.1	20.9	1,289	38.2	46.5	14.4	0.5
Harlan	38.9	16.1	1,423	0.0	100.0	0.0	0.0
Hubbard	45.5	21.0	1,037	50.1	33.1	16.2	0.5
Hyde Park	31.8	43.9	2,780	0.0	99.8	0.2	0.0
Juarez	50.1	21.1	1,900	3.3	1.6	94.9	0.1
Kelly	64.8	15.6	1,685	52.3	1.1	46.1	0.2
Kennedy	31.8	27.2	1,338	51.6	37.4	10.8	0.3
Kenwood	15.2	54.0	2,084	21.0	73.9	2.2	2.9
Lake View	46.9	23.3	1,123	25.6	21.2	48.1	4.7
Lane Tech	12.0	69.5	4,603	51.3	15.2	17.3	15.9
Lincoln Park	28.9	48.3	1,491	36.9	46.6	12.2	5.4
Lindblom	14.4	64.8	2,172	0.0	99.2	0.0	0.8
Marshall	47.5	9.9	1,825	0.0	100.0	0.0	0.0
Prosser	23.1	35.3	1,337	32.1	32.2	1.1	34.5
Roosevelt	50.7	21.5	1,764	44.1	8.7	27.6	19.0
Schurz	49.4	16.0	3,249	36.6	15.2	45.0	2.6
Simeon	23.3	28.7	1,834	0.0	100.0	0.0	0.0
South Shore	55.7	8.0	1,820	0.1	99.9	0.0	0.0
Steinmetz	36.6	29.8	2,167	46.2	36.3	14.7	1.3
Tilden	55.9	8.0	1,576	7.7	77.0	15.1	0.1
Von Steuben	**11.5**	**64.2**	**1,048**	**38.0**	**26.0**	**15.3**	**20.5**
Westinghouse	32.2	16.1	1,560	0.0	99.7	0.0	0.0
Whitney Young	**8.0**	**66.0**	**2,497**	**17.4**	**61.2**	**13.5**	**7.5**

SOURCES: Chicago Public Schools, "Chicago Public High School Dropout Profile: A Report on the Class of 1988," 1990, Box Dept. of Research, Evaluation and Planning, School Dropouts, Chicago Board of Education Archives; Chicago Public Schools, "Racial/Ethnic Survey: Students as of October 31, 1984," Box Dept. of Research, Evaluation and Planning, Racial Ethnic Survey: Students, 1969–1995, Chicago Board of Education Archives.

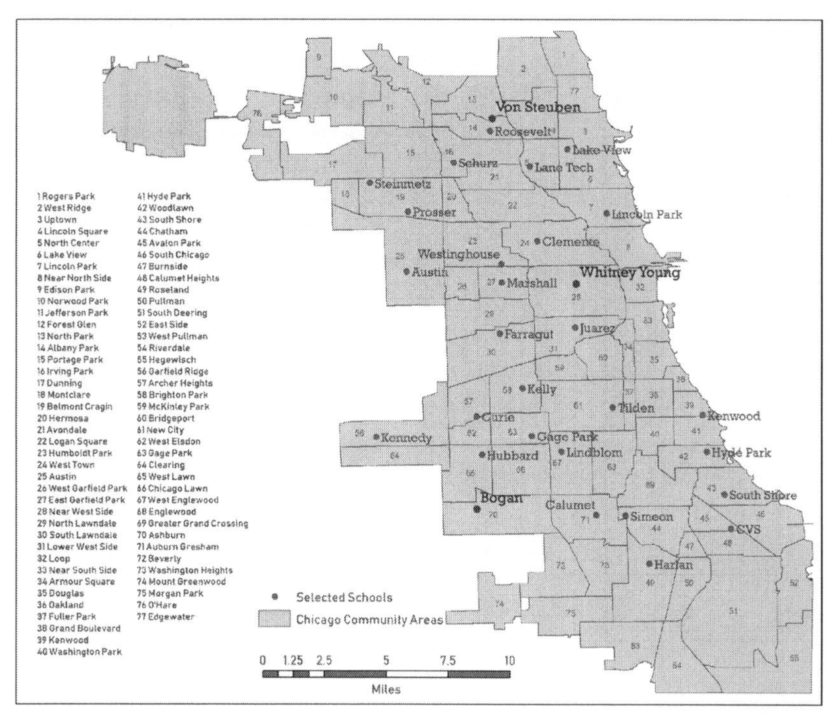

MAP 3.1 Participants' high school options

Perceived Negative School Environments: Participant Experiences

Participants' views of their neighborhood schools reveal one of their primary reasons for taking part in school desegregation through school choice. If students were satisfied with their neighborhood schools, they were less inclined to choose schools farther away from home, unless the new school's curricular focus was particularly appealing. Of all the schools mentioned, participants were unified in their negative image of Farragut. Words like *stuck*, *bottom*, and *low* were used to describe the atmosphere. Located on the West Side of Chicago in the South Lawndale community (later renamed Little Village; map 3.1), Farragut had had problems for years.[20] In the 1960s, teachers, students, and community members organized against an ineffective principal and voted him out. The school was run as a community-control school for one year.[21] Despite the teacher-led struggle to reform the school, Farragut remained challenged. By 1984, the once predominantly Black school was transitioning to predominantly Latino. Both Latino and Black participants mentioned Farragut as the school to avoid, with one participant saying, "Nobody wanted to go *there*."

Maria, a Latina from Bogan, had disparaging remarks about Farragut. "And the high school that I actually had to go to was Farragut, and that wasn't the greatest school to be at. Anybody and anyone who didn't have anywhere to go was at that school. And you didn't want to get stuck there." She also discussed the perception that teachers feared their students and stated that "all the gang bangers went there." A Black Bogan participant, Angela, said Farragut was "not one of the best schools to attend." While she had a strong elementary education in her neighborhood, she knew she would not go to her neighborhood high school and never bothered to register there. Angela stated, "There'd be too many issues with the gangs and whatnot. And who has the best this and the best that. It was too much stress. So I knew I was gonna have to go to another school outside of my neighborhood." As at all schools, at Farragut, students' abilities varied. The school's top students did not have access to the same education as those who attended selective schools. Yet the perception of the environment, presence of fighting and gangs, and stories of students' families or friends who attended the school added to its poor reputation.

Black Von Steuben participants spoke of their poor perceptions of Austin High School. Terrace stated that "Austin was completely not a good school." The comprehensive desegregation plan called for a variety of specialized programs at schools that would not be desegregated. Teresa mentioned that her sister went to Austin believing that they would have a nursing program.

> Well, she told me that they sent a recruiter, and they told her that they had a nursing program. She wanted to go into nursing. Well, when she got there, she found out the program wasn't everything that they had promised that it would be. And we didn't know anything about the West Side or Austin, or anything or how to pick a school, none of that. And Mom was absolutely no help! She just told me where I couldn't go. She told us that whatever high school you pick, you gotta stay there for four years. You're not gonna be transferring in and out and all that. So [my sister] got stuck. So that's where she went. I was like, "Sucks to be you!" I was not going to Austin, I'll tell you that much!

Austin High School underwent a rough racial transition in the mid-1960s as Blacks, many coming from the South as part of the Great Migration, began to populate the community. As the Black population increased, racially motivated fights occurred in the school. The Chicago Board of Education decided to change feeder school patterns between the North and South Austin neighborhoods, which led to schools in South Austin (including Austin High School) becoming predominantly Black. White residents who fought against school boundary changes and for federal revitalization funds to improve the declining community abandoned both the school and the surrounding community when their struggles failed. As city and school officials abandoned both the community and high schools, the area declined further.[22]

Another West Side high school, Marshall, faced similar criticism from Jacquese, a Black participant from Von Steuben, who could have gone to Marshall. She said of the school, "Well I really don't see a whole lot of people that are graduating from Marshall at that given time [or] had a lot of college opportunities." Jacquese compared Marshall's environment to that of her alma mater, Von Steuben, and said she believed that Von Steuben had higher expectations. "It seemed like by me going to Von and everybody at Von, it seemed like the kids we[re] more geared . . . towards finishing. Like, you know, 'I can't wait 'til prom, I can't wait 'til graduation, I can't wait 'til college.' There was more of that aura going around." According to Jacquese, others in her neighborhood did not have the same focus, as they were caught in the negative trappings of inner-city life.[23] Jacquese compared her opportunities and experiences with those of her West Side neighbors attending Marshall High School. She noted the high expectations set for her at Von Steuben, which she believed would not have been the case at Marshall, particularly because she heard about neighbors who dropped out or joined gangs. For an academically focused student like Jacquese, desegregation gave her the opportunity to choose a school with better academics, an emphasis on graduating, and a better overall school climate.

Other neighborhood schools on the South Side of the city did not fare well in the memories of participants either. A Black Whitney Young graduate, Cassandra, said of Chicago Vocational, Simeon, and Calumet High Schools on the South Side, "I mean the image, I never went up to them, but the image was a lot of fighting basically going on." Marc, a Black Von Steuben graduate, said of South Shore, "It just wasn't touted to me as a school known for its academics." Marc had also applied to Whitney Young and to Lindblom. He stated, "I got into Lindblom but my mom had concerns about my safety going to Lindblom. But she had concerns about me going to Von Steuben, but that wasn't quite as bad as going to Lindblom, which is perceived to be a very rough area of town." Lindblom and Von Steuben had similar test scores, but Lindblom was in a lower-income, Black neighborhood.

Raul, a Latino graduate of Bogan, remembered that when he visited Tilden High School, he thought it was more like a prison than a school, as there was a noticeable police presence. According to Raul, Tilden "was well known for racial wars, you could say. I did have a couple of friends that went to grammar school with me that ended up attending there. . . . I used to get out of school early in Bogan, and I would go pick up my friend who went to Tilden. To me, it was kind of weird seeing police [on] the block." He visited the school with his former elementary school gym teacher, who was Tilden's head football coach. Raul noticed that "the way the inside of Tilden was compared to the other two, there was more freedom in Bogan and CVS [Chicago Vocational High School]," the latter two of which he had attended. Carlos, a Puerto Rican

Bogan graduate, like many others, recalled the increased gang activity in his neighborhood high school: "There was a high school called Kelly High School that was three blocks away from where I grew up. I didn't want to go there because what had started happening as I started getting older, in my neighborhood, a lot of gangs started coming in—mainly Latinos. There was a really heavy influence of gang bangers in my neighborhood. That basically translated into the area high school, which is Kelly High School."

Ralo, a Latino from Von Steuben, described the image of Clemente on the city's North Side: "I grew up in a real bad neighborhood. I'm the only one in my entire neighborhood that made it out of high school and went to college. A lot of our friends were killed, some of them went to jail, and then some of them were lost in the shuffle with drugs, but I'm the only one that made it out of there." Annette, a Latina graduate from Von Steuben, remembering a fight she witnessed near Roosevelt High School on the North Side, stated, "A group of kids attacked another child on the bus. And I remember seeing the bus driver try to help him out and other folks try to help him out. But that's what you thought of when you thought of this other school." She believed that Roosevelt was "just a school where our local gangsters went. . . . You were college bound and that's not what you thought about Roosevelt."

South Side Whites who attended Bogan thought it was a better school than their neighborhood schools. Debbie recalled, "Bogan was actually better than the school I *was* gonna go to. . . . Bogan wasn't the school I was supposed to go to. It wasn't in my district."[24] Linda also refused to attend her neighborhood school (Hubbard), because she remembered that "there were a lot of fights there," and she "just didn't want to go there." Finally, Peter noted, "Curie, Kennedy, Hubbard didn't have the greatest reputation."

Each of these schools varied in selectivity and dropout rates, but most were less selective than Von Steuben, Bogan, and Whitney Young, based on their lower test scores and higher dropout rates. While the perceptions of these schools may have been exaggerated in some instances, safety concerns were real determining factors in students' school choice. In every neighborhood school that was perceived negatively, there were students who tested well and could have potentially gone elsewhere; however, limited space at top schools prevented this. It is also clear from the selectivity of Von Steuben, Bogan, and Whitney Young that they recruited the top students from the neighborhood schools, further contributing to the schools' negative perceptions. School desegregation measures opened opportunities for a precious few to escape neighborhood schools with poor reputations, but they did less to improve the opportunities of those who remained, regardless of their academic potential.

It is also quite possible that if the participants had attended these neighborhood schools, their perceptions would have differed. Because they attended diverse schools, two of which were in predominantly White neighborhoods, their reflections on predominantly Black and Latino schools more than twenty years later raise the question of whether participants negatively perceived their neighborhood schools because the schools were Black and Latino. This is particularly true of those who never visited the schools they denigrated. Black and Latino schools tend to have a more negative reputation, regardless of their quality. Robert Sampson argues that neighborhoods with poor reputations serve to reproduce inequality. Similarly, the negative reputations of the schools participants avoided led to increased inequality as the top students left those schools. Kate Phillippo and Briellen Griffin have determined that geography of opportunity is illustrated when schools are considered safe or unsafe based on the race and class of the students. Middle-class North Side schools and neighborhoods garnered greater reputations for providing high-quality academics even when comparable schools existed in other areas of the city.[25] However, CPS school data for the class of 1988 indicate that the students' and their parents' assumptions about the academics at some of these schools might indeed have been correct, even if they may have overemphasized the safety concerns. Furthermore, many Black and Latino participants attended segregated elementary schools that they revered, and Whitney Young was still a predominantly Black school. Finally, participants lived in the same neighborhoods as these schools and had family, friends, and neighbors who attended. Their negative perceptions were not solely the result of race.

Recruitment Efforts

As participants' perceptions of neighborhood schools indicate, school desegregation choice initiatives meant an escape from high schools that had long been underfunded, were simply unable to offer the type of schooling that led many students to college, or were viewed as unsafe or in unsafe neighborhoods.[26] Although some students found success regardless of the schools they attended, high achievement was far more possible at a select number of schools. As participants prepared for high school, they were made aware of their choices through a variety of CPS recruitment efforts. Recruitment was part of the district and individual school efforts. District efforts included distributing thousands of brochures and letters about Options for Knowledge to parents and students, advertising in newspapers, communicating with principals at schools that were predominantly Black and Latino, encouraging open houses and assemblies at receiving schools, and having staff recruit students from sending schools.[27] Recruitment efforts were highly successful for study participants, as they and their parents became aware of the options beyond neighborhood schools.

Von Steuben and Bogan staff served as recruiters and went out to predominantly Black and Latino schools. Additionally, school staff at participants' junior high or grammar schools helped to steer students to Von Steuben.

Several participants recalled visits from recruiters; this demonstrates the success of recruiting. Von Steuben was on the North Side of the city, far away from the predominantly Black neighborhoods on the South and West Sides of the city. Most Black participants had little or no knowledge of Von Steuben before being recruited. The school's recruiters targeted the best and brightest students and often only spoke with those students on their recruitment visits. Three Black Von Steuben graduates recalled a visit from the school's recruiters that directly led to their attending the school, which they had not previously known existed. More than one participant stated, "I had never even heard about Von Steuben." Recalling her choice, Teresa stated, "Von sent a recruiter to my elementary school. And I said, 'OK, well I'll go here.' I didn't know where it was!"

The participants often felt special, as they were among the few at their school who spoke to Von Steuben's recruiters. Ed recalled, "We were the only two from our elementary school. And if I remember, it was one of the school counselors who came to our school to recruit both of us, to get us there because we had good grades. . . . I guess they were wowing us about Von Steuben. . . . And they're the only ones who, I think, reached out and said, 'Look, we want you to come to this school up here.'" Like Ed, Anthony cited recruitment as an important factor in his decision to attend Von Steuben, and he remembered how significant the recruiters' visit was:

> I remember recruiters coming to our school when I was in elementary school in '84. . . . You know, I guess to sell their high school. . . . And I remember . . . being raised in . . . inner city over there on the West Side where I've never really been exposed to non-Black Americans. Everybody was Black. So here are these White people, as we call it, in our school. . . . We figured they were important, you know, for something. But they were talking about high school. I didn't know what school I wanted to go to. I was valedictorian. So I could have went to pretty much any school I wanted to go to.

These few selected students' experiences personify both the deliberate process of brain drain that occurred and the level of Von Steuben's selectivity, as only the best students were targeted by recruiters.

Latino participants who graduated from Bogan were also recruited. Bogan staff who came to their schools stressed the computer-based curriculum the school offered, which attracted these participants. Paul recalled that he learned about Bogan because recruiters from various schools visited his school when he was in eighth grade. He attended a grammar school with a computer-based curriculum and wanted to continue; Bogan provided that opportunity. Von Steuben and Bogan staff successfully drew students from predominantly Black and Latino schools to attend their once predominantly White schools.

Recruitment was still active in 1984, two years after the initial desegregation plan was created, illustrating individual schools' and the CPS district's commitment to desegregating these schools.

While recruitment from the high schools was an important part of the process, so too were the informed staff at participants' grammar and junior high schools, as they made students aware of their high school options, particularly if the students showed promise. Ralo, a Puerto Rican participant, recalled that he was planning to attend Clemente, his neighborhood high school. His principal encouraged him to attend Von Steuben and did the necessary legwork to ensure he got into the school. Ralo wanted to escape his neighborhood gangs, yet he and his parents were unaware of his schooling options. "I was supposed to go to my community high school, which is Roberto Clemente High School. And judging just by its name, of course it's a Latino school in Humboldt Park, Chicago, and that was an all–Puerto Rican high school. And when I told my principal that I was going there, he said, 'Nah, you're not going there.' And he wrote a letter of recommendation to the Von Steuben principal, and a week, a week and a half later I guess, I got my letter saying that I'm going to Von Steuben, and that's how it happened." Like Ralo, Melissa, a Black participant, noted that she had "dropped the ball on applying to school." Failing to apply typically meant students would have to attend their neighborhood school. Her counselor stepped in and forwarded her grades and test scores to Von Steuben, and she was accepted. In both cases, the school staff was knowledgeable about the school options and worked on behalf of students who might not have had parents who were actively seeking out options for them or whose parents were unaware of Von Steuben. Recruitment efforts for these participants certainly worked in their favor and made navigating the process far easier. It also put the schools on students' radars as they were applying to high school.

These recruitment efforts also helped to perpetuate the underdevelopment of segregated Black and Latino schools, as the top students were selected while doing a disservice to the rest of the students, who had no real choice or access to the top schools. It was ultimately a strategy for the denial of equal resources to segregated Black and Latino schools, as well as a justification for the funneling of greater resources to desegregated, formerly White schools. In a real sense, the recruitment strategy served as a brain drain and undermined racialized communities, while providing additional resources and top students to privileged White communities.

Parental Choice Work and Family Influence

As participants' families learned more about recruitment efforts, parents did what Lois André-Bechely terms "choice work."[28] Participants' parents were actively involved in finding the best schooling options for their children. That meant informing their children about schools they could not attend, having conversations with them about potential school choices, seeking information about their options and reviewing the recruitment literature, visiting prospective schools and attending school fairs, encouraging their children to apply, and consulting family and friends for advice. Parents and students who were aware of the district's desegregation policy through Options for Knowledge leveraged it to their advantage.

For participants whose families had successfully done the choice work, the types of work varied. One Black participant, Jacquese, remembered that her parents would not allow her to attend Marshall High School. They visited open houses held by receiving schools, including Von Steuben. Her parents felt comfortable with one of the school counselors and the school's strong academic reputation and therefore decided that she would attend Von Steuben. Other Black participants also visited Von Steuben or attended school fairs to get a better idea of the school and make an informed choice. For instance, Elizabeth initially planned to attend Lindblom, a highly touted Black school on the South Side, but after attending a school fair and learning about Von Steuben's academic focus, she and her parents decided that she should attend Von Steuben instead. "They did not want me to go to the neighborhood high school for sure. But they were not that interested in the two well-rated high schools on the South Side that I could have gone to. I was going to go to Lindblom, and I thought Lindblom and Hyde Park; I might have even registered at those schools. At least one of them I did. But when I found out about Von Steuben and that it was a math and science school, we switched." These recruitment efforts had limitations, as those without access to transportation or free time may have found it difficult to travel from the West or South Side to the North Side to attend an open house or a school fair. Consequently, parents' opportunities to fully engage in choice work were sometimes limited.

At times, parents' choice work entailed more than just school visits or discussions with their children. On some occasions, it meant using influence to gain access for their children. A Latino participant, Edgar, believed that his father's political involvement with an alderman may have assisted his efforts to gain access to Von Steuben. Edgar stated, "My father was involved with politics a little bit, and he used to help an alderman. And he didn't care for the other school's reputation too much, and understood that Von Steuben had some strength academically and helped me get into Von Steuben." In Chicago, politics certainly influenced outcomes for the politically connected. Similarly, Trey, a White participant, stated, "Through the application process, I was . . . actually not admitted to Von Steuben because they were trying to admit classes that had a certain proportionality to them [in order to desegregate]. . . . So initially I was accepted at Lane Tech High School and not at Von Steuben. Academically, I was qualified to go there, but just based on race, was not accepted."

He thought that his father's stature as a professor may have helped him get into Von Steuben. According to Trey, the racial quotas at Von Steuben did not automatically mean that local students would have access to the school. Von Steuben's metropolitan mandate meant school officials were rather strict in maintaining a certain racial balance. Whether these parents' influence led to their children being accepted is unknown. However, these parents conducted choice work to make it possible for their children to have a chance to be among the students who could be chosen. The schools were left to decide whom to accept.

Other family members or family friends were at times instrumental in helping participants become aware of schooling options. Some participants had an older sibling or other relative who attended the schools they chose. Other times, because their siblings attended schools with lower academic profiles, they sought other options. Two Black female graduates of Whitney Young had older siblings who had also attended the school. Josephine recalled, "My sister kind of helped guide me through and that's how I wound up there." Josephine attended Whitney Young's academic center for seventh and eighth graders, then matriculated to the high school. Maleta, a Black female Von Steuben graduate, had siblings who had attended that school before her. Maleta said, "I knew I wanted to go outside of the box, out of my community to go to school. I knew that that was my goal." Parents likely conducted the choice work with the older siblings, who then served as an influence for participants.

Family and friends were instrumental in the choice process for Black Bogan participants. In choosing Bogan, Kelly recalled that a family friend suggested she go there when she was deliberating her choices. Kelly recalled, "I went to a school that was out of my district. . . . I was valedictorian so I had great grades and everything, and that's how I could get out of my district. 'Cause my district school was Calumet; I was not going to Calumet. My mother wanted me to go to Simeon. I was not going to Simeon. So a friend of my mother suggested to her that I go to Bogan. And would you know I got accepted. They let me in." Angela and Charlotte had family members who had gone to Bogan and recommended the school, while Ken had friends from the neighborhood who were going to Bogan. LaDonna remembered it mostly being her parents' decision. Bogan was much closer than Whitney Young or Lindblom, the two other schools to which she had been accepted. She was "all geared up" to go to Whitney Young, but her parents wanted her to go to Bogan.

Students and their families became aware of the choices through CPS recruitment efforts, choice work, and family or friends. This awareness was only the first step. For a student to actively seek acceptance to a school meant that parents or other family members had been involved in evaluating the choices available. Conducting choice work did not guarantee a seat in these schools, but not doing the work certainly meant that there would be no opportunity to get in, unless CPS staff recruitment efforts directly influenced students. If students wanted to attend Whitney Young or Von Steuben, they needed to be highly qualified, meaning that they had to have done well on their standardized tests and attained good grades. The application process still gave most of the power to schools to determine who would be accepted, and there were usually more qualified students than there was available space.

School Curriculum

Participants overwhelmingly expressed the importance of academics in their decisions regarding the schools they attended. Desegregation was hardly mentioned as a factor, since many did not view their attendance at these schools as participation in desegregation. They simply remembered trying to make the best academic choice they could make. Framing school desegregation policy as school choice served to focus on merit rather than desegregation. This made the policy more palatable for all who engaged in the process. School curriculum was therefore among the reasons they chose their schools, as each school had a special curriculum or program (Von Steuben, science; Bogan, computers; and Whitney Young, magnet). Von Steuben became a metropolitan science center as a result of desegregation and a viable choice for participants who were interested in science. Its science curriculum played a role in Elizabeth's choosing it over highly touted Black schools on the South Side. Cornelius, a Black male student who transferred to Von Steuben after his first year at Curie, remembered, "I always wanted to go into the sciences." His first choice was Whitney Young, but he was not chosen for that school. He transferred to Von Steuben his sophomore year and recalled, "I knew I needed the foundation in science and math as opposed to performing arts for a career in science." Two White male participants also mentioned that the science curriculum was among the reasons they chose Von Steuben. One stated that he was "kind of geared toward the engineering and technical," so he decided to attend Von Steuben.

Whitney Young participants chose that school because it was among the top schools in the city; its magnet program was especially attractive. Cassandra, a Black participant, said of her choice, "We . . . wanted to go to the good school, the magnet school." Unlike Von Steuben and Whitney Young, Bogan was far more career and technically focused. Three graduates from Bogan chose the school because of its computer class offerings. Linda, a White participant, recalled choosing Bogan because of "the curriculum, the computers." She stated, "You know, what I learned then is of no use now. [*Laughter.*] I had four years of computers there. I just liked the education you could get there." The curriculum, among other things, was a draw for students, and each school provided a unique curricular focus.

Other Choice Factors

Other factors influenced the participants' school choices: attending the same school during the seventh and eighth grade, avoiding the financial costs of private schools, and having the convenience of the school's location and small size. Some Whitney Young and Von Steuben participants attended their school in seventh and eighth grade as part of the school's academic center or upper grade center (junior high). Josephine attended Whitney Young's academic center, as did Craig, a White student, and both eventually attended Whitney Young High School. Annette, a Latina, and Ben, a White participant, both attended Von Steuben's upper grade center. Their successful attendance helped bolster their case for high school matriculation, though Annette mentioned that the racial and ethnic quotas almost cost her a seat at Von Steuben.

Seven participants attended private or Catholic schools for some period during their K–8 education. The many choices that were opened up through school desegregation made it easier for parents to forgo the financial constraints of private schools. For example, Lourdes, a Latina, and her family had financial issues that caused her to go to Bogan. Her father was injured on his job, and they could no longer afford Catholic schools. Lourdes recalled,

> Well initially I was supposed to go to a Catholic high school. But my dad, 'cause he worked at UPS, he hurt his back and he was told that he had two slipped disks. . . . So my mom didn't want us to continue going to private school because of the money. . . . So my sister and I looked at each other and we were like, "Well let's just go to Bogan." We had heard it was a good school. My dad was very against it . . . because he really wanted us to focus on school, and he felt that if we went to a girls' school that we would focus more on school and not on guys. . . . But financially we weren't sure what was going to happen, my mom went ahead and signed us up at Bogan.

More financially able parents might have considered private schools if their children had been forced to attend neighborhood schools. Being chosen for slots at good public schools meant that students could avoid having to make that decision. Few other families possessed the financial wherewithal to debate about Catholic school attendance.

Convenience was another reason participants choose their schools; but this reason was a luxury afforded mostly to White North Side participants. While the numbers of high-quality schools on the North Side and South Side were similar, schools on the North Side tended to be far more diverse than those on the South Side. Southwest Side Whites would not have seriously contemplated crossing segregated boundaries to attend predominantly Black schools like

Lindblom or Kenwood, though Kenwood was 21 percent White. First, attending those schools would mean traveling through Black neighborhoods on the South Side. Second, the Southwest Side's White residents were more likely to have protested Black students' attending White schools. In fact, when CPS tried to desegregate White and Black schools in the past, some White parents refused to send their children to a nearby Black elementary school.[29]

Unlike their Southwest Side counterparts, White North Side participants who attended Von Steuben had the privilege of contemplating how far they were willing to travel to attend high school. They would not have to worry about crossing the boundaries of predominantly Black neighborhoods unless they left the North Side. For example, John lived across the street from Von Steuben and had considered attending Lane Tech. But when he weighed his options, he said, "OK, do I want to wake up an extra hour early and take two buses to get to the school?" Similarly, Melanie lived close to Von Steuben and recalled, "It was the only high school in my local area. I could have gone probably to a different school had I wanted to travel, but I didn't want to travel." Meanwhile, Black participants traveled on public transportation for up to an hour and a half to get to Von Steuben. Only one White North Side participant attending Whitney Young traveled a great distance to get to school.

A second convenience factor was Von Steuben's size. Many White Von Steuben participants mentioned Lane Tech as a school choice. However, Lane Tech had 4,600 students in 1984 and Von Steuben only had 1,000. Nicole's family had gone to Lane Tech, but she and her twin sister wanted to go somewhere different. They liked the fact that Von Steuben was smaller than Lane Tech. Size influenced Nick as well. "I applied at Von Steuben and Lane Tech. I was accepted at both, but I chose Von simply because it was a smaller school. Lane Tech . . . was huge. It was just enormous." The discussion of convenience was certainly unique to North Side Whites who attended Von Steuben. They rarely considered safety issues when choosing schools. They could attend Von Steuben, Lane Tech, or even Lincoln Park, which had an International Baccalaureate program. Even though there were other good schools around the city, Whites on the North Side had a variety of good high schools with strong academic programs from which to choose. This privilege meant that their reasons for attending desegregated schools were focused on personal comfort and convenience, unlike those of Black and Latino students, and White students from the Southwest Side.

School choice was a result of school desegregation policy, and for study participants, this meant that they could take the reputations of neighborhood schools into consideration. Once participants determined that those schools were not viable options, they capitalized on different educational options as a result of their choice work, information from other family members and friends, and the recruitment efforts of CPS. These students, like Michelle Obama, were fortunate, as many others were refused spaces at these and other high-quality schools and were relegated to schools with high dropout rates that top students avoided. Participants put great effort into their school choice, but effort was not enough to secure a spot in these top schools for everyone who wanted a high-quality education in CPS, leading to continued segregation for many students.

Community Reactions

While many Black participants saw their neighborhood schools as subpar, their neighborhood friends and acquaintances proudly stayed in their neighborhood. Black participants' neighbors responded to their attendance at schools outside the neighborhood in several different ways: they called participants traitors, categorized them with terminology associated with "acting white," or viewed their attendance at White schools as an indication of weakness; they took pride in participants' ability to go to better schools; or they were curious about the long commutes. Von Steuben and Whitney Young participants were more likely to remember negative comments from neighbors, while Bogan participants recalled a more competitive response. Only Black participants remembered negative comments. South Side White and Latino participants only recalled their neighbors' attendance at private schools as part of the White flight from public schools, and many Whites on the North Side found better schools near their neighborhoods. Formerly White schools were, for the most part, the schools that opened spaces for desegregation and school choice. Black participants, particularly girls, were more likely to feel estranged from their neighborhood peers once people knew they were attending school outside the neighborhood. They paid the price for crossing boundaries.

Ethnic or racial boundaries can be used to determine who is in and who is out of an ethnic group, by those within the racial or ethnic group or by outsiders. As students crossed boundaries to go to schools outside their communities, their perceived behaviors were sanctioned by their peers. Richard Alba describes the stigma of "assimilation" to White cultural norms that comes with crossing boundaries, including a "growing distance from peers, feelings of disloyalty, and anxieties about acceptance."[30] In essence, boundary crossing means one has to adjust to the norms of the dominant group to succeed, but if the adjustment is too successful, it is perceived negatively within one's own group.

Some Von Steuben and Whitney Young participants reported being told they were "acting white." This has been a misunderstood phenomenon in academia. Signithia Fordham and John Ogbu popularized this problematic interpretation in part to explain Black youths' underachievement.[31] They have argued that Black underachievement is partly a result of a cultural belief that academic excellence is associated with whiteness. Numerous scholars have rebuked this interpretation. One major critique is the largely ahistorical association of academic achievement with whiteness and a lack of recognition of the value Blacks have historically placed on education. Many critics acknowledge that young people accuse each other of acting white in an effort to "sanction" Black youths who seem to reject Black cultural markers, such as those of language, dress, and music preference, in favor of White cultural attributes.[32] Prudence L. Carter argues that there is a gendered dynamic associated with acting white, but she also recognizes it as "a form of social control in within-group interactions." In her study, Carter categorizes acting white in four ways: speaking Standard English but sounding like Whites, dressing like Whites, primarily associating with Whites, and acting "uppity" or superior to peers.[33] Based on student responses, it was mainly Black girls in Carter's study who were accused of acting white.

Studies of acting white often explore in-school dynamics. However, the present study differs in that it focuses on how neighbors responded to students leaving the neighborhood to attend other schools. In designing this study, I was curious about whether students caught flack for going to desegregated schools. My purpose was not to reignite the debate but rather to see whether there was any reaction at all from their neighbors. Participants were asked, "How did your community respond to your attendance at a desegregated school?" Community members, as far as participants recalled, were responding to their own perceptions of attending school with Whites, rather than to what was happening in those schools. Whitney Young was predominantly Black and therefore could not be considered a White school. Von Steuben had a sizable number of Black students (26 percent, with Whites only 38 percent in 1984), and participants' neighbors knew little to nothing about the school. As later chapters will show, the Black participants ridiculed by their neighbors mostly had Black friends at their desegregated schools. Most were not perceived as acting white at their schools. So their neighbors' responses were largely about participants leaving the neighborhood schools.

Black female participants who attended Von Steuben and Whitney Young were more likely to mention negative comments from neighbors, confirming Carter's gendered analysis of acting white. There are various ways in which Black youths interpreted Blacks who left neighborhood areas and crossed boundaries to attend schools with Whites. Participants recalled being seen as traitors, called nerds and stuck up, and told they talked "proper." When asked how the community viewed her going to Von Steuben, Terrace indicated, "They didn't take it too well. They looked at that as almost like a betrayal." She further stated, "Well first of all when they found out what high school you go to, they like, 'You go all the way up north,' and then they look at you as being White or a snob. That was kind of their view of things." Her most painful experience, Terrace remembered, was being told that she was "stuck up" and "talked white."

Other Black female participants who attended Von Steuben recalled their neighbors' negative reactions. Sylvia said people thought that she believed she was better than them for going to a White school. She often heard comments like, "Why you got to get out the neighborhood? Why you think you better than us? Why you want to act like a White girl? Why you got your own friends? Why you got to go so far? Why can't you go to school with us? . . . Your school ain't no better than ours." She rarely associated with people outside and had not attended the neighborhood schools since fourth or fifth grade. People were used to her going away for school. Her few neighborhood friends also attended Von Steuben, and they often carpooled to school. People in Octavia's neighborhood wanted to know why she was attending a White school. "A lot of them was like, 'Why are you going all the way up there to that White school?' 'That's where I wanted to go. That's where I chose to go.' But that's how a lot of them were, but to each his own."

Melissa, from Von Steuben, and Eve, from Whitney Young, emphasized the value their parents placed on education when dealing with neighbors' critiques. Melissa had other friends from the neighborhood and elementary school who went to Von Steuben with her. According to Melissa, people "called us nerds and all kinds of stuff 'cause we went to a school that's super smart as opposed to Marshall and Westinghouse. . . . Well they always told me I was a nerd even in elementary school. But I took education as important 'cause that's something that my mother and my father really stressed. So I used to always tell them that 'I don't know what your parents stress, but that's what my parents stressed. So you call me a nerd, that's what I'll be. I'm gonna be a real good nerd!'" Like Melissa, Eve thought people viewed her family as odd for not attending the neighborhood school after elementary school. But her parents pushed her and her siblings to excel. These participants often coped with the criticism by dismissing it and stressing the values their parents instilled in them. The support they received from parents allowed them to withstand the views of their peers.

Accusations of "talking white" or "talking proper" were part of the critique of acting white that participants faced. Trénace, a Black participant, was always accused of "talking white." She grew up outside Chicago in a White community and attended schools with Whites before moving to Chicago, so she "sounded white." Trénace stated, "Going through grade school, I was picked on a lot because of my voice. I was not, as they call it, 'Black enough.'" People told her, "You just talk so white!" The constant judgment of her speech made her withdraw a bit. "At that point, I didn't say much of anything just because I got tired of hearing that." The way she spoke was not a problem at White schools, but when she went home, she still had to prove her Blackness. "So what I went to a school that has White people in it, I'm still Black. . . . I never responded because it was what it was."

Josephine, who attended Whitney Young, was told she spoke "proper," which was just another way of saying she sounded white:

> I think my community always saw me as different. The predominantly Black neighborhood—I lived in K-Town . . . I think I was seen as really studious. And for some reason . . . I don't know how I wound up talking the way I talk. Some people would say, "Oh you talk so proper," or "Oh you talk so white." And what's interesting is that my parents are from the South and they have a southern accent, which I conjure up on a dime. Then I had some White teachers and then some Black teachers. All my friends all the way through sixth grade were either Latino or Black. But I always, quote, "talked proper." And so I would get a little bit of grief.

"Talking proper" was the way Blacks growing up in segregated communities often referred to the speech of Blacks who did not speak Black Vernacular English. For some Black Chicagoans, the perception of authenticity was awarded based on how one sounded rather than on what one said. Talking white was about using Standard English and sometimes sounding white while doing so. This included the tone and quality of a person's voice as he or she pronounced words. Michelle Obama tackles this issue in her autobiography. She was asked, "How come you talk like a White girl?" She did not believe she talked white but indicated that her parents stressed using proper diction and corrected her grammar. Obama writes, "We were expected not just to be smart but to own our smartness—to inhabit it with pride—and this filtered down to how we spoke. Yet it could also be problematic. Speaking a certain way—the 'White' way, as some would have it—was perceived as a betrayal, as being uppity and denying our culture."[34] Boundary crossing was not always easy but at times was necessary to get ahead in the larger society. People accused of talking white were unfairly stigmatized and castigated. However, most participants still had Black friends and lived in Black communities.

Black participants who attended Bogan received less grief for attending Bogan than Black participants attending Von Steuben or Whitney Young. Since many participants came from the South Side and went to school on the Southwest Side, they were more likely to have neighborhood friends who attended Bogan with them. Some Black students experienced teasing, and except for Darlisa, the teasing seemed to be directed at the White school they attended rather than at them for acting white. For some neighbors, White schools appeared weak, because they were White. Darlisa faced questions and criticism from her brothers about her choice to attend a White school: "Oh, my brothers used to always talk about me[, saying,] '[You're] going over to that White school, thinking you all of that.' But, you know how brothers are! But as far as everybody in the community, they never knew what school I went to, because I never talked about it, you know? I didn't really hang outside." Stanford viewed his community as the members of his church. He and his church friends would make fun of each other for the schools each attended. "We teased and ragged each other because of the school you went to, but that was just all in harmless fun. I don't have any deep-rooted emotional scars because somebody talked about what school I went to."

Rayshawn said Bogan was called weak because White students attended. Though she had people nearby who also attended the school, people still made fun of Bogan.

> There were a lot of people that stayed around Damen Avenue, so maybe about half a mile away, all in that vicinity, they went to Bogan. So all of us were fine with it. The rest of the city, at least in our culture that went to the other high schools, when we said we went to Bogan: "Ew! You go to Bogan?" I said, "No, Bogan is a good school." "Bogan is weak!" So we had that kind of competition, and I think it was because it was so mixed. . . . I looked at it as that was their lack of knowledge. They didn't understand it, and they were missing out in the long run. So I didn't take it to be anything personal.

Neighbors or family members who made fun of Bogan students for attending a school they thought was a White school viewed association with Whites as a weakness. Neighbors took pride in attending Black schools and often expressed that pride by making fun of students who attended schools with Whites. They essentially took pride in the racial and neighborhood boundaries, though these boundaries were largely imposed from outside.

For other Black participants, neighbors were simply curious about why they traveled so far to go to school. Marc, who attended Von Steuben, said, "I think people were surprised. It's like, 'Wow, that's quite a trip, isn't it?' 'Oh yeah,' I said, 'it takes about an hour to get there on a good day.' Besides that sort of incredulity regarding the travel time, I don't think anyone mentioned to me personally, say, 'Oh, what are you doing that for?' or 'Why?' I never got those sorts of questions." Ed, who also attended Von Steuben, had a similar sense about the neighborhood response. "I don't think it was negative. . . . I believe that they felt it was positive that I was going to school 'up north.' That's the term that we used, 'up north.' Yeah, still hanging out with people and just telling them what school I'm going to or whatever, they thought it was kind of odd, but, you know, just the fact that I'm traveling so far."

Some Von Steuben participants rarely connected with people in the neighborhood, because of limited time, because they were introverts, or because they had strict parents. Elizabeth stated, "You don't see your neighbors much when you leave. I took the six o'clock bus, and I didn't get back till, you know, six o'clock at night, so you don't see your neighbors." Tracy said people mostly questioned why she attended Von Steuben and not Marshall. "Well at that point I think I found myself more so focusing on my school work. . . . But I was always more introverted or just stuck around my close net of people who I have communication with. So I think it seemed odd to a lot of the people in my community that I went outside our community to go to school. But at the same time, I wanted a decent education. I knew that that would be happening at Von Steuben. So I didn't care." Teresa's mom was strict, so she missed the opportunity to hang out with neighbors. "I didn't have any friends in the neighborhood. I don't think they cared one way or the other."

Von Steuben was less known because it was on the North Side and not an athletic powerhouse like many of the city's popular schools. Charman's friends had not heard of Von Steuben either. "A lot of people never really heard of it. They like 'Who, I ain't never heard of that school.' So they really didn't know about the school." Anthony's neighbors were also unfamiliar with the school. Anthony observed,

> They didn't know what Von Steuben was until we played basketball and then everybody was identifying Von Steuben. "That's that school you go to up north?" "Yeah." They didn't know we were like two or three in the city with academics. They didn't know that we had been on the map a long time in that area. They never heard of Von because Von wasn't a basketball mecca. But when Von started playing basketball—I remember that. We went to the final eight in the city. And here's this little school from up north, playing against King High School, which is the number one high school in the *nation* at that time . . . and we got crushed! [*Laughter.*] But we were so happy to be there! And it kind of put Von on the map. But it was one of those things where the kids around my neighborhood, they knew I went up to a school up north. . . . But they didn't know exactly what or where until Von started doing good in basketball. And all of a sudden it was "Oh, I heard of Von, I play basketball." "Yeah, yeah, we read too. We kind of do a little math every now and then."

Sports were certainly the best way for a school to be known in the city, the metropolitan area, and the state. Athletes and those who followed sports became familiar with other schools through sports, particularly those schools that reach the conference, city, and state championships. While Von Steuben was known for its academics, it was so far geographically from the Black neighborhoods that it would have to stand out in other ways to be familiar to those neighborhoods. The fact that Anthony and others had to be recruited to the school demonstrates how unknown the school was in certain communities.

Von Steuben's rigorous academics were more locally known, while a school like Whitney Young was known throughout the city because it was a magnet school and was more centrally located.

For other Black participants who attended Von Steuben, like Angela and Maleta, and Cassandra, who attended Whitney Young, neighbors had positive views or there were other neighborhood kids attending the same schools, so boundary crossing did not carry a negative stigma for everyone. Angela spoke of how neighbors were proud of her and mentioned how early she had to get up. "They pretty much knew that I wasn't gonna go to the neighborhood high school. So they were very proud of me, you know, kind of like breaking the cycle, stepping beyond the boundaries. If there was something I ever needed help with, I had full support." Her family only teased her about getting up early and having lots of homework. Maleta had friends who attended Von Steuben and other desegregated high schools. She said, "Nobody really seemed to mind. I grew up on the West Side of Chicago, so . . . a lot of my friends from the neighborhood were being bused to a desegregated school. And so a few of them did go to . . . high schools that were desegregated like Steinmetz." Cassandra received positive feedback from her neighbors: "They were happy because at the time, [Whitney Young] was number one. . . . They'd say, 'Oh you're going to Whitney Young, that's good!'"

Latino participants from Von Steuben thought they were fortunate to attend that school. Yet they received no negative comments from neighbors. For example, Ralo's neighborhood had several people affiliated with gangs. Ralo remembered, "They actually protected me. Yeah . . . it was weird, not weird, but they saw greater potential there. So . . . they always encouraged me to continue on. And they never said, 'Hey why don't you transfer to my school?' You know, it was never like that. They were like, 'Just keep doing what you're doing.'" Often, people who grew up in "bad" neighborhoods and excelled received protection from gang activity so that they could achieve.

Latino students who went to Bogan did not experience any taunting from neighborhood friends for doing so. Raul attended Chicago Vocational High School (CVS) before Bogan, and people in his neighborhood commented on that choice. "Well actually, they responded differently because I was going to CVS. So they were like, 'What the hell you gonna go do in a Black neighborhood?' . . . And everybody was telling me that I was crazy. . . . I'm just going to go learn. I could care less [about] anything else." Raul chose to go to a vocational school that happened to be Black, and because of the segregation in the city and the perception of Black schools and neighborhoods, his friends thought he was making a poor decision. Despite their concerns, Raul's only issue attending CVS was the long commute. He transferred to Bogan after a few months. Among Latinos, only Raul reported being questioned for attending a Black school. Others were not questioned about their school choice because the school was in their neighborhood, they knew few of their neighbors, or their neighbors supported their choice.

Whites, however, focused more on their neighbors' decision to abandon public schools altogether. White participants from Bogan noted that several neighborhood friends attended private schools, whether they were in the immediate Bogan area or not. One of school administrators' fears since the early 1960s was that desegregation would speed up White flight. However, despite limited desegregation, White flight had already occurred in Chicago.[35] There were predominantly working-class White neighborhoods on the Southwest Side and the North Side, and often Whites who worked for the city resided there. However, more Latinos (and at times Blacks) began moving into those communities. Once the federal government forced the Chicago Board of Education to desegregate, many Whites who remained in the city and were financially able sent their children to private schools. But as Michelle Obama's story indicates, Blacks and Latinos also did the same when they could afford it.

Nora, a Latina who grew up near Bogan, mentioned that neighbors who had protested Blacks in her elementary school made a choice to attend private high schools. "It seemed like it was a whole other world just being across the street. It's like, we don't want them with the grammar school, but we can't help it with the public school. It was really weird. And all the kids in our neighborhood—most of them went to private schools if they could afford to go. They wouldn't go to Bogan. I guess the grammar school kids who couldn't afford to get sent to private school wound up going to Bogan."

Peter, a White participant who attended Bogan, said, "I think the bulk of the neighbors went to Catholic high schools." Likewise, Tracy commented, "Bogan was this huge school. And I think there were maybe, at the most, eight students from my grammar school who went there. . . . Lots of girls went to Catholic high schools, boys too. And I think the rest of them ended up going to Hubbard [a public school]." Chicago had one of the largest private Catholic school systems in the world.[36] At the time when participants attended high school, Chicago was seeing significant declines in enrollment in the public and Catholic schools from their historic highs in the mid-1960s.[37] Between 1970 and 1980, the Catholic school enrollment dropped from 174,100 to 117,150, with White enrollment declining from 131,994 (76 percent) to 66,768 (57 percent). Public school demographics also changed in the ten-year period; school enrollments went from 577,679 to 458,497, with White enrollment dropping from 34.6 percent to 18.6 percent. The city's White population declined 32.5 percent from 1970 to 1980 as the White school-age population shrank 54.4 percent.[38] Still, many remaining Whites thought of Catholic and other private schools as important educational institutions and chose them when they could afford it.

Neighbors' negative reactions to some participants' attendance at desegregated schools indicated the costs associated with attending such schools, particularly as it was associated with school choice. When students chose to do so, attending desegregated schools and crossing segregated boundaries led to an additional burden. Black female participants faced a double marginality, as they revealed painful accusations that kept them feeling like outsiders or marginalized in neighborhoods where they grew up. This seems to confirm Carter's view that acting white was largely associated with girls, softness, or "weak[ness]."[39] In the end, Black participants faced the greatest burden for attending schools outside their communities.

Travel to School

Unlike elementary school students, who were bused to desegregated schools, thus drawing great ire from some White communities, high school students used public transportation to travel to desegregated schools because it was more financially expedient. Students entering communities on buses and trains to attend the schools of their choice were much more palatable than the images of yellow school buses transporting students for the purpose of desegregation. Chicagoans, and others around the country who made desegregation optional or focused on school choice, effectively quelled much of the opposition by removing the target of their rage. School choice brought options to students of all races who had heretofore been forced to attend neighborhood schools. While the policy's reach was limited, it gave the illusion of meritocracy and broader opportunities that school desegregation seemingly failed to represent. As students embarked on their high school education, their travel to school was an interesting, often underexplored element of desegregation.

At some point, most study participants took CTA buses and the "L" to high school, joining students from all around the city, including college and private school students. Participants took one or more buses or trains or a combination of buses and trains, along with walks to or from CTA stops and stations. Students received a student discount from the CTA but otherwise had to pay their own way. The rides to school could take anywhere from a few minutes to two hours, and bad weather conditions could lengthen the trip. Except for those who lived in the immediate area, few participants walked to school. Black participants typically traveled the farthest, especially if they lived on the South or West Side of Chicago and attended Von Steuben on the North Side. Some South Side participants typically had an hour-and-a-half commute depending on the weather and how far south they lived. Participants of all racial and ethnic groups going to Bogan typically traveled less than an hour, largely because they tended to live closer to the school. Those traveling to Whitney Young came from the North, West, and South Sides, so their commute times varied as well, but they were typically no more than an hour and a half. The CTA rides could be informative, annoying, overcrowded, fun, or scary for participants. Some were driven to school for part of their high school tenure, while others, in their later years, got their license and cars to drive themselves. The commute to school exemplified the sacrifice students made for a better education and the segregated boundaries they crossed on their way. Because they often traveled the farthest, Blacks were most likely to bear the burden of school desegregation. Sometimes, Whites and Latinos at Von Steuben recognized the sacrifices that Black students made in traveling these distances and acknowledged their dedication.

The initial transition to public transportation could be nerve racking or liberating. Sylvia, remembering riding the train to Von Steuben, said, "It was hard at first going home by myself because everyone else was gone on the train.... I traveled an hour or more every day. And I was kind of nervous about that." Eve, who traveled from the South Side to Whitney Young, said that in the summer her mother showed her how to get to school so that she could be confident in her commute. Eve took two buses and had to walk about twenty minutes to get to school after the second bus. She had a middle school friend who would often join her on the bus at a later stop on the way to school. Josephine perceived her transition to the CTA as a part of growing up. When she was at the Whitney Young Academic Center, she would take the school bus from her elementary school. It was a relatively short ride to school. She said, "High school kids aren't truckin' it on the school bus in ninth grade. It was like, 'Ew, never mind!' So I took the train most days."

As Michelle Obama experienced, the bus and train rides were extremely informative. As participants passed through different areas and crossed segregated boundaries, they got a bird's-eye view of the cosmopolitan city. Ed was exposed to people headed to work and to other areas of the city that he might not have seen going to a neighborhood school.

> It helped me see a lot of people get on and off the train; so I was able to see a lot more than if I went to an inner-city school. Most of the inner-city schools are in a Black neighborhood going to a Black school and that was pretty much the interaction during the day. So I think it was different for me [because] I was able to go through a lot of the neighborhoods, especially the cultural neighborhoods in Chicago, and just to see different parts of Chicago as I went back and forth from school every day. What shaped my experience was just the fact that I was able to see most of Chicago.... The biggest advantage I had was the actual getting back and forth to the school using the public transportation, just being able to see everybody from every background and know the world is bigger than just my local community.

Elizabeth took the bus from the South Side to the North Side daily. Though one of her friends regretted spending so much of her high school life commuting, Elizabeth, like Ed, found the train rides culturally stimulating.

> It definitely shaped my experience of high school because we spent a lot of time commuting. I talked to someone who I'm still friends with, and she said she resents all that time we spent on the "L," all that time we spent commuting because we could have been doing other things. But I liked it. It got us out of the South Side, even though we still lived there, and it got us through downtown. . . . Most of us in high school worked somewhere downtown Chicago after school. . . . We were exposed to all the museums, and everything that presented itself, and we wouldn't have had that going if we had lived up north or if we went to our neighborhood school. We didn't get a lot of sleep, but it was a good experience. We slept on the trains.

The downtown rides led to a job opportunity for Craig, a White participant from the North Side who attended Whitney Young. He had to travel to the West Side, a reverse trip from those who traveled from the West Side to Von Steuben. Craig recalled,

> I lived on the North Side up by Rogers Park. And Whitney Young . . . it's just west of downtown. So a lot of my time that I might have spent . . . on an "L" train. I had a commute of about an hour or so one way and an hour or so back. . . . What I did do, as a result of having to commute from the North Side to downtown and then West, was I got to know downtown very well, which is why I was hired on at the time as a messenger for a law office. I got to know . . . the different layers of the downtown streets. I got to know those very well. It was kind of fun.

Some Bogan participants who lived within a fifteen-minute drive of school still took forty minutes to get to school, and at times they had to take more than one bus. Occasionally, there were fights on the buses or at neighboring schools that affected the commute. If buses were too full, students would be passed up at the bus stop. Gina lived about three or four miles from Bogan, but it took her two buses and forty-five minutes to an hour to get to school. "I remember the buses would be packed and they wouldn't stop. That happened sometimes. That was an ordeal." From time to time, Gina stayed after school to miss the crowded commute. She also recalled "kids drinking [alcohol] on the bus. . . . It was kind of nuts." Often the CTA added buses to accommodate the large number of students trying to get to school, but the additional buses did not always accommodate all students. Lourdes observed, "It seemed like if you weren't one of the first ones on the bus, you had to pretty much stand. And there was a lot of people, it was loud. But occasionally there was a little bit of pushing. But it was always in a joking way; it was a lot of fun with people that you knew. I just remember it being really crowded and thinking, 'Oh, great! I wish I had a car so I could drive home.'" The bus rides could be simultaneously fun and annoying. Debbie, a White participant who had to take two buses, said, "That was actually fun. I mean it was a pain at times, especially in bad weather; but it was actually fun 'cause I mean there was a lot of other kids on the bus, too. So it was like a big party on the bus."

The long commutes symbolized dedication, according to White Von Steuben students. Dave observed a classmate and noted, "This guy lives really far. He must really want to go here because he takes three buses or something." Erin also noted the sacrifice students made. "We had some kids . . . who would get on a bus and get on a train and get on another bus and take an hour and a half to get to school in the morning so that they didn't have to go to a school in their neighborhood. I would *not* have done that." Karen stated that she lived about a mile from Von Steuben and had a ten-minute bus ride or a half-hour walk. "But there were kids that took the bus like way south! Like when I think about it now, I'm like, 'Why did they get on the bus to come all the way up [here to school]?' . . . If you wanted to get a decent education out of the public schools . . . then you would make that sacrifice. You'd put yourself on the bus for an hour and a half a day, to come out." Brett, a participant who is half White and half Chinese, said, "I thought it was kind of heroic to come that far, and it made me think that this school was worth it because our school had a particular academic emphasis on science. I thought at least nominally that they had some interest in doing that." Like his White counterparts, Ralo, a Latino, said, "I can tell you one thing, a lot of the Black people that went to Von Steuben lived a lot further south than I did, and every day they were on that bus with me. And every day, we hung around the back and just, 'cause that's where we could make our noise, and every day, there was hardly any absenteeism. And I think it had a lot to do with people escaping their neighborhood and going to a place where they felt safe and comfortable, and they would actually learn."

Raul was the only Latino on a bus filled with African Americans when he attended CVS. He spoke of the protection he received from his classmates.

> Because when I first started high school, I was going to CVS, Chicago Vocational. And what happened was my mom kind of didn't like it . . . just because of the travel. And the first few days was . . . more of an eye-opener there because I would have to jump on the Dan Ryan, on the "L," go all the way to Eighty-Seventh Street and then from there take a bus and go through there. And basically, I was the only Hispanic in that bus and everybody's looking at me like if I was crazy or something. And here's this fourteen-year-old kid, you know, traveling. And then I got to know a couple people from school, and they

> would tell me don't worry about it, "You ride with us, and you know, nothing's gonna happen." But at the same time, I never felt threatened, nothing like that. They actually became more of my friends because I guess they seen I wasn't too worried about going to somewhere else for a school like that.

Raul provides another unique example of how crossing boundaries in Chicago was not only a Black and White issue. Once he transferred to Bogan, his experience was different, since he and his sister lived farther than most of their classmates. "Me and my sister . . . were the ones that probably rode the bus the longest. So as we're going along, we're picking up everybody else. And then on the way back, everybody else is getting dropped off again and we're the last ones to get off. And pretty much, the people that we saw on the bus, I sat down and ate with them because they were the ones that I dealt with more. So that's who you kind of stick to." It took him about forty-five minutes to get to school depending on the bus drivers, "'cause some of them would fly and some of them wouldn't pick up no more kids and just go! So I was lucky that we were like the ones that got picked up right off the bat." Commuting students often formed communities with fellow travelers on the buses and trains.

As students crossed boundaries on their way to school, the world they viewed outside the bus and "L" windows provided unintended educational experiences. Bus and train rides could be fun or exhausting, but the participants riding long distances on the CTA demonstrated their commitment to getting a better education than their neighborhood schools could offer, even if it meant some were unable to participate in after-school activities. The long commutes also highlighted the privilege given to many Whites as a result of desegregation policies, as their schools were desegregated. As a result, mostly Black, and sometimes Latino, students typically had much longer commutes and were more likely to cross segregated boundaries.

Choosing to attend schools with high academic rigor like Von Steuben and Whitney Young, and schools with specialized curricula like Bogan, was important for many participants; their long commutes proved their willingness to sacrifice for a better education. Whether they were recruited, counseled, or influenced by family and friends, participants, regardless of race or ethnicity, recognized that they received an education that was better than what most of the city's high schools or their neighborhood schools provided. Their decisions to go to one of these three schools laid the groundwork for a better, college-ready education and a brighter economic future. While some of their neighbors may not have understood their sacrifice, others did, and those neighbors supported and protected participants' choices. Participants who left the neighborhood still faced estrangement from their peers, another form of sacrifice necessitated by boundary crossing in a segregated city.

The many educational opportunities available to these students also spoke to the educational inequality in Chicago, as few schools received the same quality of resources allotted to desegregated schools. Those left behind in other schools had to fight harder to get to college and to avoid the pitfalls of urban life. The differences among schools were so pronounced that very few students had the opportunity to go to better schools, despite their abilities. Spaces were unavailable at the once predominantly White schools or excellent Black schools, and some parents were unwilling or unable to send their children far away to acquire such an education. This meant that the majority of the city's Black and Latino children received an unequal education, and though compensatory funding was to be given to these segregated schools, the funding was insufficient and did little to turn around high schools with extremely high dropout rates.[40] Despite the privilege participants had in attending desegregated schools, some noted the differentiated treatment they received from teachers, and while most were not conscious of it, the curriculum remained unchanged despite the changing school demographics.

4

"I Don't Know If It Was a Racial Thing or Not"

Academic Experiences and Curriculum

Maria took a French class at Bogan High School with an extremely condescending teacher who belittled students. According to Maria, the French teacher called her students animals while constantly praising French sophistication. After putting up with the constant abuse, Maria wondered, "Why are you here? You honestly hate everybody here. We're animals to you. You love France. Why are you here if it is such a bad place for you to be, why are you here?" To make matters worse, the teacher assumed the Latinas in the class had stolen her wallet.

> I remember one time she left the room and left her purse, and she came back and she started saying that somebody went into her purse. And it had to be a Hispanic because they would be the type of people that would do it. And that was the only time I remember feeling like "Oh my God, you got to be kidding me! Who would go in your bag?" I mean, there are so many people in there, you would think somebody is going to tell on you. . . . There was no way I would even get near your bag to even be associated with even standing close to it.
>
> She took us to the principal . . . four Hispanic girls, and . . . said . . . "They stole my wallet out of my bag." . . . And the principal interviewed everybody . . . and the dean talked to us, and we're like "Nobody touched her bag. Nobody

> went up there." We were in there probably at least . . . an hour to two hours talking about this. She finally came back; we missed class, other classes, and said her wallet was in her car. . . . She did not apologize. She was just like, "I got the wallet. Thanks. You can go to class, you can stop this." And the principal was just horrified, 'cause he had sat there, like, saying, "Somebody just [confess]. You're going to get in trouble, but just say we know you did it." And they took her word that somebody had stolen her wallet, and it had to be one of us. And she came back and said she had it in the car, and that was it. . . . You felt like this small. 'Cause after that everybody in class was looking at you like "You stole it" and even though you came back and said she found it in her car. . . . She never apologized.

Fed up with their mistreatment, students from various class sections got together when they realized this was happening in all the French teacher's classes. They wrote letters detailing the teacher's numerous appalling statements and incidents and created a petition to demand her removal. She finally left, though Maria was not sure whether she was fired or forced to resign. The environment the teacher created made it difficult for students to feel welcome. Her assumptions that Latinas were criminal and must have stolen her wallet and the principal's attempt to coerce a confession both signified the ways in which certain students were automatically assumed to be guilty. Even in desegregated spaces, Latino, Black, and Asian students were ostracized and segregated from the rest of the student population. Maria was racialized and marginalized by the teacher's actions, and she suffered humiliation as a result of her ethnicity. These internal forms of segregation through microaggressions preserve boundaries and stratify students within schools.

Students faced microaggressions and racism in numerous ways at desegregated schools. *Microaggression* refers to "the everyday verbal, nonverbal, and environmental slights, snubs, or insults, whether intentional or unintentional, which communicate hostile, derogatory, or negative messages to target persons based solely upon their marginalized group membership." Microaggressions tend to demean, belittle, and "other" those from marginalized groups and "relegate them to inferior status and treatment."[1] People experience microaggressions in various places in society and even from those of their own race or ethnicity. Especially in predominantly White spaces or desegregated schools, these microaggressions serve as an unwelcoming factor, creating a hostile environment, even when attributed to just a few people. Microaggressions are reminders that racial boundaries exist even in spaces meant to eliminate them.

School desegregation brought students together, but barriers like stereotypes and prejudice still existed, making students feel unwelcome. Most institutions may not have truly planned for how to best accommodate diverse student bodies. Chicago school desegregation plans called for the training of administrators, teachers, and counselors to prepare for the implementation of school desegregation. A number of these important professional development trainings covered classroom management, equitable discipline, cross-cultural communication, working with diverse cultures, and multicultural curriculum. Yet desegregation reports indicate that there was difficulty in determining who received training, what the training entailed, and whether it effectively helped teachers and other school staff deal with the diverse student body.[2]

Most school staff adjusted well to diverse student populations, but participants mentioned some teachers and counselors who favored White students. Teachers' or counselors' inability to treat students fairly limited Bogan's, Whitney Young's, and Von Steuben's potential for greater integration. Instances of discriminatory treatment by teachers and counselors meant that a truly integrative experience was prohibited by structural barriers within the schools. These barriers included the limitations placed by counselors or teachers on what students could do based on the latter's race or ethnicity and teachers' microaggressions, which made students feel uncomfortable or unwanted.

In addition to how school staff treated students, the curriculum was an important aspect of the school culture. Desegregated schools often continued with the traditional academic curriculum, which focused mostly on White and European culture and contributions to American society and the world. These schools failed to make a concerted effort to include the contributions of other racial and ethnic groups in coverage of subjects like history and English or in the overall school culture. Though the district provided some professional development workshops in multicultural curriculum and bits of information on the contributions of diverse groups, the curriculum was unaltered at Bogan, Whitney Young, and Von Steuben.[3] Multicultural education was gaining popularity in the 1980s, but it would take some time for schools to make more consistent changes in the curriculum. Participants viewed the school curriculum and school culture as normal or traditional, which translates to White.

Interaction with Teachers and School Staff

Chicago Public Schools desegregated its teachers and other school staff beginning in the 1977–1978 school year in response to federal pressure. The consent decree led to further teacher desegregation.[4] Of the three schools, only Bogan's teaching staff was over 80 percent White in the 1980–1981 school year. By the 1985–1986 school year, its faculty was below 67 percent White, 28 percent Black, and 4 percent Latino. Von Steuben maintained a similar percentage of White (68 percent), Black (27 percent), and Latino (4 percent) teachers between 1980 and 1986. Whitney Young had the greatest percentage of Black teachers (43 percent), White teachers were 53 percent, and Latinos teachers less than

1 percent in 1986.[5] Desegregation of faculty meant that racialized students, particularly Black students, had access to teachers who looked like them. An increased number of Black and Latino faculty could ease desegregation for students.

The diversity of the faculty certainly helped students from diverse backgrounds feel more comfortable and gave White students exposure to diverse teachers. Participants of every race and ethnicity appreciated the Black teachers they had. Diversifying the faculty was an important part of desegregation, but microaggressions continued. Nonetheless, teachers, counselors, and administrators from all three schools were generally remembered fondly. Participants believed that they were pushed to excel, mentored, and treated fairly.

Among the participants who recalled a good relationship with teachers was Raul, a Latino from Bogan. He remembered a Black English teacher who pushed him to achieve and made learning fun. "I have a teacher that I kind of thank every time I see her there. I saw her about two years ago, and she came up to me and she recognized me right away. I thank her a lot because she's one of the ones that made English interesting for me. I never used to like to write. But she kind of made it fun. And she didn't care [about] your color and everything. She actually would get down on you whether you were Black, White, Hispanic." Likewise, Nick, a White participant from Von Steuben, most fondly remembers one teacher: "The teacher that impacted me most in my life was my high school band teacher. He was great, and he's Black, great guy! Loved him, actually loved him. And he taught us lessons, he was hard and he was tough, but twenty years now looking back, I'm grateful for him." Finally, Marc, a Black Von Steuben participant, confidently stated, "I can't recall a single instance where I was mistreated or perceived to be mistreated."

Teachers and other school staff left an indelible mark on participants. However, remembering positive interactions with school staff does not negate the negative interactions with teachers and counselors who failed to provide the same level of inclusiveness. Amid supportive and fair teachers, there were teachers or counselors who treated participants differently because of their race, ethnicity, or gender. The microaggressions and discrimination participants endured symbolically separated them from other students by limiting their ability to feel fully integrated into the school, and they also helped to keep the racial boundaries in place. Black and Latino participants recalled the various ways they were mistreated or felt slighted by their teachers. Teachers and counselors viewed students as criminals (as in Maria's case), had low expectations, made racist remarks, distrusted them, disciplined them more severely, or discouraged them from applying to certain colleges. The discomfort participants felt because of their race or ethnicity decreased the potential integrative experiences the students had and at times made them feel like outsiders, even if most of the teachers made them feel welcome. A few teachers were enough to remind students that they did not fully belong.

Teresa, a Black student from Von Steuben, had a driver’s education teacher who stereotyped her because she was Black. Students from Von Steuben went to Roosevelt High School for driver’s education. The instructor asked Teresa if she was in a gang. “Why would you think I’m in a gang?” Teresa asked. He responded, “’Cause I thought all Black kids were in gangs.” Flabbergasted by the comment, Teresa said, “No, I am not in a gang, my mother would not allow that. And furthermore, I would not want to ever be in a gang.” After the discussion, she wanted him to “just teach [her] how to drive a car and shut up.” Teresa, like Maria, endured negative racial stereotypes. They had the additional burden of being viewed as thieves and gang bangers.

Along with stereotypical assumptions, teachers at times made racist or inappropriate comments. Josephine, a Black student from Whitney Young, recalled one such comment from a White teacher she thought was arrogant.

> The White kids of course didn’t pick up on a lot of his stuff and they just thought he was so great. He said some things about . . . an African American baseball player named Razor Shines. . . . I don’t know how it happened, but somehow he was talking about him and then was like, “Yeah, and something, something Monkey Shines.” And I was like, “Huh?” And then there were other things that other Black kids picked up on. . . . And again, for the most part I liked him because I felt like he was a good teacher and he was inspiring. But again, as I look back on it, I’m like, “Wow, he said really inappropriate stuff!” And I don’t know how much he got reprimanded for it or called on it because he was so beloved and gave a lot to the program.

Black participants had issues with a few of their teachers. Teachers’ mistreatment of Black students in many ways isolated them within the classroom, regardless of the diversity of the class. In subtle and not so subtle ways, these teachers made Black students feel as if they were not as smart and did not belong; they were often unsuccessful at providing assistance to students. Some of these same teachers responded differently to White students in the same classes.

A few Black Von Steuben students had difficulty with teachers who treated them differently. Anthony believed one teacher acted as if Black students were not very smart when he explained things in class.

> I don’t know how Von was in the seventies. . . . But you could still see there was a transition with the teachers, with the influx of African Americans coming into the school because a lot of them were apprehensive . . . like I was this new creature or something. I’m not gonna name teachers, but I remember

> specifically looking at one of my algebra teachers, talking to me as if I didn't understand them the first time. And I remember going, "Why'd you talk to me like that?" And he's like, "I'm trying to explain it to you." I said, "But you explained it while we were sitting in class and I understood it then." He's explaining it; he's like looking at me or looking at other African Americans. It was very obvious that he was looking at the African American students like talking like . . . "You understand what I'm saying now?" And I remember sitting there and we're looking at each other like, "Why's he doing that?" But I think it was just a transition for us all. I was being exposed to them for the first time and a lot of them were being exposed to me or my culture for the first time.

While Anthony's teacher, though condescending, tried to make sure his students understood, Tracy thought her statistics teacher failed to help her when she had trouble in the class. Though she struggled to definitively state whether it was associated with race, she certainly felt ostracized.

> There was only one teacher that I would say I was concerned about in terms of a racial impact, felt as if maybe he didn't like me, or really wasn't fairly giving me a chance. . . . I knew that I wasn't really getting the material. And so at that point early on I sought the help. . . . I was pretty much blown off. . . . I realized that it had nothing to do with the class or the material. I felt like it really was about me and the color I was. . . . I could be wrong because I don't know how he treated other students. But our one-on-one interaction was not the most positive. I don't feel like I got the help that I wanted or was seeking.

Octavia also had a problem with her math teacher. "I think I might have had one teacher that I really . . . thought was maybe a little racist. . . . It was one of my math classes, but I can't remember which one and he was kind of nasty and kind of talking down to me. So he wasn't the best teacher, but you know, I dealt with it and kept on going." The teacher treated students of different races differently, according to Octavia. "He was nicer to [Whites]. He was explaining the problems to them when they had issues, when they couldn't understand something. And to me, he'd be like, 'Figure it out.' So he was more willing to help them."

Ed had problems with White male teachers who he believed asserted their authority over him, and he often felt as though most of his teachers did not care for him. "I'll be honest with you, I don't think I had an extremely good relationship with the exception of two teachers. . . . I'm from . . . the West Side of Chicago, you just assume everybody there's bad. . . . Keep in mind, I was one of the smartest kids from my elementary school, but they treated me like I was never meant to be there. That's how I felt." One of his teachers would simply tell him he had the incorrect answer but showed White students how to get the correct answer when they were wrong. Ed thought his teacher's interaction with Whites was preferential. "When they answer, you see the smiles; you see the laughter and interaction." This same interaction was not part of his experience with that teacher. Teachers could play a critical role in making integration work by treating students with respect, helping them learn, and providing them spaces to interact. But if teachers hardly put forth the effort to help racialized students succeed, they promoted symbolic segregation. In some ways, it could lead to actual segregation, since failure or poor performance restricted Black students' opportunities to be in higher-track classes with White students.

Ed had the expectation that a teacher who cares corrects a student so that he or she can improve. Despite his difficulties in English classes, Ed had an English teacher who helped turn him around. He said, "[She] worked on English, she didn't work on people and that's why I had a respect for her." For Ed, a good teacher challenged all students regardless of their race. Participants who were pushed to achieve valued those teachers who pushed them; when they were treated differently from White students, Black and Latino participants perceived this as racist.

Latinos, particularly those from Bogan, also faced problems with teachers who made assumptions about them or had low expectations of them. Sirena had a teacher who thought she already knew Spanish: "I guess because they assume that because you look Hispanic or you have a Hispanic name that you speak it. And so when I took Spanish, my teacher thought that I was lying . . . and probably thought I was taking . . . an easy class. And he's like, 'You know you're . . . Mexican. You're just ashamed to speak Spanish,' or whatever. And it really wasn't the case, you know. I just didn't know it." She was embarrassed by the teacher's response in front of the class and felt that she was being picked on. "I thought it wasn't fair because you're really judging somebody by their appearance or their name. But I would ask my parents why we didn't speak Spanish or whatever. They just said that we just didn't. I guess it really wasn't a big deal for us because in reality all of our areas were predominantly White. So it was not like we were in a certain area where a lot of Hispanics are, like maybe like Twenty-Sixth Street or what have you." Like other Latinos who spoke only English, Sirena sought out Spanish when she was older and made a choice to learn it on her own.

Other Latino participants believed that they or their fellow students were treated differently. For Paul and Eric, being Latino seemed to invoke differential treatment. Paul thought his biology and computer teachers treated him differently because of his mixed race/ethnicity (Puerto Rican and White). He also believed that he was graded and treated differently and received less attention than other students in his class. Like Paul, Eric thought teachers believed he had limited potential based on his ethnicity. "Some of the teachers, sometimes I guess because of my background or maybe because of the way I looked, thought that I wouldn't be able to do a particular job or a particular homework assignment, or even be successful in the class."

Carlos also highlighted teachers' racist assumptions about Asian students and their expectations that students should act White in order to get attention from the teachers. "What I actually heard several times, 'You're Asian, you should be taking these classes.' That was kind of a little bit of a shock. I've heard that several times. . . . I'm talking about teachers saying this to students in the class. Like, 'Oh, what do you mean you can't figure that out, you're Asian, you should be really good in math.' That was kind of a shocker." The model-minority stereotype of Asians as smart kept some teachers from helping Asian students.[6]

Participants had diverse experiences with teachers, but counselors at Von Steuben were often viewed as discriminatory. There were a few participants who remembered counselors trying to discourage them from applying to certain colleges. The field of counseling was designed to help track students in school and sort them for their future positions in society.[7] Most counselors are overwhelmed with high student-to-counselor ratios, and on average they see each student at least once a year. Students rely on counselors more heavily when their parents are unaware of the role of academic tracking or the requirements and application process for college. Counselors provide students with information that they think the students need. While most students, regardless of race, expect to go to college, those on the highest academic track, mostly Whites and Asians, are given the most information about how to make college a reality. They are encouraged to apply to highly ranked schools and provided with financial aid information.[8] Counselors often discourage students in the regular tracks from applying to prestigious universities. While this is partly a reality check, students of color are more often discouraged.

Participant experiences with counselors at Von Steuben seemed to confirm the research on counselors. Melissa wanted to attend the University of Illinois at Urbana-Champaign, but her White counselor told her, "I don't [know if] you will be able to make it there. Try some other state schools." Elizabeth also remembered her counselor telling her not to set her sights too high.

> The only person I had a problem with was I had a really bad guidance counselor senior year. She was racist, and I actually didn't really recognize it as racism until after it was over. But you'd go in your senior year and they want to know are you going to go to college? I remember her telling me that she thought that maybe I had set my sights too high, for the colleges I was applying to. . . . I felt really weird during that meeting with her, but I didn't listen to what she said. But afterwards and especially once I actually got to college and . . . I thought about [it] several times over the years, and I realized, "Oh she was just being

racist." And I actually after the ten-year reunion a couple of other people told me they had similar experiences with her.

While other students recalled bad college advice from counselors, Annette, a Latina, remembered her counselor's advice to limit her course selection in school.

> I had an experience where I was at my senior level, and I had taken tons of classes. So by then I wanted to take—I think it was a college science, college biology. And you know I think I was at 3.0. I was an average student. I did well. Never got in trouble. As and Bs and what not. I was certainly qualified to go to that class. And I remember being told by a counselor that "you should really leave these types of classes to the smarter Asian kids. You know they'll excel better than you."
>
> [I] didn't feel as encouraged and I got lazy. So I didn't fight it. I could have fought it. I could have gone because there was nothing wrong with my grades. They were As and Bs. I did well. . . . I just said, "You know what, just forget it. It's my senior year. I've got three more classes and got only a few classes that I need." After homeroom, I go to work, and that's what I did.

Annette was profoundly disappointed by her interaction with the counselor. "You know the whole point of going and taking the early high school biology course was so when you got to your senior year or junior year you could start taking the accelerated courses. That was the whole point. And to be told that really you should reserve this for someone, you know the Asian kids are a lot smarter than you, it kind of stung." Annette's experience demonstrates how the perception of her ethnicity limited her ability to take accelerated courses. Based on the comment about Asians, it was clear that her counselor's discouragement was about more than just her grades. The assumption that Asians were the model minority not only infringed on Annette's choices but also asserted that all Asians were the same. Asians were considered the only racial or ethnic group outside of Whites that was capable of high-level classes. When they needed help, as Carlos described, they were less likely to receive it.

Counselors have quite a bit of influence in determining the classes students take.[9] They often encouraged or discouraged participants based on issues that went beyond students' abilities. Based on the comments Annette received from her counselor, race, class, ethnicity, and gender served as important factors for the courses recommended to students. Students were in the same building, but their opportunities to truly learn together were often negated when White and Asian students were disproportionately placed in the upper academic tracks and Black and Latino students were overrepresented in the lower tracks.[10] Academic tracking is a process of sorting students into groups within the same classes (ability grouping) or in different classes based on perceived abilities. Students may be tracked by remedial, general, and honors classes, or they may be tracked by vocational, general, or academic programs.[11] Scholars have demonstrated the use of standardized tests and grades, along with counselor and teacher recommendations, to determine tracking. The process appears meritocratic; however, in some studies, students with similar qualifications were given dissimilar access to higher-track classes or gifted programs.[12] Students have historically been tracked as a result of race, ethnicity, social class, and gender.

Participants at the three schools had overwhelmingly satisfactory and even great experiences with teachers, counselors, and administrators. They believed teachers genuinely cared about and encouraged them. However, Black and Latino participants acknowledged that some teachers looked down on them and made inappropriate comments, or failed to challenge them academically or provide the help they sought. Some teachers held stereotypical assumptions about the intelligence of Asians, the trustworthiness of Latinos, or the intellectual ability of Blacks. Others subtly favored White students over Blacks and Latinos. The limited diversity training may have been part of why teachers failed to adjust to the needs of a diverse student body. Desegregation itself was not enough to change widely held beliefs about the capabilities of Black and Latino students or to stop microaggressions from occurring, and it certainly was not enough to make teachers, counselors, or administrators treat all students fairly. The boundaries persisted, making integration difficult.

Curriculum

Amy Stuart Wells and colleagues note, "Racially diverse schools, for the most part, operated on White people's terms of whose knowledge and experiences were valued and who had greater status and prestige socially. Had the goal for these schools been to create greater integration, the educators would have made more of an effort to value and embrace traditions and experiences that Black and Latino students brought with them."[13] Wells and colleagues view the schism that existed for students of color in prominently White schools as a continuation of W.E.B. Du Bois's double consciousness. Participants in their study, they conclude, "have learned that in a White-dominated society they are more likely to gain access to the resources and opportunities they need to compete and succeed when they are in close proximity to Whites—no matter how much these Whites resist their presence or try to make them feel inferior. These schools and the classrooms that were predominantly White carried the reputations and the connections to take these students on to the best colleges and universities or job opportunities."[14]

Participants in the present study understood the significance of the schools they attended for their future life chances. In subtle ways, they recognized that they had to learn to navigate negative interactions with teachers and staff and master the curriculum and culture they were taught in order to be successful. Mwalimu Shujaa argues that in heterogeneous societies with one dominant cultural group, schooling perpetuates "the maintenance of existing relations of power and privilege. . . . The existence of a politically dominant cultural group ensures that schooling and education can not [*sic*] be assumed to be overlapping social processes." Unlike schooling, which reaffirms the dominant culture, education is cultural transmission and "affirms the cultural identity" that students bring to school.[15] The curriculum in desegregated schools reaffirmed the dominant culture and did less to affirm the culture that students brought to school.

Von Steuben, Bogan, and Whitney Young High Schools all offered a traditional history and English curriculum largely focused on Whites. During the late 1960s and 1970s, as students at colleges and universities were pushing for ethnic studies, high school students in Chicago (and elsewhere) had similar demands.[16] Chicago students demanded Black history courses in 1968, and the superintendent obliged them by adding such courses at predominantly Black high schools.[17] There is little information about the curriculum of these courses or where and how often they were taught. As Black and Latino students entered desegregated schools in the 1980s, the curriculum, for the most part, did not reflect their cultural backgrounds. The participants who remembered any ethnic or racial studies or such an emphasis in history or English found these classes at Bogan (which had a Black history course), ethnic or language clubs, and Black History Month celebrations. In 1990, after most participants graduated, Illinois passed a state law requiring public schools to teach African American history. Though these courses were taught haphazardly for decades, Chicago finally organized a systematic curriculum in 2013.[18]

Though Black students gained better resources at desegregated schools, scholars and parents both recognized the loss of opportunity to fully transform schools in a way that would fundamentally recognize the wholeness of all children.[19] William F. Tate, Gloria Ladson-Billings, and Carl A. Grant argue that "with a growing social consciousness that was further enhanced by the passage of the Civil Rights Act [1964], African American people also wanted to see their boys and girls and other students of color, as well as White children, experience a curriculum that celebrated culture, accurately told of their ethnic group's deeds and contributions to society, challenged the status quo, and promoted their personal and ethnic group's membership by accepting and affirming them as full members of American society."[20] The lack of an inclusionary curriculum in desegregated schools meant that students of color would have to adjust to the schools, even though the schools were not required to adjust to them. Their contributions to American society would not be fully acknowledged, and as Carter G. Woodson surmised in 1933, Whites would continue to believe that they were superior, even if students were in schools together.[21]

Segregated Chicago schools also failed to be exemplars of inclusionary curriculum. However, many participants who attended segregated elementary schools remembered more efforts to include Black history and culture in Black History Month programs, in art and pictures on the walls of the schools, and in their classes. The lack of access to multicultural curriculum was district wide. Yet in a study of desegregated schools, it is essential to note the parameters of boundary crossing and efforts to achieve integration.

Participants were asked, "Do you feel the school curriculum reflected your racial/ethnic group?" At times, they were asked follow-up questions about what they learned in history or English classes, whether they were taught Black history, and whether they learned more about their ethnic group in elementary school than in high school. Several participants said the curriculum did not reflect their racial or ethnic group; some participants believed that it failed to represent any ethnic group. A few acknowledged that the school's curriculum was already rigorous and therefore sufficient. This was an unconscious admission of the belief that learning about groups beyond Whites was somehow less rigorous. Some participants thought that ethnic studies could offer more cultural reflection than would be provided by incorporating such information into the regular history and English courses. One participant surmised that "curriculum inclusion" meant separate ethnic studies classes and consequently believed that it would defeat the purpose of desegregation. Bringing diverse students into desegregated schools did little to correct the dominant beliefs and ideologies in society, schools, and the curriculum.

Desegregation provided Black and Latino students with resources and opportunities that their neighborhood high schools lacked, and consequently gave them opportunities their peers in other Chicago Public Schools likely missed. But as scholars have shown and as Black opponents of desegregation predicted, there was still much work to be done to improve the integrative experiences within schools. The curriculum did little to acknowledge how Asians, Latinos, or Blacks were also fundamental contributors to American history and culture. The desegregated schooling environments still elevated whiteness as normal, standard, and traditional, perpetuating the maintenance of the dominant culture.[22]

In 1990, Von Steuben conducted a self-study for accreditation from the North Central Visitation Committee. Both the Social Studies and English Departments recognized their inability to fully meet the needs of the diverse student body with the current curriculum. The Social Studies faculty recommended that "new courses should be developed to meet the growing needs of Von Steuben's multi-cultural student body," while the English Department wanted more "minority literature" because there was "little study" of such literature.[23] Moreover, both departments mentioned that the Chicago Board of Education curriculum and the textbooks were outdated. This indicates that teachers recognized the need to provide a culturally relevant curriculum to the diverse student body but were hampered by the curriculum and textbooks. Although teachers at the time recognized the need for a more multicultural curriculum, study participants rarely understood the importance of a more inclusive curriculum when they attended high school. Still, many believed their education at these desegregated schools had served them well, even if it focused on Whites.

For many participants, there was little consciousness about the missing aspects of the curriculum while they were in high school. Additionally, some believed the curriculum reflected the trends of the decade. As far as they were concerned, their responsibility was to master the materials provided by their school. Black Von Steuben participants remembered little in the way of ethnic or racial inclusion in their high school curriculum, and few thought it was even an option then. Anthony noted, "I never really thought about it having any type of parallel with me being Black. I just thought you get the grades, you performed, you were given the opportunity to be placed in other classes. And I think that was simple as that." Trénace believed the curriculum was "modeled as best as it could at that time period." Reflecting, she said, "It was almost like we were nonexistent, or we didn't play a role in anything." For Octavia, there was no reflection of different ethnic groups, except maybe in history class. When thinking about the books, she said, "Yeah, they didn't really talk about Black people. It was all just basically a lot of White folks that they talked about."

Latinos at Von Steuben noted that there were no ethnic studies courses or much inclusion of other groups in history classes either. For example, Annette stated, "I guess looking back, I didn't hear as much about Mexican culture, I didn't hear about African American culture, I didn't hear about race relations much. . . . I can't say that culturally I learned anything, not even in the Spanish classes I took while I was there."

Like Black and Latino participants, Whites remembered little in the way of ethnic studies or multicultural education. At Von Steuben, David, Ben, and Dave saw little recognition of other racial or ethnic groups, including their own. David recognized that the curriculum was not very ethnically varied. "You didn't hear a lot about Frederick Douglass. You didn't hear a lot about Nat Turner, you didn't hear a lot about Malcolm X, you didn't hear a lot about Cesar Chavez. . . . I don't think people deliberately tried to cut [them] out." Ben thought the curriculum favored White Protestants and Western civilization. "I think that most of our subject matter, especially at least in the English classes, was based on probably like the classics kind of by the White Protestants, so your typical high school reading, so like Shelley, Keats, things like that. I don't think that it was very diverse, but I didn't really think about it at that time. . . .

But actually, now that you mentioned it, like even history classes, it was basically Western civilization history, history of America. And again, that just seemed like, that's what we should be learning." Dave, a Jewish participant, agreed that Protestants were favored, stating, "I don't think my heritage was reflected."

When prompted, many Bogan participants, like Von Steuben participants, recognized the limited curriculum, even if some viewed it as normal. Black students were aware that curriculum on other cultures was missing but found ways to justify its absence. LaDonna believed the curriculum was not based on her race and stated, "I didn't have an issue with it." Stanford had an interesting take on the issue, even though he wished he had learned more about diverse groups in high school. He said, "I didn't come in there looking for [the curriculum] to reflect [me], but if it did not reflect [me], I was not upset with it. I just thought that I was learning something different." Reflecting on his schooling, Stanford remarked, "I go to school to learn, and I don't care if they tell me that it's going to be White power today. It's going to stir some emotions, but I have to learn it because I need to know where you coming from to try to get where I'm trying to go." As he discussed the electives, he mentioned, "I think that this is just more of a bigger variety, and I don't think it was racially spurred or ethnically empowered." For Stanford, school was a means to an end. Looking back, he understood that he had to learn what schools offered him, even if he lacked access to information on his own Black history and culture. From this perspective, students simply needed to learn what was taught. Participants, like most other high school students, were not very conscious of the lack of diversity in their school's curriculum.

Rayshawn doubted the curriculum reflected her culture, but she and other students remembered a Black history class being offered at Bogan. She noted, "I wouldn't say that the school made a strong concerted effort to add in any new extra things with it, but there was an African American history class. There was a good balance and blend of teachers of various ethnicities. And so that helped." The Black history class conflicted with the academic requirements Rayshawn had, but she felt she learned about her culture at home. "I think it conflicted with another class that I wanted every time I tried to take it, and I just never took it. And besides, I said, well I've got a bunch of books [on Black history]. . . . My mom and dad made sure that we had enough. . . . What he was teaching, I pretty much knew a lot of it anyway." Rayshawn believed her parents filled the gap for what was lacking at school, so missing the chance to take a Black history course was not as important.

Latino participants at Bogan also noticed the lack of diversity in the curriculum. Maria saw a general curriculum: "I don't remember them getting in depth into the Incas or the Mayas, or anything like that." When asked whether the lack of diversity bothered her, she said, "I mean, that's what they taught. I felt like there was nothing you [could] do. This is their curriculum. This is what they want you to know. Why we need to know this, I don't know, but you had to learn it and try to get with the program. . . . I don't think there was ever a time when anybody stood up and said, 'Well, why do we need to know this? Teach us something.' We went with the flow. If that's what they taught, then that's what we needed to know."

Raul stated, "The classes I took, I don't think there's actually any difference between Black, White, and Hispanic. Algebra, you've gotta learn algebra." Although one of his favorite English teachers was Black, the course was still traditional. They read Shakespeare and *The Canterbury Tales*, but the teacher made it interesting. Raul remembered, "She put the twist on it, and she told us, 'Think about how it reflects right now.' And she made it so it fit our generation. Not Black, White, or Hispanic. But she did it in the sense of what we deal with today and how we live." Bogan's curriculum was likely limited, but Raul's English teacher and others found a way to make the traditional curriculum relevant to the students, even if they failed to incorporate more diverse materials.

Whitney Young was the only predominantly Black school, but its curriculum still lacked diversity; participants who attended recognized this shortcoming. A White participant, Craig, focusing on history, briefly stated, "It was definitely a dead-White-guy history curriculum." Black participants Eve and Cassandra thought their history was minimized. Eve said, "It was just the average curriculum. . . . I mean it's going to give you the glossed-over history of our people. . . . But as far as . . . the literature classes, it wasn't like African American literature. It was the general stuff that most people would kind of be like, OK this is fine, I'm just going to accept it. You don't think about it." For Cassandra, there was little difference between high school and elementary school when it came to diversity in the curriculum: "Neither one of them really did extensive history on African Americans. But I think that was just commonplace. And if there was like an African American history class, I didn't take it. I wasn't a big fan of history. But it was just general education curriculum more so. They rarely focused on Black folks."

For each of these participants, whether they recognized the lack of multicultural curriculum at the time they were in school, most still felt they benefited from their education. Either they received the knowledge elsewhere, such as at home, or they believed that their responsibility in school was to master the information given rather than question what was left out. This was certainly different from the stance of their parents' generation, which was full of calls for changes to the curriculum. In the late 1980s and early 1990s, there was a resurgence of politically conscious music and Afrocentric ideas, as well as a growth of multicultural education, but most schools failed to adapt the curriculum, and most students were conditioned to receive the information without questioning it. This is likely due to an emphasis on back-to-basics curriculum, the publication of *A Nation at Risk* in 1983, the growth of culture wars, and an increase in national conservatism as part of the backlash from the leftist movements of the 1960s and 1970s.

When participants were asked whether the curriculum reflected their ethnic group, some White, Black, and Latino participants said they believed that the curriculum failed to actually represent any culture or ethnic group. A White student said, "We didn't really have much in the way of like racial education, I don't believe. I think it was all just educating ourselves. I think you just had the basic classes. . . . I mean it could have been mixed in maybe history . . . but there really wasn't much emphasis on it." Latino participants stated, "It was American history, it wasn't dealing with other ethnic groups," and the school "didn't focus as much on culture." Black participants said things like, "Most of the educational system don't have a curriculum that's based off of your race group," and "Education has not stemmed from an ethnic background." Many of these participants lacked a conscious recognition that much of the history and English curriculum focused on Whites. In fact, the status of Whites as a racial group went unacknowledged; participants seem to have perceived race or ethnicity as belonging only to non-White racial groups and non-American Whites. These participants' responses probably vary little from what most Americans would say, but they certainly are at odds with what Von Steuben teachers recognized as a need in the self-study the school produced in 1990.

School language and culture clubs were places where students could learn about different cultures. These clubs often provided a space for various groups to feel comfortable and share common interests, and they were not exclusionary. Because few students belonged to them, the clubs could not serve as a substitute for curricular changes in courses like history and English. Still, Eric, Eve, and Jacquese each believed the clubs provided cultural opportunities. Eric thought the clubs offered an atmosphere to learn about different groups.

> I mean they did have a Spanish club but because I didn't take Spanish, I didn't participate in it. But, the club itself did kind of focus on enlightening people about the Spanish culture. They promoted that for all of the cultures. They did have like Asian clubs, Latin, and like I said Spanish, French. I guess it kinda gave somebody the ability to be able to learn about it and also participate. They didn't limit it to—you know, for example—if you were not Asian, you were not allowed to participate in the Asian club. They left it open for everybody if you wanted to participate in it, it was there for you to join if you chose to.

Like Eric, Eve said, "I think we had an African American club to supplement that." While Eric and Eve were not part of these clubs, Jacquese recalled receiving some Black history in the Afro-American Club at Von Steuben. The schools should certainly be credited for fostering these types of extracurricular activities, even though providing a multicultural curriculum would have been more beneficial.

A White participant from Bogan mostly remembered a standard curriculum but thought the addition of curriculum on other cultures or ethnic classes would separate students. "It was just core curriculum. In retrospect, I think it was just a very general broad curriculum. I don't recall there being any African history classes or anything that would essentially segregate students. I don't think that's desegregation at that point. I think that's segregating. But the only thing that I remember that was different, other than the language classes, and I believe Spanish and French were the only languages offered, was a Latin class. But there weren't any ethnic-centered classes whatsoever." This participant's assessment that a multicultural curriculum was not the point of desegregation may have been correct. Many advocates of school desegregation were far more concerned about eliminating the segregation and isolation of Black and Latino students. While others recognized some of the value of segregated schools and knew that all would not be well with desegregated schools, desegregation advocates went full speed ahead to eliminate the gross inequality of segregated schools. However, the challenges to desegregation (e.g., White resistance in the form of White flight, boycotts, and policy changes) meant that advocates spent much of their time focusing on how to achieve racial balance rather than integration. The general curriculum provided little information on the contributions of various groups. While the addition of ethnic studies courses could be an important step, infusing the regular curriculum with the diverse contributions of other groups would have been a far more productive way to integrate the curriculum.

The recognition of the curriculum as essentially "dead-White-guy history" does little to affirm many non-White students in desegregated schools. The entrenched nature of institutional racism makes it easy for all students, regardless of race or ethnicity, to see this limited curriculum as normal and to be unaware of its exclusionary teachings. This type of desegregation affirms whiteness and avoids integration. Underlying the lack of a reaffirming curriculum was the need for participants to understand the ways of the dominant culture in order to eventually be "successful" within that society. Students recognized schooling as a means to an end and knew that mastering what was taught was an essential aspect of social advancement. However, if they just mastered what was taught, the society remained largely unchanged.

The mistreatment, microaggressions, and racism directed at students by some teachers, counselors, and administrators, and the lack of a culturally inclusive curriculum, were some of the ways school structures limited integration. Desegregation was an important step in providing Black and Latino students with the resources and opportunities their neighborhood high schools may have lacked. The expectations of supporters of desegregation were high, but as shown by several scholars and predicted by Black opponents of desegregation, a lot of work was still needed to improve the integrative experiences within schools. Boundaries remained difficult to cross, and the structural limitations meant that students themselves were tasked with furthering their integrative experiences through interracial interaction and the development of interracial friendships.

5

"We Were from All Over Town"

Interracial Experiences in and out of School

Karen was fully immersed in the diversity at Von Steuben as she made all types of friends, brought friends to her home, and made the most of her cross-cultural experiences. Her mother referred to her friends as "the Rainbow Coalition." Fred Hampton, the leader of the Illinois chapter of the Black Panther Party, started the original Rainbow Coalition when he united the Panthers with the Young Lords and Young Patriots Organizations. This brought together Blacks, Puerto Ricans, and Whites for political organizing.[1] Jesse Jackson founded the National Rainbow Coalition in 1984, also utilizing the name to signify interracial coalition building. Karen's mother interpreted the parade of people who came through her doors as a similar interracial grouping. Karen described her friendships:

> A car would pull up, and some kids would come in, and I wouldn't be ready to go or whatever. They'd say hi to my mom. . . . One of my best friends was an Indian girl, like first generation. I'm first-generation American. My parents are from Ireland. But I'm still first-generation American. . . . One of my best friends at school was a Jewish guy. . . . I had a bunch of like Asian friends because I was in kind of accelerated classes and so were they! . . . My group of friends seemed

> pretty well mixed. It's like a couple little Black girls, a couple of Asian girls, and a couple of White girls and an Indian girl, a Jewish guy.

Karen represents the full richness that integration can embody, though others were unable to move beyond a simple association and polite tolerance. Those who did largely maintained friendships in school. Few were able to interact outside school.

Advocates of school desegregation sought to create integration by putting students of different races into the same schools. The larger goal was an end to inequality, but a by-product was that students would overcome their stereotypical ideas of one another, learn to see each other beyond race, and perhaps even create interracial friendships. Students from segregated communities who attended desegregated schools were presented with the novel opportunity to integrate with fellow students of other races. Collegiality and camaraderie tended to emerge when these students were placed in common social settings daily for several hours—classrooms, the cafeteria, buses, athletic teams, social clubs, and so on.

Study participants themselves made integration occur at their schools despite the limitations of school structures, society, and Chicago's segregated neighborhoods. Their classroom interactions and extracurricular activities fostered interracial friendships that were also visible in school cafeterias, in neutral locations outside school, and in cultural exchanges that occurred when they visited each other's homes. A few went beyond friendships and dated interracially, much to the chagrin of some parents and classmates. When students interacted interracially outside school, they carried integration with them to meeting places and homes, countering the norms of their communities and families.

Most participants revealed that their closest friendships were with others in their racial or ethnic group. Still, some participants reported forming and sustaining interracial friendships beyond superficial acquaintances. For instance, athletes found substantial connections, as team sports brought them together. Those who formed meaningful friendships visited the homes of friends from other racial and ethnic groups. This provided cross-cultural experiences and elicited awareness of the socioeconomic class differences between neighborhoods. Students' interracial friendships and relationships spurred integration at desegregated schools. Yet despite their best efforts, societal limitations and the spatial distance between students' communities curtailed their efforts to maintain friendships and hindered their dating relationships. Sometimes participants were successful in subverting societal norms, but other times the norms of their families and communities influenced their efforts to integrate. Maintaining interracial friendships while living in segregated environments meant challenging community norms by disregarding their parents' and community members' attitudes as they ventured into segregated neighborhoods. Crossing racial boundaries transformed their cultural understanding, but it did not bring an end to those boundaries.

Interactions in the Cafeteria

At most schools, lunchtime provides students a reprieve from the structured day and permission to freely associate with their friends, most of whom are of similar racial, ethnic, or cultural backgrounds. Participants viewed separation by race and ethnicity in the cafeteria as a result of individuals' preference and comfort rather than of hostilities between groups. In desegregated schools, the question often arises (which also happens to be the title of psychologist Beverly Daniel Tatum's book), "Why are all the Black kids sitting together in the cafeteria?" It may be easiest to recognize when Black students are sitting together, but this means that White students are sitting together too. Tatum argues that students are in search of their identities when they reach adolescence. They begin to identify racially in middle school as a result of puberty and awareness of how society views them racially.[2] In predominantly White schools, students cling to their own racial and ethnic groups.

Participants mostly ate with other students who shared their racial or ethnic background, though there were some notable exceptions. Blacks and Latinos, athletes, and those who had the same classes or participated in the same activities sat together. Though the cafeterias at Bogan, Whitney Young, and Von Steuben High Schools were remembered as segregated spaces, Blacks, Whites, and Latinos acknowledged that they all got along. A few participants experienced in-group pressure to sit with their own racial group in the cafeteria instead of other racial groups. The internal racial and ethnic boundaries were structured in a way that determined the boundaries of acceptability and sanctioned those who appeared disloyal. Those who had trouble crossing boundaries simply avoided the cafeteria or sat with their own group to avoid ridicule. Cafeterias still served as important spaces for integration for those who sat with interracial groups of classmates or friends from extracurricular activities.

The ways participants interpreted sitting with their own groups in the cafeteria defy the view that separation is automatically negative. Tracy, a Black Von Steuben participant, exemplifies this in her understanding of why the friends she sat with were mostly of her own race: "As much as we had classes together . . . most people kind of just had a comfort. I mean they've done studies. Just had a comfort, you gravitate toward your own. And so, not to say that you won't sit with someone else, but you kind of develop those connections with people. There were a couple different people that I gravitated to that I had lunch with that looked just like me . . . for the most part." Ladonna, from Bogan, sat with mostly Black friends and summed it up best: "I sat with people like me . . . who were my friends. [*Laughter.*] . . . There are cliques everywhere. You basically come from . . . some commonality. In a racial school back then, the commonality was your race."

Two White Von Steuben participants, Trey and Ben, noticed the segregated nature of the cafeteria and explained how they interpreted the racial and ethnic separation, though they themselves mingled with other racial groups. Trey thought students sat where they were most comfortable: "Like in most places, people gravitate to what they feel comfortable with. I mean there was no . . . tension or animosity or anything along those lines. I think it was just was the natural evolution of . . . people . . . conversing or being with people that are like them. . . . But there's certainly . . . that aspect to it of being segregated in terms of ethnic groups, for sure." Ben also saw groupings based on race. "I actually found it to be somewhat segregated in practice in the sense that when we'd go into the cafeteria . . . you'd get a group of White kids all together, you'd get a group of Asians whether they're Korean or the Filipinos would all kind of hang together, and . . . Blacks would all kind of be together, and I found that they just grouped themselves by . . . their own particular race or ethnicities, and I just found that to be somewhat strange." Although students crossed segregated boundaries to integrate, many still found comfort within the confines of their own racial groups.

White participants who attended Bogan thought racial divisions in the cafeteria were not inherently negative since students were cordial to one another and shared academic spaces. Tracy assessed her cafeteria experience and thought people mostly ate with their own groups. "Well I think . . . that it was again a social versus academic thing. And I think socially, everybody kind of congregated during lunch time, during study periods, on their own . . . and within their own groups. But academically, across the board, I really don't remember any divisions." Then again, Tracy only ate in the cafeteria freshman year. "After that you were a dork if you ate in the lunch room!" Jennifer thought that people got along but did not necessarily socialize with one another. She said, "It was just like we all got along and, I mean, we didn't necessarily hang around . . . outside of school. We didn't sit together at lunch. But, we didn't not say hello if we had someone in our class." Jennifer's response indicates a view of getting along characterized by tolerance, as students accepted each other, even spoke when they saw each other, but never created interracial friendships or even meaningful connections. Tolerance is the most limited form of integration, in which people accept others in their space and, if there is no hostility, everyone interprets it as getting along.

Like members of other groups, Latino participants sat with other Latinos. Lourdes recalled, "During lunchtime, mostly . . . like the Hispanics would stick together. . . . But you could see a couple of them here and there just kind of intermingle." On days that she did not go home or to White Castle with her friends for lunch, Oralia sat mostly with Latinas in the cafeteria. White and Latino participants from Von Steuben and Bogan who lived near their schools were more likely to eat lunch outside the cafeteria. Few Black participants mentioned leaving for lunch; this could be because they lacked the financial means to do so or because Black Bogan students were uncomfortable in a community that was once so adamant about keeping them out.

While many used their lunch break to catch up with friends from their same racial or ethnic groups, there were many participants who sat in mixed groups. These interactions served as important forms of integration, beyond participants' simply tolerating one another. LaDonna, from Bogan, stated, "Every now and then you have someone . . . from a different race, who bonds with you, and they were a token in the middle of your crew." A token is typically nominally accepted or treated as an insider but also serves an integrationist role as a symbolic bridge between groups. Marc and Teresa, Black participants from Von Steuben, sometimes sat with mixed groups of friends with the same lunch period or with the same extracurricular activities. Marc sat with friends from the band and in mixed groups depending on whom he "felt like talking to that day." He never made a "conscious decision" about sitting with any racial or ethnic group of friends; it depended on whom he saw. "If there were any folks from band, I would often sit with my band friends. . . . If the band teacher was . . . on duty that period we would all sit and chat." Teresa also moved around at lunch, and she played card games with her White friends. "I taught them how to play spades. And they hated playing spades with me. Because [my friend] told me that my whole demeanor changed! [*Laughter.*] He said, 'You were just so nice until we played cards!'"

Latino and White participants from Bogan and Von Steuben and Black participants from Whitney Young sat with mixed racial and ethnic groups, mostly from their classes. Nora either sat with the so-called nerd herd, a group of students in high honors classes at Bogan, or her Black friend Jamise. Debbie ate with her White, Chinese, and Mexican friends. Roger, who sat with people from his classes, remarked, "I just tried to sit with different people every day. If I could I'd sit with different groups of friends, tried alternating. It kind of gets boring sitting with the same people every day!" Whitney Young was predominantly Black, and Eve recalled that the cafeteria was mostly grouped by race. She sat mainly with Blacks and a few White friends. Cassandra chose to sit with White students because "there were so many of us [Black students]." Josephine sat with different racial groups over the years. She found her one-on-one relationships with her half-White/half-Filipina friend and Black friend more meaningful, so she ate with them.

Blacks and Latinos from Von Steuben and Bogan sat together in the cafeteria and learned about each other's cultures. Ralo, from Von Steuben, sat mainly with Mexicans and Puerto Ricans but observed, "There was a lot of segregation in the cafeteria and you could tell that it was only the Latinos, the Puerto

Ricans, and the Blacks that mainly hung out together, or they interacted with each other the most." Similarly, Rayshawn, from Bogan, sat mostly with Black students but also remembers sitting with Latinas. "I probably would say, anybody that were part of the group, that tended to blend together . . . they were Blacks and Hispanics. We would buddy up. And they would teach us their language and they would teach us different words mean different things in different cultures. So they would try to enlighten us about a lot of things." Cultural sharing was an important aspect of integration and a way to break down barriers between groups.

When students chose to sit only with others outside their race, they often experienced a backlash from their own racial group. These experiences call into question the level of tolerance that existed. One Black participant, Elizabeth, felt like an outcast and consequently avoided the cafeteria because it was segregated. She said, "I was a lab assistant in the science lab or doing some extracurricular activities, so I wasn't often in the cafeteria. But probably the reason I wasn't often in it, because I probably didn't feel that comfortable. . . . If you're Black and you're not sitting with the Black people all the time, there's going to be issues. . . . Back then people call you 'Oreo' a lot.[3] You don't . . . hang [with] Black[s] enough, that was definitely an issue." For Elizabeth, boundary crossing was a difficult endeavor. The distinct racial divisions meant that students who wanted to move in multiracial circles or who appeared to prefer White friends were often taunted.[4] Some Black participants made a conscious choice to sit with other Black students; otherwise they would not be seen as "Black enough" and were ridiculed and pressured to be loyal. In-group pressures to conform made boundary crossing tenuous. While the boundaries were forced from the outside, internally, there was an acceptance of them and the criteria for how one performed within the confines of a group.[5]

A Von Steuben student wrote a feature story about Oreos in *New Expression*, a high school–run, citywide publication. In the story, another Von Steuben student was interviewed and stated that she was called an Oreo because she had "White friends and achieve[d] like White people do."[6] This student's statement harks back to beliefs about "acting white."[7] Sociologist Karolyn Tyson notes that Black students in high tracks "spend most of the day in the company of Whites, away from the vast majority of Black students."[8] This often limits their ability to make friends with other Black students. Being called an Oreo has more to do with broader issues of racial identity and friendship networks that form in schools than with academic success. The students were ridiculed for reasons beyond their being "smart," and more likely because they seemed to prefer to associate with Whites over Blacks. A multiracial group of students formed the Oreo Club to end the hostility that their friendships created.[9] Indeed, the multiracial Oreo Club was an ingenious attempt to delegitimize a negative label and form a new group in which students could associate.

An Oreo symbolizes "both racial separation and racial integration."[10] Those who use the term value group loyalty and those called an Oreo are criticized for their attempts to integrate.

Where Elizabeth found problems in the cafeteria, Anthony found a welcoming environment:

> People sat with me. And that is the honest-to-God truth. I could sit at an empty table and by the time I'm halfway through my plate it could be one Black guy, one White guy, Hispanic guy. It was just like that. That's just how it was. There was no cliques. . . . I can't remember cliques. And even if there were cliques, they weren't cliques that superseded the overall friendship of others. You know, it wasn't the cliques that couldn't be infiltrated. If I saw a bunch of White guys, oh, it was nothing! . . . It was nothing for us to see a bunch of White people go over there. We'd go, "Let's go sit with those White people."

Anthony was popular and social, and he cared little what others thought of him. His ability to sit with whomever he chose seemed unthinkable for Elizabeth. It likely made him unaware of other people's difficulties.

Athletes often had the easiest time breaking the color line in desegregated schools, as they maintained bonds that were more likely to endure beyond the athletic activity itself. The interdependence, solidarity, and collective achievement inherent in team sports made it more likely that athletes would break down the barriers of racial separation and form interracial friendships.[11] Melanie, a White Von Steuben participant, had memories of a White athlete who "totally clicked with [Black members of his team]." Gina, from Bogan, thought people had their separate groups but athletes mixed. "I mean everybody had their own little groups, except the athletes, the jocks. It was just a mix of everybody. But everybody else had their own little groups. . . . I kind of floated."

Sports also serve as a way for even nonathletes to cross racial lines. For instance, Nick's love of basketball gave him common ground to share with other students interested in sports, regardless of their race. He recalled the fun they would have supporting different basketball teams.

> My buddies, my group, my guys that I typically hung around with were Black, were Hispanic, Middle Eastern. . . . I've sat down at a table there's Black kids all around and, we sat down and they were yelling at me and I was yelling at them. And I was a big basketball fan, I was a big Celtics fan at the time and the Celtics were doing great and the Bulls weren't. . . . Every time the Bulls would lose, I'd let 'em all have it, everybody there I saw, I'd let 'em have it, regardless of their color. And, of course, every time the Celtics lost, they were letting me have it, regardless of the color! So but . . . that's about what I can recall from the lunchroom.

People who crossed racial boundaries in the cafeteria often did so when they had common classes and interests and participated in sports and extracurricular activities.

School Activities

Extracurricular activities fostered interracial collaboration at the three schools, though certain sports, clubs, and cultural groups were less diverse.[12] Based on the 1986 Von Steuben yearbook, sports like track, cross-country, volleyball, and cheerleading offered a greater mixture of Blacks, Whites, Latinos, and Asians. However, soccer tended to be mostly Latino and White, basketball was predominantly Black, and boys' tennis was mostly Asian. According to Bogan's 1986 yearbook, football, wrestling, tennis, cheerleading, and baseball were more diverse. But volleyball, swimming, bowling, and softball were predominantly White, and basketball and pom pons were mostly Black. While the band and choir at Von Steuben were very diverse, at Bogan, the concert band was diverse, but the choirs, particularly the mixed chorus choir, were mostly Black. At both schools, Asians were more likely to participate in academic activities like math teams.[13]

Socioeconomic status was one factor that determined student participation in school activities. Those who worked had limited opportunities to stay after school. For instance, Anthony participated in a few activities but eventually stopped because he had to work after school. He was a member of the African American Club, sang in the school choir, and took part in theater. Anthony said, "I didn't get involved with too many other things because I had to work from sixteen on. So when I got out of school I went to work. I missed a lot of after-school activities [after] my sophomore [year]. . . . I didn't have much money growing up. So I didn't have the luxury of time." Paul was unable to participate in any extracurricular activities because of the cost. "It's always something about money. . . . I also didn't have the encouragement from my mother and her husband either." Students having to work and their parents' inability to pay the costs associated with some activities (e.g., uniforms and fees) were socioeconomic factors that limited participation.

Long commutes also hindered student participation in after-school activities. Because participants often took public transportation, they got home very late and often in darkness. Angela, from Bogan, was involved in choir for four years and was briefly on the cheerleading team, until her mother made her quit because she was coming home too late after games. "I literally only did that for a couple of games and then I had to . . . quit. And I think when I left cheerleading, I was on the pep squad. So that was during the games." Like Angela, Melissa, who attended Von Steuben, participated minimally. "I didn't do a lot of activities 'cause my mom and dad did not want me to have to travel [home] by myself. I'm like, 'I'm not traveling by myself!' They just [were] like no." Melissa managed to attend some games and events despite her parents' apprehension. Erin, a White student from Von Steuben, recalled,

> I really didn't do anything. There was a couple of reasons for that. One, I was too busy being a juvenile delinquent. Two, it was not a good neighborhood. . . . I remember freshman year I joined the swim team, and as soon as the time change [daylight saving time] on the clock hit, and I'm standing out in the middle of the street waiting for a public bus—'cause we didn't have school buses—at eight o'clock at night in that neighborhood. My mother went, "Not a chance." And my father was a cop, so there was no way I was going to be out.

The Albany Park community, where Von Steuben is located, was considered a good neighborhood. Her parents likely feared her taking public transportation alone at night. Another White student, Jennifer, from Bogan, was more involved in community activities because of the long commute, although she participated in French Club for two years. She said she was not involved "because it was so far from home. It was two bus rides home." However, she also noted that this made her more active in her own neighborhood. "So . . . in my community I was involved in more things. Like I was a girl scout until I was sixteen. [*Laughter.*] It's a little embarrassing. I really enjoyed it!" Desegregating in a segregated city through school choice made it more difficult for students of different racial groups to participate in after-school activities because so many had to travel farther to get to school.

While some parents were concerned about the distance, others were strict about their children's responsibilities in their homes. For example, though Annette, a Latina, lived close to Von Steuben, she had to go home after school because her mother was so strict. "There wasn't a whole lot of going out, because there was coming home, doing homework, cleaning the house." To Annette's mother, extracurricular activities were not as vital to her child's development as academics.

Students who participated in after-school activities found that the participation of members of different racial and ethnic groups varied by activity. Trey's experience as a basketball and baseball player for four years and as a member of the concert choir for two years at Von Steuben is a great example of the different racial and ethnic representation in each activity.

> I was the only White guy on the [basketball] team. . . . My nickname was White Lightning because I was the fastest White guy that most of 'em had ever seen. . . . They gave that to me, obviously. But so that was certainly . . . segregated and then . . . I played baseball. That was sort of a different, more Hispanic, you know Latin, type of thing. There were more . . . Caucasians that

played on that team or in the program as far as that goes.... There weren't certain neighborhood people [in these activities], so most of the people that I hung out with in school lived in other areas. I really didn't spend a whole lot of time with the basketball guys outside of school, or the baseball players 'cause they lived in different part of the city. So that was kind of a little bit of the aspect of segregation ... geographically.

Concert choir ... was sort of a representative group of different ethnic backgrounds throughout the whole school regardless of class—freshman, sophomore, junior, senior, whatever. Through that we would go on trips to, we went to Atlanta, Georgia, we went to Los Angeles to perform and places like that. So ... then ... the people that I hung out with socially or in the lunchroom or things like that were different from people that were on the basketball team or in the baseball program. But concert choir was sort of more representative, so I did kind of have the unique position of being a part of different groups just based on activities.

Trey's participation in these activities gave him access to people of different ethnicities. Although segregation limited his friendships outside school, he still formed bonds with them.

Bogan and Von Steuben both had predominantly Black dance teams that performed at halftime during basketball games. At Bogan, the group was called the pom pons. Maria, a Latina, recalled efforts to diversify the squad:

The principal had said that he didn't want the pom pons squad to be all Black.... He went up to ... the coach in charge of the pom pons team to have open auditions for anybody that was non-Black to try out. And she could pick from those people to join, because originally ... they were always Black. And I mean, if they had the moves, then they were the only ones who could do it. It was hard. I mean, it was hard for people ... to pick up a lot of the steps that they had; they used to do a lot of moves that are difficult.

Maria acknowledged that while the coach followed the principal's request, the team sometimes had to learn two dances for each game, and some of the new girls had difficulty learning the moves with such a quick turnaround. She said,

It was sometimes a week before the next game, some two weeks that you had to learn two different routines, and they were powerful, they were fast. They were really energized ladies and the coach, she was really tough. They got all these people and in the end a lot of them were dropping like flies, 'cause it was like, this is how she runs it. And yeah, you want to have a mixed team, but if we can't keep up, you know. And sometimes if you weren't ready she'd pull you out....

> You're not going to perform because you're not ready. You didn't learn the steps and then it was back to the drawing board for the next thing.

The team never became evenly mixed. In 1986, there were twenty-five people on the team, and only seven were non-Black, two of whom were team managers.[14] Yet the principal's demands for a more diversified team led to the addition of a few non-Black girls. Principals at other desegregated schools also attempted to diversify school activities through quotas, particularly cheerleading and pom pons squads.[15] It is difficult to know whether Bogan's principal attempted to diversify other activities. The predominantly Black pom pons squad was unlikely the public representation he wanted for the desegregated school, especially if they performed at other schools.

Tracy, from Bogan, also recalled the pom pons squad being Black:

> I'll tell you specifically that I did try out for pom pons girl at one point. My girlfriend and I, she was also Caucasian. . . . We both tried out for pom pons group and we were the only two White girls who tried out. And she was the only one, the only White girl who made it. The rest of the team was Black. And I thought that was interesting at the time. . . . I guess I thought it was strange that no other White girls wanted to try out—that were motivated to try out and . . . I remember the whole pom pons squad being Black. Maybe it wasn't, but that's what I remember.

As other studies demonstrate, when a tipping point was reached at which Black students accounted for a particular percentage of an activity's participants, Whites often withdrew.[16] In other words, Whites felt comfortable in activities where they were the majority, and when that changed, they abandoned the activity. Despite Bogan's pom pon team having seven White or Latino participants in 1986, fewer Whites tried out for it over time.

Some students participated in activities that few others in their racial and ethnic groups joined. Eve, from Whitney Young, joined the Key Club and discussed the diversity of the club: "I think that the perception was that that was kind of a quote-unquote 'White' thing, or not a Black thing. It was probably three of us who were Black . . . that were in the Key Club." Roger, a White participant from Von Steuben, joined the Korean Club because he "just tried like mixing with different cultures or whatever and just trying to learn different things . . . about different people." He noted, "They were pretty accepting. So I went to picnics and volleyball games and stuff with them and everything." Although the group was accepting, they often spoke Korean when he was around. "But the language was something where you kind of . . . feel a little bit awkward. 'Cause when they start talking Korean and you don't have no idea what they're saying. I don't think it was really intentional, per se, but it was just more of a familiarity and just comfort level for them just to do that. 'Cause it is after all the Korean culture. Right, you know what I mean? It's my bad if I don't speak Korean! [*Laughter.*]" Roger's experience demonstrates the cultural adjustments made by students when they were the minorities in activities. The students who made up the group's racial or ethnic majority were there so that they could be themselves.

Josephine felt like an outsider with the more affluent Black students at Whitney Young. But she found a place in extracurricular activities. "[I] found my comfort zone in the . . . theater group called the Company that I participated in quite a bit doing stage management or sometimes being a part of the chorus when we did musicals. And the kids in those groups were . . . White kids, Latino kids, kind of—I don't want to say misfit Black kids, but they were definitely not from the mainstream Whitney Young kids. So that's kind of where I found my niche."

Interracial Friendships in School

Participants at Bogan were more likely to discuss the subtle distance that existed between racial and ethnic groups, though students remained cordial and tolerant. For many, the racial boundaries remained. A few White participants had acquaintances of other races from their school activities or classes. Tracy, Jennifer, and Debbie said they had no problems with students of different races but had limited friendships with them, particularly with Black students. This was the result of both the social distance within school and the segregation outside school. Tracy's friends were all White, but she was friendly with some students from different races and ethnicities in her class. "I didn't really have a lot of friends like that. I mean I had some academic acquaintances, but I didn't really have any friends that were Black or Asian or even Hispanic." She thought it was a function of segregation within school. "I mean you got along with other students in your classes. . . . I remember I had a *friend*, I guess, for lack of a better word. She was somewhere between a friend and an acquaintance, on yearbook staff, who was Black. I couldn't tell you her name now. But I remember her, and I remember she had me in the grab bag [gift exchange like secret Santa] one year. But she wasn't a friend that I had outside of school." Tracy acknowledged that there was a difference between being "friends" because of a class or activity and forming real friendships, particularly when geographic and social distance in the larger society limited the continuation of friendships outside school.

Like Tracy, Jennifer was friendly with a classmate of a different race. "I never had any problems at all and everybody was always very nice—even if we didn't hang out. Like OK, I had [a friend] that I had drivers ed with, and she was Black, and I was White. And we didn't hang out maybe at school, but we had a great time at drivers ed. It was just like we all got along and, I mean, we didn't necessarily hang around outside of school. We didn't sit together at lunch. But we didn't not say hello if we had someone in our class." Their friendliness was a function of convenience that rarely went beyond the class they took together. Outside that space, they managed to speak, but that was the extent of the relationship. This is a typical high school interaction, as students change classes and may only have contact during one class period. However, Jennifer's use of double negatives signifies that there was little expectation that friendships would go beyond these amicable, space-specific interactions. Friendships are not an expectation of integration, but the extent to which they formed demonstrates the meaningful connections that could occur.

Debbie had a Chinese and a Latina friend and felt as though she was accepted into Latino and Asian groups; but she had no Black friends. "I mean even the Black students . . . were always very nice to me, the ones that I did know. I mean I wouldn't say that I hung out with them socially, but they were always nice to me. They were always decent. . . . I don't think I wasn't like *welcome* to go hang out with them after school or anything. But while we were in school, we got along fine."

A Black participant, Rayshawn, talked about the difficulty of being more than "surface" friends with people of other racial and ethnic groups while at school.

> Some were a little distant, and I guess like me initially, and some remained this way throughout their experience at Bogan. A [few] seemed to be a little unsure or a little unsteady as to how to approach a relationship or as to how to develop one. So it was more surface level hi and bye. . . . My locker partner was Mexican . . . and we were also in the same division room [home room] of course. So . . . the first couple of years, we were good as gravy so to speak. We communicated a lot. We shared books and everything was fine. But then something happened and then she just kind of changed on me. I don't know if she gradually grew more and more towards her own culture and less and less from other cultures. I don't know, maybe subconsciously I did the same thing. I don't know. But then our relationship just became more of respectful and cordial but nothing really beyond that. It really became surface level, and by the time we graduated, it was a kind of a superficial hug goodbye. We signed each other's yearbooks with very general statements and that was it. Nothing deep, nothing that showed four years of a friendship.
>
> Being a segregated city, it was almost like when it came to the outside activities, Bogan was segregated. When we left school, a lot of the times, we went our different ways. And there were a few students, Blacks, who had friends of Caucasian descent come to their houses and vice versa. But then there were still some families who could not accept us, White families. I do

> remember that, and the kids would tell us that. Their families made comments that, you know, don't bring us home, or don't bring Hispanics home. They would make some comments, a few of the families would. You can kind of sense it too when those parents would come up to the school. You might not even know it, but you could just see from their body language that if they didn't speak to you when you spoke, you knew.

Some parents, many of whom protested desegregation in the late 1970s and early 1980s and lost that battle, were unwilling to let go of segregation. Once schools were desegregated, these parents discouraged their children from forming in interracial friendships. However, students often ignored their parents' views and sought to create integration. At the very least, they were tolerant of their diverse classmates.

Stephen thought the friendships were a bit superficial as well. "I mean, just, wasn't that kind of party. They didn't socialize with us like that. Did I have White friends or Mexican friends? Yeah, but no, we didn't visit each other's homes." Both Rayshawn and Stephen noted the underlying tensions that still existed at Bogan. Rayshawn's experience with her Mexican locker partner could simply have been an instance of people growing apart over the high school years; however, her and Stephen's discussions of the distance between them and White students indicate that there were more barriers at Bogan that inhibited a truly integrative experience. Since Bogan was a difficult school to desegregate, not everyone was readily accepting of interracial friendships. Desegregated schools brought the students together and gave them an opportunity to develop tolerance and respect for each other, in some ways chipping away at the divisions created by the segregation in the outside community, but friendship was not guaranteed.

Some participants recognized people from different racial and ethnic groups as their friends, but the friendships were still largely limited to school. Edgar, a Latino from Von Steuben, said, "I had friends of different racial groups, yes. But as far as coming home, there was only like one or two pals that ever kind of hung around the house. They were both Hispanic. But I certainly had friends at Von Steuben that were non-Hispanic." Likewise, Maleta, a Black participant from Von Steuben, had friends of different races in school. She said, "I hung around mostly Blacks. I did hang around some Hispanics and mostly Blacks. . . . I guess I was part of a clique! I did hang around some White people, but not as often 'cause I mean I still lived in my neighborhood!" Diana, a Latina from Bogan, also had diverse friends in school. She noted, "I definitely had two different sets of friends. I had the set of friends that I grew up with that I went to grammar, elementary school with, mostly Hispanics. Then I had my other set of friends who I met solely at high school, and they were very diverse. They were Hispanic. They were Black. They were White. I mean, they were combined.

And that's actually who I spent most of my high school years with [more] than with the first crew because they were in, all in different classes than I was." Anthony had a friend whom he only saw at school, but this did not diminish their friendship. Seeing his friend at their twentieth class reunion reminded him of how close they were in school. "Even though we were from two different cultures, two different backgrounds, I never went over to his house; he never went to my house." Yet they were close friends in school because they had a lot in common.

Connecting meaningfully across racial and ethnic lines was often difficult for some students, particularly at Bogan. This may be due in part to the racial tensions in the community, which have since simmered down but for so long caused some of the unease. Von Steuben participants appear to have been more likely to form connections with students of different racial and ethnic groups, but even when they did not, the conversations around interracial friendships were not the same as at Bogan. For some Bogan participants, interracial friendships seemed less favorable. Those who were able to maintain intimate friendships did so at school, in the lunchroom, in classes, and during school activities.

Interracial Friendships outside School

Long commutes to school often negated opportunities to maintain the interracial friendships formed in school. Most participants admitted that the distance to friends' homes was the main reason they lacked interaction outside school. Chicago's segregation exacerbated those distances, making it difficult to cross racial boundaries. Craig, a White participant who attended Whitney Young, stressed the distance: "Well because we were from all over town it never occurred to me to ever invite anybody. 'Cause we were all the way up, practically on the Chicago/Evanston border. Anyone who would have come with me would have had a long trip back. I wouldn't do that to someone." Ben, a White participant from Von Steuben, also acknowledged that the distance made it difficult to sustain friendships outside school: "Because everyone was taking public transportation, I don't think you knew where everyone was coming from. And also I really haven't kept in touch with very many of my classmates from high school, I'll admit, because I only saw them at school. Like, when I would go home, I would go miles up north and they would go, like, west or south or whatever, so we didn't really see each other after school quite so much." Finally, LaDonna, from Bogan, said that she brought home people of different races from her job, but not from her school. "First of all, most of the Latinos and Caucasians . . . [who] went to Bogan lived around Bogan. And I lived a good distance away. . . . Once we left school that really was it. . . . I know my clique pretty much lived around my house."

Families of other participants were relatively strict, preventing them from having friends over. Nora said her mother's strictness and desire to appease their White neighbors kept many friends away. "No, I never really did [have many friends from different races over] . . .'cause my mom, like I said, was so strict. And you couldn't go and do stuff. So that made it kind of difficult to have friends 'cause everyone was coming from different neighborhoods. . . . It would be far to go see them. So that became like difficult to do." Nora also remembers her sister worrying her mother by having Black friends over. "Well it was difficult 'cause my sister's best friend, one of her really good friends . . . was Black. . . . So now we both have these girls coming to stay over. . . . I only think she would worry what the neighbors would say. 'Cause we would walk to school . . . when they stayed over. So that was like a big problem and that was in high school. Yeah, well she was kind of like, they're gonna have a fit!" Nora lived near Bogan in the Ashburn community. Ashburn remained predominantly White for some time, as residents fought against Black encroachment and desegregation at Bogan. After initially facing discrimination, Latinos were eventually accepted in the community, but bringing Black friends home could lessen that tenuous "acceptance." Community pressures at times stifled integration outside school, but Nora and her sister balked at their mother's strictness and the neighborhood's expectations.

Other participants also had strict parents. Strictness served as a form of protection (sometimes overprotection) for girls in neighborhoods where trouble could easily be found. Additionally, religious or familial values limited the possibility of visiting or being visited by others. Gina, a Bogan participant who is half White and half Puerto Rican, rarely had friends visit her home. "I didn't bring many kids to the house. . . . My dad . . . was a Chicago cop [and an] alcoholic. [He saw] way too much bad stuff to give anyone a fair chance. There [were] some guys that he just flat out told them to leave. He would sit outside . . . in the squad car and run their license plates. He would wait till I got home from my dates to make sure they brought me home, which I can understand. He was something else."

Parents who are most successful at raising children in neighborhoods with few resources and ample vice typically segregate their children from neighborhood peers, monitor and control their behavior, and determine acceptable friends.[17] Trénace, from Von Steuben, was forbidden from visiting friends: "Oh, my mother didn't have that! She's like, 'I don't have my children going off to other strangers' houses.' Uh uh! Momma didn't have that. [*Laughter.*] 'I don't know their mother, I don't know their dad, I don't know what they're doing. I'm sorry, you won't go.'" Kelly, a Black participant from Bogan, also had a strict mom. Kelly remembered, "Nobody came to my house. They weren't allowed to. My mother was very strict. . . . And I also couldn't talk on the telephone. So they weren't allowed to call my house. But when my mother went out, I would get on the phone to sneak and call them so I could talk to folks if I chose to. So it just didn't work. People weren't allowed to come to my house and I couldn't talk to folks on the phone." Charman, a Black participant from Von Steuben, talked about the strictness of parents in general at that time. "Most of my friends were Black and Hispanics. But like during this time parents were more strict and the Hispanic friends they were like, 'Naw, I can't come 'cause my mom was like blah, blah, blah.' So that was basically it."

Participants usually met up at neutral sites outside school. This way, they could circumvent both their disapproving parents and the distance between their homes. Nora and others recalled the mall and other locations being common meeting places. "We . . . would meet at Ford City or at the movies 'cause the movie theater was brand new. We would just all meet there. Or if we didn't meet there, and we saw you there then we'd all just sit together." Nora's father preferred that she meet her friends at Ford City Mall, which was closer to home; but by sophomore year she chose to go farther away to Evergreen Park Mall. Eric, a Latino from Bogan, also met friends in a central location closer to school. "We did some after-school stuff like if it was somebody's birthday, we'd go out to like a nearby restaurant and just maybe buy the person lunch and probably somebody would pitch in and get 'em a cake." Roger, a White participant from Von Steuben, met friends away from home as well. "In high school, I think it was, most of the time we just hung out, not really at each other's homes per se. We just hung out in a central area . . . for the most part." Lourdes, a Latina from Bogan, also met up with friends near school: "After school a lot of us would get together and we'd go, there used to be a Pizza Hut down on Pulaski. . . . And it would be . . . Arabians and the Hispanics, and you know, the Blacks. I mean it was pretty much, and then Chinese and a couple of them were Japanese as well. But we would just all go eat. Have a good time. It wasn't, there was no[t] just one race."

In the 1980s, many Chicago high school students attended parties around the city that featured house music and other musical genres. Julian, a Latino from Bogan, described partying in segregated neighborhoods with friends from school:

> It was more of a mixed crowd I would say. Back in our days . . . there used to be a lot of parties happening like almost every weekend. And depending [on] what neighborhood it was in, that would determine what type of people you would probably get. Chicago is really segregated as far as the neighborhoods are concerned. So if there was a party going on in a Latino neighborhood, then almost everybody in that party would be Latino. You'd get a few people from out of the group, but not really. And then if the party would be in a White neighborhood, then the majority of people that . . . would attend would be the White people.

Julian never had a problem attending parties with people from other ethnic groups. While some people may have been surprised by his appearance, he was comfortable because he always attended parties where he knew people from his classes. Meeting in central locations helped to sustain integration beyond schools.

Despite the circumstances that limited participants from visiting one another's homes, many managed to visit friends or had friends of different racial and ethnic groups over. Michelle, from Bogan, talked about traveling to see friends in different neighborhoods. "It kind of depended like what groups you were in. You know what I mean? I kind of got along with everybody, so I don't think I'd be part of the norm. I hung out with the Latino kids, I hung out with the African American kids, I hung out with the kids from the neighborhood. I would even travel to other neighborhoods to see my friends. I'm not sure if that was the norm or not?" Peter, from Von Steuben, thought his parents were probably surprised when he first brought home friends of different races. "I think at first maybe they were a little shocked but . . . they didn't seem to respond any differently to any of the other friends that I brought around the house."

There were times when participants employed extraordinary measures to visit friends in different neighborhoods or to get them to attend functions. Marc, a Black participant from Von Steuben, had a friend going out of his way to pick him up. "I remember one of my colleagues, he brought me to a youth group meeting, and he actually came and got me; he and his brother, I think, could drive at the time. So his brother made the trip all the way from the northwestern part of Chicago to get me to take me back to the northwestern part of Chicago for a church meeting and then brought me back home!" Marc rarely brought friends to his home, because he "didn't want people to see how [he] lived at home per se." While admitting his home was nice, he also recognized that it was probably not as nice as the homes of his friends on the North Side.

Anthony had friends visit after a performance at a nearby church. "Friends came over from my choir. We had White people that loved to sing Black gospel music. And we had an outing at a church, an African American church in the city on Chicago Avenue." He said they had a "great time singing, great time praising God. [They] came to my house a little bit 'cause I stayed not far from around [the church]. Love them. And they were comfortable because of who they were with. And we made them feel comfortable. We didn't place fear in their mind. We didn't say, 'Y'all better get out here!'"

Crossing segregated boundaries to visit others came with perceived safety concerns and sometimes unwarranted fear. Media discussions of crime in Black and Latino neighborhoods, and lingering reputations of racism in White neighborhoods, caused many to fear for their own safety or the safety of others who visited them. With such extensive segregation in the city, most were unaware of what they might encounter if they chose to go beyond the segregated boundaries.

Even when they were unaware that they should be afraid, venturing into segregated neighborhoods often surprised neighbors who saw few people of other races or ethnicities in their neighborhoods. Carrying friendships outside schools not only served to extend integration but also highlighted how students took integration into their own hands. While participants crossed segregated boundaries almost daily on public transportation or in cars, venturing into communities was different from passing through them.

Some participants had safety concerns about bringing White friends to Black neighborhoods. Jacquese, for example, talked about not only the distance but also the possible danger of bringing White friends into her neighborhood. She had White friends with whom she sometimes sat in the cafeteria, but when asked whether she brought friends from different races home, she laughed and replied, "No, not in the hood. [*Laughter.*] I couldn't bring 'em home in the hood! Ooh no! I knew they couldn't come to my house 'cause I lived way in the West Side, deep in K-Town. I was like, 'No!' They would get hurt. So no, I didn't want to be responsible. [*Laughter.*]" Cornelius, another participant from K-Town, had a similar reaction: "To my house? . . . No. . . . They would have got beat up! I was sitting on the West Side. I was in the ghetto! [*Laughter.*]" He visited the homes of others and felt, "It was more acceptable for me to go to [their] house than for them to come to mine." The area dubbed K-Town is on the West Side of Chicago, where the streets all begin with the letter *K*. Anthony also lived on the West Side but disagreed that his classmates would have any problems visiting him. Jacquese and Cornelius were unwilling to the take the chance, whereas Anthony saw no reason for his friends to fear his neighborhood. Neighborhoods on the West Side were not all the same, and neither were people's perceptions of them.

Though some Black participants thought their neighborhoods were safe, their classmates believed the opposite. Elizabeth, a Von Steuben participant, was unable to convince her classmate to come to her house on the South Side for a class project. "I was trying to get him to come but he wouldn't come. He refused to come because he was afraid like he would get jumped [beaten up by a group]. And I kept trying to reassure him like, 'No, that's not going to happen.' But he never did. So he ended up doing his own part of his project on his own. And then when we got to school, he ended up, you know, we all got together, and we were able to complete it. But he didn't come to my house. Everyone else did but him." Black and White perceptions of Black neighborhoods as dangerous places limited integration. Either Black participants refused to be responsible for what could happen to a White visitor, or White friends were unwilling to risk finding out what dangers awaited them in those neighborhoods. Of course, not all Black neighborhoods were unsafe, but the widely held perceptions meant few wanted to test it. Neighborhood reputations often persist even when the reality is different.[18]

Lourdes, a Latina from Bogan, invited classmates to her home to work on a group project, but a Black friend refused to go. Once he found out she lived in Marquette Park, the friend responded, "No, I can't go there." Her friend's response helped Lourdes understand why her own family had a hard time when she first moved to the neighborhood. Her classmate was aware of the community's racist reputation, and whether the problems had subsided was irrelevant; Lourdes's classmate was unwilling to test the segregated boundaries in the same way Elizabeth's classmate was unwilling to go into a Black neighborhood.

Jaime, a Latino from Bogan, on the other hand, managed to get his friends to visit. He recalled that many people had assumed that his predominantly Mexican neighborhood was bad. "One of my Black friends would come over here. This was more towards like junior year. . . . He had a commute though. It was more of the pressure, but . . . even a couple of White girls would come over here too to visit. They always said that they wanted to visit the Little Village, and then everybody would say it was a real bad place. But when they got over here, they were like, 'Oh, it's actually not the way they said it [would be].' [*Chuckling.*]" Predominantly Mexican and Puerto Rican neighborhoods were feared and perceived as dangerous, much like Black neighborhoods. Most of the time that students visited neighborhoods with negative reputations, they found that their fear was unwarranted.

Ralo, a Latino from Von Steuben, invited over school friends of different races and ethnicities, and his White friends were "surprised" by his surroundings. Many refused to come back because he "grew up in the ghetto," where many of his neighborhood friends had difficulty avoiding urban pitfalls. Few people dared cross the real and perceived boundaries that existed in Chicago. The almost complete segregation of neighborhoods, along with media coverage of crime in those areas, made integration extremely difficult.

A few participants recalled their neighbors' reaction when friends of different races visited. Safety was not an issue, but their friends were often seen as a spectacle because of the rarity of certain racial groups in segregated communities. Cassandra, a Black participant from Whitney Young, remembers her neighbors' reaction to her two Asian friends dropping by her house. "I had a really good friend that was Asian and this one Asian guy that I liked, that was his friend. And they just showed up at my house one day and we weren't there. But my neighbors were trippin' out; they don't see Asian people where I lived. But . . . my family members didn't trip out 'cause my brother had friends—he went to Whitney Young too—he had friends of different races that he used to bring home. So it wasn't a big issue." When Maria brought Black friends to her Latino neighborhood, people wondered why they were there:

> We had people come over. It was funny because at first, like I said, in the neighborhood they'd be like "Oh, why is that Black guy coming here?" . . .

> [I would tell them,] "This is my friend from school." . . . They're still apprehensive about it. Or we would go over there, and you hear the moms talking to each other in Chinese or whatever and it's like "Who's that?" "Oh it's a friend from school." . . . They're stuck in the neighborhood, that's all they've been, so they had apprehensions about it. But once they knew that the person was fine and it wasn't any big major thing, they were OK with it.

The city's segregation meant some Chicagoans rarely saw people of different racial and ethnic groups in their neighborhoods. Crossing segregated boundaries led to different racial groups being easily identified and seen as "other," strange, and out of place.

John, a White participant from Von Steuben, had a best friend at school who was Black but identified as French Indian. "So my best friend . . . was African American. If you would ask him he would say he wasn't African American." His friend's family hailed from New Orleans, and he refused to identify with the "negativity" in his South Side community. Hence, he referred to himself as French Indian. John believed that no one challenged him because he was big. "We were the *Miami Vice* guys. And if you see the pictures in high school, you know back then *Miami Vice* was hot so I always wore like white. He came as the opposite. He had the dark clothes on. It was funny to see actually. It was comical." Since John lived across the street from school, his friend would come by and wake him up every morning. John's other friends from his apartment building would say, "Who's the big Black guy always coming to your house?" Though John said it was his best friend, he knew that they probably saw the two of them as "an odd-looking" pair.

Interestingly, some participants ventured into Black neighborhoods and housing projects to visit friends and had no problems. Keith, a Von Steuben participant who was half Mexican and half White, recalled going to a Black friend's house on the West Side in elementary school and learning from that experience. Though his experience was in elementary school, it is pertinent to the ways in which crossing racial borders to visit friends from different racial groups can be instructive. Keith stated,

> Even in grammar school and high school though, I felt that we were always aware that there was difference. Like, we were very aware that my neighborhood was different from your neighborhood. . . . My best friend in grammar school, his name was Marcus and he lived on the West Side in K-Town. And, believe me, when I went to Marcus's neighborhood and he came to my neighborhood, we realized there were differences in our neighborhoods. But . . . Marcus did not come from a poor family though. His family had been living in K-Town since like the twenties. And his grandfather retired from the steel mills when retiring from the steel mills was good and his grandmother retired from

AT&T. So you could imagine, they lived on Kostner right by Harrison, and it was crazy going down that block because it was literally like: burned-out building, vacant lot, burned-out building, some kind of drug-dealy house, and then their grandparents' building was a three-flat. It looked pristine, it had a big high fence, and his grandfather drove a very nice Cadillac. And so it's kind of weird 'cause going into his house, they had a big-screen TV and I didn't have a big-screen TV. . . . You know, they had nice things but they lived in a really crappy neighborhood. But they had been there for fifty years. Whereas, where I lived, was a quote-unquote "nicer neighborhood," but you know, we didn't have a Cadillac and we didn't have a big-screen TV in the eighties, where they did. But looking back at it, I never really thought of it as a matter of class. It wasn't until I got older that all of a sudden it started hitting me.

Keith managed to visit his friend in K-Town with no problems. While he learned a valuable lesson about class and the differences among neighborhoods, his story exemplifies the ways in which Black neighborhoods often had mixed socioeconomic classes living together.[19] Those who had migrated earlier and were longtime members of their community often remained in their neighborhoods despite the deterioration that occurred around them. They simply lived well among neighbors with fewer means.

Dave, a White participant from Von Steuben, visited a Black friend who lived in a housing project, not realizing that he should be scared.

My ignorance was my bliss. I found out later some of the Black guys I befriended—they were in some pretty bad neighborhoods. There's one from the projects. I don't think he was in the gang. He was Black, he was in the projects, and it was certainly different. And I went to visit him and I didn't even know that I should be scared out of my ass by walking in one of these projects. My parents freaked out when I told them where I was. I don't think I even knew it was called a project, I don't think. It's just where this guy happened to live.

Chicago housing projects had a notorious reputation as a social experiment gone terribly wrong.[20] Many people, regardless of race, feared entering them. Both Keith and Dave were unaware that they should be fearful of K-Town or the projects, and they were perfectly safe. Their naïveté allowed them to continue their integrated friendships beyond schools and into neighborhoods that had few White, Latino, or Asian visitors.

Unlike other participants who freely visited friends or had friends over, Stanford, a Black participant, admitted that his parents were against it. While at Bogan, Stanford hung out with his really good Asian friend, but he was not allowed to bring home friends of different races. He believed his mother's southern roots prevented her from being more open:

> Because they wanted a better way for us and my mother knew that in order for me to grow and to go to Bogan, I needed to know everybody and do everything. She still didn't allow it in her house. . . . I was never allowed to—I actually had a little Mexican girl that, the same girl that was like I wish that we had dated. I was going to bring her home for Thanksgiving. My mom said, "Naw, I don't want you to do that." It wasn't a big old argument, because at that time if my parents made a statement and that's what it was. You don't ask why. She was like, "Naw, I don't think you should do that." It was like, "OK." I found out later . . . that they didn't have no White friends. They had no White people to come through. We had a couple of White teachers, and they were cordial with White people when you'd go into stores and businesses, attorneys, you know those type of things. But no, no White friends.

Parents, regardless of race or ethnicity, often refused to change their beliefs and accept their children's friends of different races. Yet other parents were more open to their children's interracial friendships. Teresa, a Black participant from Von Steuben, remembered being close with a White friend and his family. "[We] would have sleepovers. His mother, she absolutely loved everything about me, and she said, 'You come over anytime you want, honey!' She practically gave me a key to the house." The race of a parent did not automatically determine how that parent would interact with his or her children's friends.

A few participants who visited the homes of others learned about different foods in their friends' homes. One of the first times Keith noticed the differences in neighborhoods was during elementary school. "When I was in grammar school, this one girl used to . . . come every morning with a pickle, a hot pickle. And I couldn't get those hot pickles in my neighborhood. I could get pickles, but they weren't hot. So I started giving her a quarter to bring me a hot pickle. I would have never had a hot pickle [*laughter*] if it was not for kids on the bus." Once he got older, Keith dined at friends' homes. "In high school, I learned what Korean food was, I learned what Indian food was. You know, I got to go to different people's houses. People's houses smell different based on what they eat. Greek people's houses smell different from Indian people's houses from Filipino people's house from my house." Tracy, a Black participant from Von Steuben, also recalled visits to friends' homes. "I remember one young lady, I think she was Chinese, her background was Chinese. And I just remember her house was set up a little bit different. Then another person I remembered, their mother was cooking, and the scents smelled differently. It was good, don't get me wrong! But it was different! You know, it's like, 'What's that?' Now I know it's garlic!" Visits to the homes of others facilitated cultural learning. In the foregoing examples, food became one of the primary vehicles through which people learned about each other's cultures. Participants came to both appreciate and differentiate among various types of foods based on the interracial friendships they formed.

Because Chicago's segregated neighborhoods meant that students from different races and ethnicities lived far apart, it was often difficult for students to maintain friendships with students of different races outside school. Other issues, such as parental influence and real and perceived safety concerns, added to the difficulty of maintaining such friendships. But participants often found ways to meet outside school and at one another's homes nonetheless. Interracial dating was another avenue for interracial relationships.

Interracial Dating

Staunch southern segregationists often touted separation of the races as the best guard against sex between Black men and White women. Fearing miscegenation, Alabama state senator Walter Givhan claimed that the motive for the desegregation advocated by the NAACP was "to open the bedroom doors of our White women to Negro men."[21] Sex was often used as a reason to avoid desegregation. Beneath this opposition was an underlying belief that bringing people of different races together would automatically lead them to the realization that they were not so different, and they might even be attracted to each other. Interracial relationships were not always perceived positively by participants' parents of all racial and ethnic groups. Though each situation was unique, it tested the limits of society's approval.

Some Latino parents opposed their children dating Blacks, and vice versa. Anthony remembered his girlfriend's father was opposed to their dating.

> My first girlfriend was Puerto Rican. . . . And I was crazy about her and I had no shame about it. . . . I remember her father threatening me, telling me that I couldn't be her boyfriend, but he wouldn't ever tell me why. And that was my . . . first exposure to racism, toward me. And it was outside the school, at her house. And that crushed me. 'Cause that was the best he could come up with; that I can't be with your daughter 'cause I'm Black. And I remember, she said, "He doesn't speak English." Well I said, "Well ask him how do I change this?" [*Pause.*] And she's like, "Come on." And I didn't want to come on 'cause some things you can't change.

Anthony's girlfriend's brother mentioned his father's disapproval of the relationship, saying, "My parents are not too kind—about Black guys." Anthony responded, "But I wouldn't have to marry your parents." The two laughed about the situation because they were friends. Despite her parents' disapproval, the two dated for a year until she went away to college.

Jacquese thought parents had the biggest problem with interracial dating. She recalled the parental involvement in an interracial relationship. "One of the guys in our class was dating a girl, she was Hispanic. She got pregnant. And the parents would not let him see the baby." Although she wondered whether the parents softened up after graduation, she said, "During the whole time [of high school], he could not [see the baby]. We were like stunned. We were kind of behind him, like, 'What?' She was like a year before him. But they really interfered with that. And I think they kind of made everybody like, 'Wow,' you know."

Diana, a Latina from Bogan, knew her mom would have a problem with her dating a Black guy: "I love my mom to death—but she's a racist. And I would have just had so many problems if I would have dated a Black guy. So I did, but behind my mom's back. What my mom doesn't know doesn't hurt her. That was the only time it became an issue with me, and it even occurred to me there was 'an issue' with Blacks and Whites was when, like, 'Oh wait. I think my mom's going to have a problem with this.'"

Cassandra, from Whitney Young, recalled that she liked a Latino but felt that his ethnicity affected the possibility of a relationship:

> I did like this Mexican. . . . That was the one time I had a weird experience being Black dealing with somebody else. I called his house and you could tell—I don't think they spoke English, first of all. But you could also sense the like, "What is this Black girl doing calling my house?" And we never really dated. And I wasn't sure if it was because I was Black or what was going on. 'Cause my friends thought he liked me too, but it was kinda weird. That's when interracial dating wasn't just real big, or whatever. So that was the only experience I had in high school that was *weird* in terms of race.

While some Latino parents disliked their children dating Black students, Sylvia remembered her mother's reaction when she brought her Latino boyfriend home. "I tried that once. That didn't sit well with my family. . . . He was Hispanic. That didn't sit well with my family. . . . Man! I was told, 'No. That is not gonna work. You are not to bring him here.' I don't know why, but after that we were kind of sort of friends from that point and then not really anymore. We would say hi and bye, but that was it. And I really liked him, but I guess, I don't know why that was a deterrent." There were limits to integration that made interracial relationships unacceptable, especially for parents.

Interracial dating was often viewed negatively or with curiosity at Bogan. Black and Latino participants made the following comments: "I don't think they liked it." "Most people were upset." "It wasn't the 'in' thing to do. They just didn't do it." Kelly thought Black students disapproved of interracial dating. "Black folks talked about them! 'Cause there was other Black folks dating the White girls. The one who I was dating, he started liking White girls. And we were like, 'What is wrong with him?! No, no, no!' But hey, that's who he liked. . . . But I was like, wow, isn't that interesting. He just liked White folks." LaDonna said, "People had their little comments about it. . . . No one treated anybody differently because they decided to date outside their race. But . . . it was kind of an eye-opener. And it made you wonder, like, 'OK. So what is it like? Tell me.' But I don't think anybody had a serious problem with it." Rayshawn believed the reaction to interracial dating was mixed. "Some people had a problem with it, and the rest of us said, 'Date who you like.' They say some dated for experience, some Whites say they dated for experience, some Blacks said they dated for experience. But for the most part, they genuinely liked each other. I never personally noticed any tension or anybody mistreating anybody else because they were dating somebody White or Black or Asian."

According to Black Von Steuben participants Maleta, Octavia, and Anthony, interracial dating was negatively perceived. Maleta observed that both Blacks and Whites viewed it negatively, and some students would say, "Man, she has jungle fever" or "He has jungle fever." She noted, "Some people saw it negatively. But a majority of people were just like, 'Oh well, they like who they like.'" Octavia thought some people had a problem with interracial dating and were not "happy about it." She said, "I don't think they really picked on people. . . . But they never got into any fights over it, but it was going on." According to Anthony, Black girls disapproved of interracial dating, although they would not say so publicly. Because Black women were far less likely to date outside the race, they viewed Black males' crossing racial dating lines as the potential loss of a mate in the pool of available Black men. While Black boys tended to cross racial lines more often, Anthony noted that Black girls who dated outside their race tended to have grown up in White communities. "I seen a couple of Black women that were dating outside the race. But it was different because most of the women . . . dating outside the race were not raised in an African American neighborhood. They were raised in neighborhoods where they were already exposed to other cultures. So it was different for them."

Sometimes interracial dating led to lasting relationships, but it also exposed Latinos' resistance to Latinas dating outside the race. Annette and John dated while at Von Steuben and eventually got married. John caught flack when he went to Annette's neighborhood to see her.

> My wife [and I] both lived on the North Side. But I lived right by the school, which most of the people that lived near that area . . . were White, Jewish. But she didn't live that far from me. We're talking maybe not even a mile. She lived closer to Roosevelt [High School], but when she got over there it was a

> Hispanic neighborhood. So here I am a White guy walking through a Hispanic neighborhood. . . . A lot of them, looked at it like well, ". . . Who's this guy think that he is." It was almost like . . . the Hispanic girl was their property. That's sort of what I got. I'd ask a couple times like, "What's your problem? Why you always have problem. I come, I never say anything to you guys. You guys are always talking garbage to me." It's like . . . "You're not supposed to be dating her. Get a clue buddy. You know that's supposed to be our girl." Now I'm like, "Why? You know I'm looking, I don't see a copyright on her. What's the deal with that?"

This situation reaffirmed the difficulty of interracial dating.

It seems as if a double standard existed for Latinos, in that, as John described, Latinos tended to have a bigger problem with interracial dating than Latinas. It was the reverse of Blacks, where females were more likely than males to have a problem with interracial dating. Lourdes recalled, "I know some of the Hispanic guys, I noticed that sometimes they would get a little jealous with some of the guys . . . [who] were trying to take their girls. There was some of that going on. But I didn't experience any of that personally. But I did see it. I did see like where some of the guys would get upset because, the Hispanic guys, because they would see that the Arabian guys were kind of moving in on their women." The same expectations were not in place for Latinos. Julian, for example, dated a White girl and his friends accepted the relationship. "Well I think everything was fine. I mean 'cause we all kind of ran in the same circles. We all kind of knew each other." The two broke up because she had a different culture. "I think it was more, later on it was a personal choice. Just 'cause there were certain things that I felt as her being White, she wouldn't understand especially going home and I'm speaking Spanish with my parents, that kind of thing. But that just, that was my own personal choice." Afterward, he decided to date Latinas.

Some students preferred to keep their interracial relationships a secret. Eve, from Whitney Young, recalled a Black acquaintance who was involved in an undercover relationship. "He didn't want it to be known that he was messing around with a White girl. And then, finally, he just told her he couldn't do it anymore. And so whatever happened, she was all [*big sigh*] just dramatic. . . . There were . . . a couple of cases that it was open, but if people were doing it, it was kind of . . . undercover." Eve noted that people were more curious than disapproving of interracial relationships. Ed, a Black participant from Von Steuben, remembered an interracial couple. "I wouldn't say that was the real [relationship]. . . . What I seen was the guy didn't really care for her and she was more using him for validation and it just reeks of phoniness. . . . I think this was one of the ones where it was just on the hush-hush. That's why I said it wasn't real." He continued, "It just wasn't real because the guy just never interacted with any Black people, and she never really interacted with any Black people either, even though she was Black." Ed's example corroborates Anthony's statement that Black girls who dated outside their race grew up in predominantly White communities.

Yet Josephine, a Whitney Young participant, dated outside her race, though she had grown up around Blacks. At the predominantly Black Whitney Young, there were norms about interracial dating. Socioeconomic class, ethnicity, and coolness all played a role in whether students dated and how their relationships were perceived. Josephine recalls being criticized by a Black boy when she dated outside the race:

> I think the cooler you were, if you were non-Black and you were kind of cool and you hung out with Black kids, I think it was considered "OK" for you to date a Black girl. . . . You'd see a lot of Black girls with, like, cool Latino boys. You'd see some of the athletes, non-Black athletes, like, they would have Black girlfriends. . . . But there was still a little bit, outside of that, there was still a little bit of like, "What's she doing with him?"
>
> This one mixed-race boy, he was African American and something else, I remember him saying to me when we were passing [between] classes. He was always a slight bully to me and then wound up kind of acting like he liked me. But I didn't like him, but then he was mean again. . . . I was dating this White Jewish guy at the time, who was also in the academic center. And he's like, "You think you're better than everybody because you date White, huh? But you're not!" And I remember him saying that. And I was like, "Wow!" You know and that was his thing, that's what he needed to say to me. But I think part of why I got a pass and people didn't give me that much grief—but I got a little bit—was because I was just a little . . . a misfit anyway. And so it wasn't like I was betraying the clan, in a certain kind of way. I wasn't quite a part of that kind of like the bourgeois, Black South Side crowd. Where like a couple of West Siders were a part of that.

A couple of Black Von Steuben participants recalled talking to Asian students about Black boyfriends being unsuitable dating partners for Asians. Teresa spoke with a Chinese classmate who told her, "Well, I could never bring a Black boyfriend home! . . . Because in my culture that's considered a disgrace." Teresa replied, "You don't know what you're missing!" Marc also remembered talking to Korean classmates and getting a similar response. "So I was speaking to a Korean gal, actually a couple of Korean gals, and they were saying why, in their family, it would be kind of frowned upon. But if they had to, if there was a choice, the perception would be . . . a Korean and a Caucasian. A Korean and an African American wouldn't have gone over very well."

Michelle, a White participant from Bogan, discussed her interracial dating experience as an act of rebellion.

> As a teenager, I used to try to bring home people that would shock [my mother]! And I know it sounds bad, the guy with the big leather coat and the long hair, you know, "Come on over to my house! Come on over for dinner!" You know? My mom is going to love this! But I did date a Hispanic guy throughout most of high school. And I asked my mom about that later on, knowing her history, and my mom said, "You know, I kind of thought if I said anything, you would become more involved with this person. But if I just left you alone, and didn't react to anything, then you would do what you really felt."

A couple of Bogan participants mentioned more extreme cases of students who dated interracially and visited their significant others in predominantly Mexican neighborhoods. Stephen, a Black participant, remembered, "It wasn't good. I can't recall this guy's [name] offhand. But, I mean, I know somebody got killed for dating a Mexican. . . . I mean they went to go visit her and didn't come back home. So it wasn't viewed well." Nora remembers another deadly incident. "And one girl I felt so badly for, she was just hanging around Pilsen too much and she got shot and killed, I think our first year. . . . Yeah, it was a dangerous neighborhood. I mean it was all gang bangers and not a place for her to be. You know what I mean, hanging out. It was sad." These incidents may not have been a result of interracial dating as much as they were a result of being in the wrong place at the wrong time. Most dating did not end in tragedy, but if these incidents happened, they exemplified the ethnic and racial tensions that existed in the city and the likely consequences of not only dating interracially but also venturing into certain neighborhoods.

Desegregated schools were often safer spaces for interracial dating; racial boundaries could not always be crossed in neighborhoods or people's homes. Crossing boundaries for dating was often difficult in the 1980s. Few dared to do so, and even fewer dared to cross segregated borders to maintain their relationships. Keith was a rarity as he acknowledged, "By the time I got to college, I think I had dated just about every race, color, and creed of female on this planet."

Desegregated schools gave many participants an opportunity to interact with people across racial lines. While not everyone took advantage of these interactions, those who did appreciated the opportunity to make friends they otherwise would have never met. What was significant about their interracial friendships was that they carried the isolated integration beyond the school walls to neutral locations, different neighborhoods, and each other's homes. Students exerted significant effort to make integration work despite the city's spatial separation, parental condemnation, and community disapproval. The tragedy of these connections was that the distance caused by segregation lessened the likelihood that they would go beyond high school. As Amy Stuart Wells and colleagues found in their study, the accomplishments for race relations that started in desegregated schools were limited by the lack of similar achievements in the larger society.[22] Segregated boundaries remained, though students were able to cross them and, at times, contradict the norms. While being together led to tolerance, camaraderie, and even friendships, conflicts and contention also emerged from such interaction.

6

"We All Got Along"

Difficulties and Differences

Mayor Harold Washington died suddenly of a heart attack on November 25, 1987, during the senior year of most participants.[1] Washington's death was just as divisive as his election; both led to racially tense experiences for participants. Trénace recounted a racial incident at Von Steuben after Washington passed away:

> I do remember when Harold Washington died. . . . I did the books for . . . basketball. . . . One of the guys from the basketball team came in and he was talking about, "Did you hear that Harold Washington died?" And I was like, "No, I didn't." And he said, "Some White guys are talking about, 'I'm glad he's dead!'" And I just looked, and he said, "I told him every Black person he sees he better say he's sorry and thank you." I was like, wow, that really made him angry. . . . The [White] guy walked around telling us thank you. And I think that lasted for about a week or two!

For Black Chicagoans, Washington's death was a time of great mourning. For those who were not old enough to have lived through the assassinations of great leaders in the 1960s, Washington's passing served as a watershed moment. As mayor, he actively worked for the communities long neglected by the Democratic machine, and he often fought public and contentious battles in city hall. He was the first Black mayor of Chicago who won two racially contested and divisive elections, with little support from White Chicagoans. In 1983, only

21 percent of Whites voted for him.[2] He was beloved by most Black Chicagoans and supported by many Latinos, and while many Blacks mourned his passing, White Chicagoans celebrated it.

Rayshawn recalled how difficult Washington's death was and the insensitivity of some Bogan students to the event. It nearly caused problems at the school.

> I think that by far the worst day though was . . . November of 1987, when that Wednesday before, the day before Thanksgiving, we had half a day. So we got out, what, eleven o'clock or so. We went on home, and then later on that day, we found out that Mayor Harold Washington died. Community was devastated. Even as teenagers, we still were quite aware of him and he had made his presence known so much in the city that many of us had had firsthand experience with him, whether he had come to speak at our church, and myself, my mom had my sister and I involved with campaigning for him at twelve and thirteen. So a lot of people had different experiences with him. So that was pretty grappling to the heart. When we returned to school, and I can say that was in God's grace that time. When we returned to school that Monday, we had a lot of White students yelling and—well, not yelling—joking and celebrating his death.
>
> There was some tension there. And if I'm not mistaken, the school had to intervene a little bit. . . . I think that was the first year that we did not have a full day of school the day before Thanksgiving. We usually would have a full day, so we said, "What if we had been in school all day this year?" That means we would have heard about it while we were in school. And if their reaction had been the same, there probably would have been something on the news that night. I know it would have been. It was just that tense; and for a while, there was some division there between Blacks and Whites after that. . . . But I also remember, I was shocked because I do recall friends and family . . . who were at work when he died, saying that a lot of Caucasian people at their jobs went out and bought champagne and popped corks right there in the office place, celebrating and woo-hoo and all of that. So I was shocked by that response, but then to come to school and see it amongst the students, I said, "Oh OK, so their parents were the ones doing that at work." So [I] think that was the most heart-wrenching, and at the same time angering, experience . . . that I had ever faced.

Rayshawn's memories of Washington's death were substantiated by *Chicago Tribune* columnist Gary Rivlin, who interviewed a man who had not voted for Washington. "The reaction was mixed among those Whites who would not for a moment consider voting for Washington. 'I don't have any grief,' a man named George Sajkick told a *Trib*[*une*] reporter looking for quotes in Vrdolyak's ward. 'It's phony for us to mourn a guy we hated.' That night, there were many public toasts to the new day that dawned with Washington's death. One bar on the far southwest side was selling buttons, Harold's Dead; We Want Ed [Vrdolyak]."[3]

In many ways, these schools were affected by the larger society; and try as they might, students often found it difficult to leave their individual, parental, or community views outside the school doors. This was particularly true during racially divisive events, which created a wedge between students who wanted to be tolerant of or friendly with one another. Segregated boundaries remained in place even if individuals had made friends with people of other racial and ethnic groups. Just as camaraderie occurred when students were together, so too did conflicts when people brought racial issues from the outside into the schools. While numerous participants indicated that students all got along well in school, some also recalled instances in which students of other races or ethnicities said or did something racially or culturally insensitive. Although participants worked to integrate their schools, the issues of the outside world—of their communities, the city, society at large—still penetrated the school walls. These racial and ethnic differences were just one level of separation.

Another level of separation was in-group identity. Some participants felt like outsiders of their own racial and ethnic groups, and consequently had difficulty with their identities. Differences between people are exacerbated in high schools because adolescents are simultaneously trying to figure out who they are and trying to fit in. For instance, a few Black participants found it difficult to be comfortable with White friends because other Black students stigmatized them for doing so. Latinos, particularly those of mixed race or ethnicity and those who grew up outside Latino neighborhoods, had the most difficulty coming to terms with their ethnic identities. For some participants, being from two different worlds but not feeling fully accepted in either caused anxiety. The divisions within groups at desegregated schools created boundaries that determined what behaviors and people were acceptable. People were asked or felt they had to prove that they were Black, Mexican, or Puerto Rican enough. Students at segregated schools also faced identity issues, so these issues are germane beyond desegregated schools. However, when participants were asked whether they faced difficulties at school, several brought up facets of their identity.

A third area of difficulty and separation was socioeconomic class. Class difference was recognizable at all schools; however, the differences were more pronounced at Whitney Young and Von Steuben, where students came from a wider range of socioeconomic classes, including a number of wealthy and upper-middle-class students. Bogan students, regardless of race or ethnicity, were more likely to be poor, working class, or middle class. Many White residents who lived in the area around Bogan in the Ashburn community and could afford private schools abandoned the public schools after desegregation. This led to fewer upper-middle-class students attending Bogan. In addition, White residents in the neighborhoods around Bogan were typically of a lower socioeconomic class than White North Side residents around Von Steuben and White families who sent their children to Whitney Young. Whitney Young was unique because there were also identifiable distinctions there among Black students in terms of class, color consciousness, and divisions between the South Side and West Side Black students. Elite Blacks attended Whitney Young, and for Blacks from families with low and moderate incomes, there were perceptible differences between them. Additionally, a group of light-skinned Black males created an exclusive group for themselves, reminiscent of the groups that elite Blacks have formed historically. Finally, South Side Blacks often had a negative view of West Side Blacks, some of it related to assumptions about socioeconomic class. Class differences rarely caused the same divisions as race and ethnicity. The combination of class and racial differences led to subtle separation among students.

The racial, ethnic, and class dynamics highlighted the complexities within many high schools. However, desegregation brought together students who were unlikely to have met or interacted with such a diverse group of students had they attended their neighborhood high schools. Segregated neighborhood schools were more likely to have students of similar race, ethnicity, and socioeconomic class. Consequently, interactions between people of different races, ethnicities, classes, and cultures were increased because of desegregation, which brought together students from all over the city. Bringing them together meant differences were exacerbated and integration tenuous.

Racial Issues

Many participants in this study, particularly those from Von Steuben, stressed that "we all got along" when asked about their desegregated experiences. Perhaps the nostalgia of the class reunion made it easy for them to remember the happy times. Although they insisted "we all got along," it was clear that this was not always the case. Students at all high schools, diverse or not, exploit the differences among students, which leads to name-calling, bullying, and physical fights. These desegregated schools were no different.

The passing of Harold Washington was certainly a defining moment in Chicago's history, as it permeated the experiences of some participants. Yet there were negative racial experiences unrelated to his death and not solely the result of actions perpetrated by Whites against Blacks. Erin, a White Von Steuben participant, remembered being called an insulting name by a Black student.

> One girl, and she was at the reunion last week. And she gave me a big hug. We had a nice little chat. . . . I remember like having it out with her over this issue. Again, we were fifteen or sixteen. I don't know why she didn't like me. She

> didn't like me. But she would see me in the hallway and we barely knew each other. But she was friends with a friend of mine. She would see me and she used to be like, "White bitch." And I just used to say, "Shut up, bitch," back to her. And I remember grabbing her one day and going, "Is that fair?" And she's like, "Well you are a total bitch." I was like, "Then so are you." But then we got to be friends after that because we were both total bitches. But I was like, "I don't attach Black to it; and like if I did, I'd probably gotten beat up." But she used to call me a White bitch. And she was like, "Well I don't mean it like that." I was like, "Well then don't say it." And then I don't remember us not getting along again after that. And I remember saying like, if I would have called her Black bitch that would have been horrible. But it was OK for her to call me a White bitch? And I don't know why, but it is kind of, it seems less hurtful maybe? I don't know. But it's no less tainted. It just really isn't. I think it's just as bad.

It was less consequential for a Black person to say "White bitch" than for a White person to say "Black bitch," as the second would easily be construed as a racially derogatory term because of Whites' position of power in society. Erin understood the double standard and chose to address it rather than have the situation escalate.

Several Von Steuben participants remembered name-calling incidents. Edgar was called "typical Latino names" instead of his real name: "In those days it was, people would poke more fun at you, I guess. Maybe they'd joke you around and call you a Julio. I remember classmates joking around with me, calling me Juan or Julio. But these are people that I knew really well. So you just threw a jab back. And I'd say that, in all fun, but not anything where I ever felt uncomfortable." Students who were called names took it in stride, but these incidents demonstrate high school students' immaturity and racial insensitivity.

Bogan participants acknowledged the racial tensions at their school. Eric believed that students were unwilling to accept the behavior.

> Everybody pretty much treated everybody the same. I mean of course there was a few exceptions. Sometimes, somebody either grew up thinking a certain stereotype about certain nationalities or a certain ethnicity. Most of the time, though, if somebody would say something as far as being racial, there was always usually somebody who would stand up and say, "You know what, don't say that" or "Why would you say something like that when you don't know it's true?" But I mean you did see a little bit of tension every once in a while, but for the most part, it was not bad.

Oralia's Middle Eastern friend was called a derogatory term. "My friend . . . is half Palestinian and half Italian. I remember hearing the term 'camel jockey.'

'What is that?' I didn't understand what that meant and why would they call her that. Then she explained it to me. And I said, 'You know what, you need to break this down for me 'cause I don't understand what that meant.' Again, very naïve. She's like, 'Oralia, this is what that means. Camels, in the desert, to get on top of . . .' 'Oh, OK!' Terrible."

Rayshawn remembered a few other racially charged experiences at Bogan aside from the Harold Washington incident. One incident centered on prom planning, underscoring the difficulty desegregated schools such as Bogan had expanding school activities to incorporate a more diverse student population.[4] Rayshawn said,

> I remember I had a couple of friends that were on the student council, and I remember them saying that during the meetings in planning our senior year, and planning prom, where it would be held and what the theme would be, in the end, none of their opinions counted. It was all about what the president wanted, and his constituencies. We didn't want prom on a Thursday. It had been on Thursday forever. We thought that was the stupidest thing. Why would you have a prom on a Thursday? I think we were the only school outside of one other at that time that had they prom on a Thursday. They gave us Friday off, we could go to Great America [theme park], but we wanted prom on a Friday. So that got turned down. I know they gave some wishy-washy excuse for it; but then the next thing was the hotel. We didn't want it there. And I don't know, maybe it was just a Black thing. But it was at the Palmer House, and we called it the hotel by the tracks. It was right by the "L" tracks, and we didn't want that noise, and we wanted it at the Chicago Hilton. And it might have come down to monetary reasons and so forth, but being teenagers at the time you wasn't looking at all that. You figured all the other high schools could do it. What's wrong with this one doing it? And then the theme music. We didn't want "The Time of Our Life," which was the theme from *Dirty Dancing*. We didn't want that theme. We wanted a Black song. And I heard it was a big to-do in their meetings, and that got voted down. In that instance, it seemed like maybe there was a little racial divisiveness going on there that nothing that we wanted seemed to have mattered.

The process of prom planning was difficult because students had different musical tastes, different preferences for the location, and different desired dates. White Bogan students on the student council were unwilling to forgo the traditional Thursday date, nor did they feel the need to make other accommodations. Because White students made up most of the student council, their decisions were upheld. This is vastly different from the ways in which desegregation occurred at primarily Black schools, where Black traditions were disregarded to accommodate White students and trophies and memorabilia were removed from displays.[5] When Black students entered traditionally White schools, these same accommodations were not made for them. In this situation, White students on the student council were unwilling to give up their dearly held traditions, even though the school no longer had a White majority population. These cultural differences were not easily overcome.

Rayshawn also remembered a few other incidents in which race was an issue:

> There was one young man, he and his brother, we thought were cool—"we" being the Black race. He liked to date Black girls. He hung out around a lot of Black guys. We thought, this is all right, Blacks and Whites getting along. It went on for a couple of years, and then one night while listening to the news, he and his brother had been arrested—the two of them along with three other White boys—had been arrested for throwing a Molotov cocktail bomb through a Black lady's house because she moved in the house about six blocks west, east of the school. A lot of Blacks had not lived there at that time. We were just starting integrating that area. And this woman moved in, and they threw a Molotov cocktail bomb. Totally changed our perspective of him. They had his picture up on the news and everything. So once that happened and he returned to school, I think he was only there for a brief while, he and his brother. And his parents shipped them off to some military school or something from what I understand.

White residents were the majority in the Ashburn community and remained so despite school desegregation. The community had a tradition of using violence against Black encroachment.[6] Rayshawn and others were confused by someone who seemed "cool," and even dated a Black girl, being involved or associated with such a racially motivated incident. The White student may have been "cool" with Blacks while at school, but he also had to fit in with family and neighborhood peers.

Rayshawn recalled other incidents that concerned racial hatred and inappropriate behaviors. One incident involved Officer Joseph Moseley, brother of Senator Carol Moseley Braun.

> He was a Chicago police officer assigned to the school. Well, one day, we got to school and on the back of the school was spray-painted the words "Officer Moseley is a N-lover." So the Black people were looking at each other like OK. Somebody is not, their tick-tocker not working too right, because, hello, he's Black! [*Giggles.*] But I think their main point was to let us know that they didn't like us there and that was maybe my junior year. And so it was a little unsettling and shocking because we had been there for a couple of years now, and we thought everything was fine. . . . I don't know if they ever found out who it was, but I remember that occasion.

> And then there was another occasion that stay in my mind. One student dressed in Blackface on Halloween. I thought they were going to kill her after school. She had to hurry up and get home. That would have been—that was no. She said she thought it was cool. "Who told you that, your mother?" We said, "This is 1985! What's wrong with you?" We said this is not back in the day. She had to take it off. They made her take it off when they discovered it.

Each of these incidents reflects White students' lack of awareness and racial insensitivity. That they occurred at Bogan was not surprising given the neighborhood's history of boycotting against busing. The participants in this study entered the school in 1984, just two years after significant desegregation was initiated. Each year leading up to their entrance saw the White population decline, from 95 percent in 1980–1981. In 1984–1985, White students made up 44.8 percent of the high school student body.[7] Whites were no longer the majority at the school, and some students and community members found explicit and implicit ways to show their discontent. White families continued to leave the school and surrounding community in order to avoid socialization at desegregated schools and to maintain White segregationist norms. At times, those who remained protested integration through racist or insensitive behaviors.

Like Rayshawn, Josephine remembered a classmate at Whitney Young whom everyone thought was friendly and popular being exposed for who he really was.

> I remember one particular kid—White kid—who lived on the North Side. All the girls liked him; he kind of had this alternative style. And he came into school one day . . . and he had this big gash on his face. And we asked him what had happened and he said, "Oh, I was walking down the street and this big Black guy came up to me and said, 'Don't make this any harder than it has to be, just give me your wallet.'" And somehow there was a struggle and the alleged "big Black man" gashed him across the face with something sharp. Later on, we found out that he worked at the, I think it was the National Rifle Club that's right on the lake, and he was trying to operate one of the skeet machines and he got too close or something and gashed his face. But he chose to tell this story because it had more cachet and potentially was more believable and less embarrassing than talking about the fact that he used a machine incorrectly and cut up his little face. . . . I always felt like he was arrogant anyway and just always had this sort of sarcastic air about him.

The White student Josephine described thought it was all right to use a racial stereotype about Black male criminality to embellish the cause of his injury, exemplifying his adherence to racial stereotypes.

Participants from each school remembered incidents of cultural insensitivity and students' involvement in racist acts. Name-calling, disrespecting the deceased mayor, monopolizing prom decisions, and participating in racist activities inside or outside school all demonstrate that progress was needed to fully bring students together. Schools were left to deal with society-wide racial divisions that often found their way into the schools. It is unclear how administrators handled the incidents they knew about, but more needed to be done to help students cross the racial divide in productive ways. Integration was not automatic, nor did it occur without problems. The isolated integration that transpired at the three schools was challenged from the outside. Bogan was understandably the hardest to integrate because of the opposition of the surrounding community. But racial stereotypes were unavoidable even at Whitney Young, a predominantly Black school.

Racial Fights

Students of different races may have fought, but it was seldom racially based, particularly when considering the more significant disturbances that occurred at other schools. Fights occur at many high schools regardless of the racial makeup; it is not unusual that fights at desegregated schools would occur for reasons beyond race. Few Bogan students noticed racial fights. Raul thought that there were such fights, "but not to the extent that they [escalated between Blacks and] Whites—it was usually one on one. It never got to that real high tension like that." For Raul, fights at Bogan were a minor issue because, comparatively speaking, Curie, a neighboring high school, had far more racial problems. On his way home from school, the bus would pass by Curie; Raul said,

> Sometimes we would get off there, take the other bus, or we would just keep going straight. For some reason or another one of my friends said, "Whatever you do, just keep staying on that bus and don't even get off." And I'm like, "Why?" And they go, "Don't worry about it." And it was a big—I mean this one was a big racial fight between Blacks and Whites there. And whoever was in between, just happened to get it. And then, the thing about that school, I would say it lasted about a month that even when they were even at their lockers, people would get attacked. But I was like, "Whoa!" But nothing like that ever happened at Bogan.

Jaime thought the fights that occurred were more likely between Blacks or Latinos and Whites. "It was more of a, like, the Blacks would fight, like, more with the Whites. . . . There was more of that than the Hispanics. It was very seldom you would have a Hispanic and . . . Black fighting. It was just more of a Black and a White, or a Mexican and a White. It wasn't too much of a Hispanic and Black." Although Jaime never mentioned why these fights occurred or whether they were solely racially motivated, his statement hints that Blacks and Hispanics were more likely to get along.

At Von Steuben, race-related fights were rare. Some participants were involved in fights with students of a different race, but they considered them frivolous. Ed had a fight with a White student. "I guess it was just one of the incidents where a bunch of White males—I knew them, but it wasn't like we were sneery-eyed, but we still took class together. And I guess they just wanted to have a fight with me, just have a fight with some of the Black guys hanging out with me and they picked me as the guy to fight with. And I guess we went somewhere and had a fight—I don't know, I beat 'em up, if that's the answer you want. I took boxing." Peter, a White participant, also got into a fight with a Black student, but the scenario was not racially charged. "I got into a fight with a student and he happened to be Black. But it wasn't because he was Black, it was because we were in gym, and we were playing volleyball, and instead of hitting the ball, he basically threw the ball at my head. So it was more of a competitive altercation than it was racial. I think the gym teacher just kind of broke [it up]. He did it on purpose and it was obvious he did it on purpose."

Anthony was once asked to squash a racial disturbance. His choir director got him out of class and brought him to the principal. Anthony had no idea what was going on but soon was "surprised to hear that there had been some fights" involving racial tension. He was asked to talk with the students and calm the situation. While Anthony had never seen himself as a leader, he had been popular with people of various races. He remembered, "I think we kind of came and kind of squashed it ourselves. We kind of saw the guys who were kind of hyping it up. And we kind of be like, 'Man, get up off that. 'Cause you're not gonna mess with him! That's my friend.' And I was pointing to my non–African American friend. I'm like, 'You're not gonna mess with him. You're not gonna mess with him. So you gonna mess with him, you're gonna mess with me.' And they didn't really want that. They really didn't want all that at all." His choir teacher recognized the role his leadership could play in potentially defusing a racially charged situation, and Anthony's interracial friendships made it easier for him to quell the potentially escalating quarrel.

Nick remembered a playful attempt at a race riot in the cafeteria that concerned teachers and administrators.

> It was a joke. It was done on purpose as a joke. It was funny. It was my buddy who was White, and my other buddy who was Black. . . . We had a division [homeroom] assignment, and we were all in the cafeteria at one time, and they thought it would be cute if they could start a little race riot—just for fun to spook the teachers and get 'em concerned they wouldn't know what to do. And the teachers did freak out, and my buddy got up there and my White buddy got

> up there and yelled the *n*-word. And everybody knew it was a joke. And then my Black buddy, he got up and he's yelling at him and the teachers were just pale as a ghost and the kids got a big laugh out of it because we all knew it was a joke. They got a stern talking-to! That was hilarious. [*Laughter.*] You don't realize it at the time how serious it could have become. . . . They were freaking out; they turned white as a ghost—the Black teacher turned white as a ghost! And it was hilarious, and they were panicking. It's funny.

The staff responses to the escalating racial fight Anthony was involved in and the cafeteria hoax indicate that these types of behaviors were not tolerated at Von Steuben. Teachers and administrators were attuned to these incidents and moved to quickly put a halt to them. The racial divisions may have slipped in with students, but Von Steuben's staff focused on order as a top priority. Fights, racial experiments, and any other incidents that disrupted the learning atmosphere were quickly handled. Regardless of the differences among students, the racial attitudes of teachers and administrators, and whether students were disproportionately punished, all students had to adhere to the school policies so schools could run effectively. The orderly focus of schools could be a hindrance to integration, but it also provided the order that enabled integration to occur.

Assimilation and Multiethnic Identities

A few Black and Latino participants struggled with their identities and where they fit in at school. Boundary crossing brings challenges to individuals who assimilate to the norms of the dominant culture. Whether a person lives within or outside an ethnic enclave, there are common internal group behaviors, languages or dialects, tastes, and so on associated with a group, and group members often sanction the behaviors of those who seem to reject group traits. When people grow up outside an ethnic enclave, they appear as outsiders to their ethnic group if they "act white" and seem less authentically Black, Mexican, Puerto Rican, or Asian, as defined by the group. If people grow up within an ethnic enclave, then their behaviors are scrutinized when they cross racial boundaries and seem to assimilate or take on characteristics associated with Whites. These internal group boundaries constrain assimilation. For many advocates, assimilation is not the goal of or even necessary for integration. Equality and access are the main goals. Sharon A. Stanley states, "While critics of integration condemn its pressure for assimilation and its corresponding destruction of institutions and spaces that foster black solidarity, its most compelling defenders insist that true integration does not simply demand the assimilation of Blacks into already-existing, hegemonic norms and institutions. Integration, they explain, is not a one-way street. Rather, it is a process of *mutual transformation*."[8] But integration invariably leads some to assimilate. If assimilation is viewed as forgetting where one came from, sanctions occur, people's identities are questioned, and difficulties arise from boundary crossing. For those who are biracial or multiethnic, their difficulties are increased as they face both internal conflicts and external pressures to determine who they are and where they fit.

As discussed in chapter 5, some Black participants felt forced into choosing one race with which to socialize. Elizabeth stated that students had "no problem" calling her an Oreo. "It was only hard a little bit socially because if you didn't really have classes with people, you didn't really know those people. So Black students today I'm sure experience the same thing. If you're in classes with all the quote-unquote "smart people," and if they happen to be non-Black, then you're hanging out with a lot of non-Black people, that can be socially difficult. It was socially difficult for me in high school."

Another Black participant, Cornelius, thought that Black students did not like him because he hung out with White students from his Advanced Placement classes. He considered it odd because he had grown up on the West Side and had Black friends. Nevertheless, he sensed a growing distance between him and friends in the neighborhood, and some from school, as he crossed racial boundaries. Cornelius felt as if he was living in "two different worlds" because he hung out with Whites in school and then hung out with Blacks in the neighborhood. He said, "I think the Blacks kind of didn't like me because I hung around the White people, only because I was in AP classes. But I had Black friends because I grew up on the West Side. I felt that probably the Black people thought I was White but the White people knew I was Black." Both Elizabeth and Cornelius felt estranged from Black students in lower academic tracks at Von Steuben. They befriended White classmates because they spent more time with them, but this was often viewed as a preference for Whites over Blacks. The difficulty of crossing racial boundaries was a reoccurring theme. It was almost viewed as a betrayal.

Outside school, Trénace, a Black student, encountered trouble because of the way she spoke. Extended family members teased her when her family moved back to Chicago from Kansas. Her mother's stepsister said that she and her siblings were "good and White." Trénace often found herself code-switching to fit in. She would shift her dialect depending on with whom she was speaking. High school was a more comfortable place for Trénace than for Elizabeth or Cornelius. Trénace was told in grammar school that she was not "Black enough" and that she "just talk[ed] white." In analyzing the differences between high school and home, she stated, "So then when you go into a school where, 'Oh, there's some White people here. Who cares how you talk?' But then in a way when you come home, you still gotta prove that—'I'm still Black' even if I went to a school that has White people in it." Trénace refused to address the teasing, saying, "I never responded because it was what it was. Because I do [sound like a White girl]. A lot of times I do."

Sounding "authentically" Black in Chicago meant having an "up south" dialect that reflected the hundreds of thousands of Black southerners who migrated to the city from the 1910s to the late 1970s. Additionally, a student's being considered "authentic" affected who his or her friends could be. There were social consequences for students who made friends with Whites or sounded white. Students' peers often determined the extent to which individuals integrated at these schools. In many cases, it was OK for Black students to make friends interracially, but friendships viewed as indicating a preference for one race over another were unacceptable.[9]

Like Black participants, some Latinos also faced problems fitting in, particularly if they were of mixed ethnicity. Gina, a half–Puerto Rican and half-White graduate of Bogan, was raised by her White mother and her "prejudiced" White stepfather, who was a cop. Instead of telling Gina that she was Puerto Rican or a Latina, Gina's mother told her she was European, and Gina grew up believing that she was White. Her stepfather also steered her away from hanging around Blacks or Latinos. When a Puerto Rican girl arrived at her grammar school, Gina faced a rude awakening.

> My friend . . . came to school when I was in fifth grade. She was Puerto Rican. And I didn't even know I was Puerto Rican at the time. My mom told me I was Spanish. So I was Spanish, Italian, Bohemian. She goes, "You're not Spanish." I said, "Well yeah I am! That's what my mom told me!" So then . . . she was trying to be top dog. She wanted to kick my ass all the time. . . . I didn't want to fight with anyone. Everyone always was just not nice, so. And that's kind of why I started keeping to myself after a while. Because I just didn't feel like I fit in anywhere. You know, so that was kind of hard.

After speaking to her mother, Gina found out that she was half Puerto Rican. Her mother thought it was easier to be Spanish than Puerto Rican. Once this was revealed, Gina became interested in her Puerto Rican side. "I wanted to like learn that whole other side of me. . . . I didn't speak Spanish, so I didn't fit in there either. Some of the kids were not nice. And they would like talk in Spanish behind my back . . . in front of me! About me! Just to be mean." In her attempt to make her daughter's life easier, Gina's mother ended up making it a little harder in the end. Because Gina initially was unaware of her own ethnic heritage, she was marginalized. Her later attempts to fit in were shut down because her Latino peers thought she was inauthentic, was unaware of the language, and was trying too hard. Her attempts were viewed as too little, too late.

Gina began learning Spanish in high school and could "catch little things here and there." But learning Spanish had a limited impact:

> In high school . . . most of my friends were . . . Hispanic. Like from freshman to probably junior year. And then I just got so sick of trying to fit in there, because I didn't. . . . Then senior year I was just like forget it. And I hung out with my cousin and made some other friends. The girls were mean. I didn't fit into any of the groups. I wasn't a stoner, I wasn't Hispanic. I mean I am, but I'm not. I'm not nerdy. I'm not a jock. Well, I was on swim team for a while. I don't know. . . . By senior year, that's when I was kind of like, I would go to school and then go to swim practice and then go to work. So I didn't hang out with anybody then. I was just kind of in and out.

Being raised unaware of her ethnicity and outside a predominantly Latino or Puerto Rican neighborhood created a social chasm that Gina had difficulty overcoming. Despite her best efforts, she lived on the periphery of her ethnic group. Her situation illustrates the power of racial and ethnic groups to define group belonging.

In adulthood, as in high school, people made assumptions about where Gina fit based on her phenotype. She attended a college prep seminar with her son and had the following experience.

> They had a room for all of the Spanish-speaking people and then a room for all the English-speaking people. And I went in there, and this woman . . . looked at me she goes, "The Spanish-speaking people are on that side." I looked at her and I said, "I speak English!" I'm like, "Can I go over there?" So they still, people still look at you and make their own assessment. . . . She was so embarrassed. I'm just so tired of that, because I've been dealing with that my whole life. People just assume that by the way I look I can speak Spanish and understand what they're saying. They'll just start talking to me. I'm like, "I don't know what you're saying." . . . But this one woman was very embarrassed. She apologized to me like three or four times during the next session.

Gina's experience provides a window into multiracial identities. Kerry Ann Rockquemore, David L. Brunsma, and Daniel J. Delgado argue that one must differentiate among racial identity (how individuals understand themselves), racial identification (how others view the individual), and racial category (the available racial identities and what individuals choose based on context).[10] In addition, racial identity may shift over time and is often based on context. Those who embrace multiracial identities often have a higher level of identity integration. Those with lower levels of multiracial identity integration often face racial distance and racial conflict. Early on, Gina's identity and racial category was White, but she was identified as Puerto Rican based on her appearance and the ways others perceived her (racial identification). She later embraced being Puerto Rican but experienced racial distance and conflict in her interactions with other Latinos. Multiracial and multiethnic people often face social isolation, as well as disapproval from family and peers.[11]

Keith and Kenneth, brothers who attended Von Steuben, also experienced issues that stemmed from their mixed heritage. Keith was asked his ethnicity and responded, "I guess I'm Mexican. I mean that's always been an interesting question just because—I look actually like I could be Mexican. My brother does not. 'Cause in high school once a year in homeroom or division, they would do the thing where they'd have to ask ethnicity. And so whenever I would say Mexican, all the kids that spoke Spanish would be like, 'You're not Mexican.' But . . . I guess for the purpose of everything on paper, I've always, my entire life, wrote down that I'm Mexican." Despite Keith's self-identification as Mexican, people were often quick to classify him as some other ethnicity. "Most people thought that I was Greek or Italian or some sort of Mediterranean."

In school, Keith's ethnicity was often questioned.

> The only time, there was once in grammar school . . . in eighth grade we finally got another Hispanic kid that wasn't my brother. And he had a very Hispanic name. He looked like what someone would consider to be Mexican, I guess. And he had an accent. And I remember the kids picking on him, but they didn't pick on me. . . . I don't remember it being really bad every day, but occasional[ly] it would happen. And then I remember telling the other kids that I'm Mexican. And they're like, "Yeah, yeah, yeah." But like somehow, I was different, and again, I didn't have a Hispanic name, no accent, you know, I didn't look like Pancho Villa, I guess.[12] I don't know what I was supposed to look like. Then in high school, the only time it was ever an issue was during homeroom class once a year where [the teacher] would do the thing, "Raise your hand if you're Mexican." And the Hispanic kids in the class would be like, "You ain't Mexican!" And I'd be like, "OK, I guess not."
>
> It didn't bother me. Like nobody ever picked on me or anything like that, but whenever it came up, which wasn't very often, it was just made very clear. I didn't live in a Hispanic neighborhood or anything like that. I don't know, maybe things would have been different. . . . I can't really think of any time in high school other than the occasional, "You're Mexican? You don't look Mexican!" Or the occasional, "You're not Mexican!" But I don't really recall it being a big deal, like, it was never a point of contention. If anything, it was something that we made fun or that I would make fun of.

Despite how others perceived him, Keith consistently claimed his Mexican heritage when asked, even if others were unconvinced.

Kenneth seems to have struggled a bit more with his identity than his brother because he looked Whiter than Keith.

> I did think there was some confusion for people 'cause they'd see my brother—my brother went [to Von Steuben] his freshman year, he was there when I was a senior. And they met my brother for the first time and they'd be like, "Who's the father of this one? Same mother? Different fathers?" So there was some confusion there. . . . I did notice, though, that some Latinos seemed a little more like, "OK he's one of us, that's cool." They seemed liked, "OK, he's different but he's . . ."
>
> In some respects, in my life it took a long time for me to accept who I was. Not because I had a problem with it, but when I look in the mirror, I don't see anything. But then I said, "Wait a minute, I'm the best of both worlds." What I would have liked to, sometimes, maybe just to say that I belonged somewhere. . . . I think I'm grateful that I was able to figure it out. But I know some people would have a hard time with it. "Well what am I? Where do I belong? Where do I go?" And I figured out, all right, I'm not White, I'm not Hispanic. I'm the best of two worlds. And that's what I finally [decided], I am the best of two worlds.

Keith looked more phenotypically "Mexican" than his brother, but people still refused to accept his self-identification; Kenneth looked White and had a hard time figuring out his place in the world. He wanted to be accepted as Mexican, but his looks and name prevented this. His struggles with being half White and half Mexican meant he felt uncomfortable passing as just White. Eventually, he had to come to terms with being "the best" of both. This was Kenneth's simultaneous attempt to rationalize ethnic marginality and come to terms with his racial identity.

Paul, a half–Puerto Rican participant from Bogan, thought he was treated differently because of his mixed ethnicity. "I'm half White and half Hispanic, so I do see a difference with certain people that treat me differently because either I'm not all White or I'm not all Hispanic. So it's definitely—there wasn't many other children or kids my age that were like me. They were either one or the other. I was much different in the sense I was carrying both races around." Like Gina, Keith, and Kenneth, Paul also recognized his difference because he was from two racial/ethnic groups. Unlike the others, Paul grew up in a Latino neighborhood and attended elementary schools that were over 91 percent Latino.

Brett is half Chinese and half White and attended Von Steuben. He, however, did not struggle as much with his identity because of how he was raised. "My mom's White and my dad is Chinese. And I would say that my dad never pushed his culture too much. So I probably would say that I grew up more White than I did Chinese. Of course, who am I, it's not something you can measure, right, 20 percent or whatever. But I would say that I did not share a lot of common interest with my Asian friends. Let me put it this way: my closest friends were not Asian." Because his father deemphasized Chinese culture in his upbringing, Brett focused on his White identity. Brett went to predominantly White elementary schools with 5 to 11 percent Asians. Early on, he chose to self-identify as White and felt less torn about belonging to two worlds. Chi-Ying Cheng and Fiona Lee note, "Formative experiences around race and multiracialism can have long-lasting effects on how multiple racial identities are managed."[13]

Beyond multiracial identities and the social isolation that some experience, Trey, a White athlete from Von Steuben, recalled his difficulties fitting into Black spaces and feeling like a minority:

> In the spring and summers, I would play on sort of the AAU [Amateur Athletic Union] basketball team. It was comprised of entirely Black basketball players and myself. I would play in tournaments where I was the only White person you would see for miles. . . . One memory I have very distinctly is playing in a tournament that was at a playground in an elementary school in the West Side of Chicago. And our team won. And the fact that a White guy had a first-place trophy wasn't exactly very pleasing to some people. So we had to take the train or public transportation there. And the guys on my team said, "Hey, listen, we'll ride with you or we'll go with you until you get to whatever [the] street was. Sort of just to make sure that you can get out and you're not troubled or hassled and . . . it's not a problem."
>
> It sort of put me in the position of being a minority. You know, which, I don't think most White people have that experience to that extent. A minority in a position where, hey, you may be in physical danger. My best friend growing up, he actually lived a half a block away from me. He went to Whitney Young High School, same time and all that, and he played basketball too and had some of those same kind of experiences. So certainly, I think it's helped me to be at ease among groups of people that are not like myself, and also have an appreciation or sort of a viewpoint as to kind of what their perspective may be.

Trey's experience highlights the privilege that most Whites have as part of the majority in some spaces. However, through this experience, he became painfully aware of how some minorities feel on a regular basis. Trey was a numerical minority, but he still had White privilege. That privilege allowed him to simply leave a neighborhood when he felt threatened.

Fitting into one group was hard for Black and Latino participants, because of either mixed heritage or the constraints of group dynamics. At such an impressionable age, Black and Latino students had difficulties maneuvering between different racial and ethnic groups and with their racial identities.

Youths struggle with their identities during high school, especially as cliques form based on mutual interests or racial identities. Because these participants were attending desegregated schools, they often felt forced to choose one racial or ethnic group over another when they would have preferred the freedom to move among multiple groups. If integration meant assimilation to White cultural norms, members of racialized groups, particularly those who grew up in ethnic enclaves, even those forged by segregation, often rejected assimilation and distanced themselves from those who assimilated. Those with multiethnic identities often found themselves on the periphery of both groups. This certainly occurred at segregated schools as well. In their desegregated schooling experiences, participants encountered people from different neighborhoods, which seemed to add more questions about where they belonged.

Class Differences

Participants, particularly those who came from poorer families, recalled socioeconomic class differences in school. Of course, class differences played out in unique ways at each school. Whitney Young had the most pronounced class differences among Black students. Some of the students who attended the school came from the city's Black elite and upper-middle-class families. Others came from moderate middle-class, working-class, and poor families. Participants from Von Steuben, particularly Blacks and Latinos, were acutely aware that they did not have as much money as their mostly White, North Side peers. Bogan participants, regardless of race or ethnicity, were most often from working-class and lower-middle-class families. As a result, the class differences among Blacks, Latinos, and Whites at Bogan were not as great as they were at Von Steuben. Additionally, many participants first noticed class differences in elementary school, and their formative understanding of class informed their perceptions of it in high school.

Whitney Young's socioeconomic class divide partially resulted from the preestablished division between the West Side and South Side of the city. The South Side typically consisted of Black communities with long-established ties to Chicago. Many Black residents from the South Side had migrated before or during the first wave of the Great Migration, beginning in the mid-1910s. The Black West Side grew after the 1940s, during the second wave of the migration, though some residents moved there from the South Side. Back then, Black West Side residents tended to have less social status and appeared more "country" to their South Side peers. Although middle-class Blacks also lived on the West Side and poor Blacks on the South Side, South Siders often thought they were better than their West Side peers.

Josephine vividly recalled experiencing socioeconomic class differences at Whitney Young:

It was the first time I had ever met and spent a real amount of time with middle- and upper-middle-class kids . . . both Black and non-Black. . . . I had never had friends who weren't like from my neighborhood and working class and who weren't working class from my church. I mean there were a few middle class, like the pastor's children and he was middle, upper-middle class. . . . But other than that, I hadn't really had any long-standing contact. So that was an eye-opener for me. Whitney Young, at the time at least, was known as kind of a fashion school. Kind of a bougie [slang for bourgeois], Black bougie school was the reputation that it had. You know, that the kids were smart, but also very sort of style conscious.

And while it was predominantly Black, there were still other races of kids, and I feel like it was *pretty* mixed class-wise. Like there actually [were] . . . a few kids, other working-class kids from the West Side, but it seemed like a lot of . . . the African American students were from the South Side. One of the things that I found challenging as a working-class kid, both of my parents were blue collar—my mom was a nurse's aide and my dad was a forklift operator . . . for Royal Crown Cola, RC Cola—for as long as I can remember. At the time I was going to Whitney Young, he had been there for at least a decade. And so having designer names and brands wasn't something I was used to, or something that I thought I could expect of my parents. And that was definitely—it felt like a scene of our school. I mean, that's where I kind of learned about all these styles and brand names—and so that wasn't something that I felt like I could keep up with. And so I felt alienated from a lot of the sort of . . . Black middle-, upper-middle-class kids . . . whose parents made more money, but also . . . who were maybe going to be . . . third-, fourth-, maybe fifth-generation college educated. And my parents . . . got high school diplomas in the Jim Crow South of Alabama. So it was a very different experience.

Name-brand clothes, shoes, and purses were status symbols for a lot of high school students. Poorer students were easily distinguished by their inability to keep up with these expensive trends. Josephine said, "I didn't even think of asking [my parents] to get me a Coach purse. I mean girls were carrying Gucci and Louis Vuitton and Coach back then. Kids were wearing Girbaud and Guess and Perry Ellis. I mean just a designer school. [I was] trying to fit in as best I could with the money I had and with the parents that I had, but doing it in a way that I could afford."

Josephine learned to shop at thrift stores from her friend who was half White, half Filipina:

She introduced me to the magic of secondhand stores. We'd go on the North Side and she would show me how to push back all the hangers and kind of go through very quickly. You could get name-brand stuff, but you know a pair of

> Guess jeans for three dollars instead of seventy-five dollars. That sort of helped me navigate the . . . socioeconomic waters of Whitney Young just a little bit better. [*Laughter.*] But still, not entirely. I found myself more connected to non-Black kids who were working class or Black kids who were working class. Or some of the middle-class and upper-middle-class kids who I just felt like weren't so caught up in all of the flash. We could just relate heart-to-heart.

Another Whitney Young student, Cassandra, recalled the class and geographic differences. "The South Side–West Side rift [was] going on. We had a lot of children of college-educated families. Like Hyde Park students coming in, whose parents might be like professors, doctors, et cetera. And we all mixed, but then there was like this rift about folks from the West Side, how they were, [and] folks from the South Side and the different culture [and] economic[s] of the two sides." According to Cassandra, those with less money wanted to hang out with those who had more money. As a result, they dressed up to fit in, "but you could see the difference."

> I don't think we had really, really poor students . . . at our school, for the most part. Everybody was kind of either like decent working class or middle class or higher middle class. But all I could say, you saw the students who had the nice cars, who dress real nice, who had Gucci, Fendi bags. All that type of stuff. And *they* would associate with one another. . . . The kids-with-a-little-bit-of-money clique. But it wasn't so different that there were like really poor kids in the projects and there were really rich kids. I don't think we had that wide range of economic class, to be honest. Again, I probably wasn't paying attention!

Cassandra noticed that class status determined one's friends. "It was just who you hung around, who your clique was. . . . Like if you didn't have certain clothes or certain bags, you just weren't hanging around certain people. That was more so, whether you fit in or not. But . . . I didn't see people picking on folks because they were poor. Or jumping people 'cause they were a few rich kids—'cause you know, it worked the opposite way. You didn't really see that."

At Whitney Young, there was a group called the Yellow Boys, which highlighted the class and color divides at the school. According to Josephine, the Yellow Boys

> were mostly African Americans who lived on the South Side. They were—literally they were all fair-skinned. Most of them went to Whitney Young. Some were friends of guys who went to Whitney Young. Then it grew a little bit into like some Mexican boys from Whitney Young became part of the Yellow Boys. And they were this kind of good-looking, cool group of guys who hung out together and hung out a lot on the South Side, dated Black girls or

> maybe some Latinas. But definitely dated like the cute Black girls. And they actually wound up developing this reputation as these kind of, like, not as punks, but they would kind of roll together at parties. And I think a lot of dudes resented them because they were stylish, they were good looking. There was this combination of light-skinned Black, and you know, Latino. And so I remember hearing about fights that they would wind up getting into with other guys and then there would be a girl in the middle of the . . . conflict. And so they were kind of their own entity. I remember three of the Yellow Boys, of the African American Yellow Boys, were mixed race. I remember they had either White moms or White dads.

Like Josephine, Cassandra recalled the reputation of the Yellow Boys and the conflicts that resulted from their group. "It was a group called the Yellow Boys—and they were all light-skinned, African American men. I think they had one dark-skinned—now there were fights between *our* school and other schools. . . . And because of that whole color-conscious thing." Cassandra believed that other people thought Whitney Young students were uppity.

> Other schools did kind of view us as the elitist, middle-class, light-skinned. That was the reputation that was out there. And they would come up to 'em and beat them up. [*Laughter.*] There were several incidences of the Yellow Boys getting beat up. I mean it was a cocky group to be in. And a lot of 'em now look back on it in complete shame. It was—our school was really the—it was the light-skinned, elitist school. It wasn't all light-skinned people there, but that was the image. And that's what the Yellow Boys were, a "pretty" group. It was like, "We the prettiest men at the school and we get all the women and we have all the fun!" That's what it was organized around. Middle-class, preppy, *Baldwin Hills*–type stuff.[14]

The Yellow Boys may have appeared to be a school club, but their colorism and elitist attitude resembled those of the historical Black elite, for which membership was often based on one's complexion, educational attainment, career and family status, and organizational affiliation.[15] The Black elite's proximity to whiteness essentially elevated them to a superior status. Whether or not the members were truly elite, the Yellow Boys acted similarly to the elites of the past. Based on the fights they were reportedly involved in, others negatively perceived their exclusivity. They epitomized Whitney Young's elite reputation, which polarized less affluent students.

Eve saw class differences at Whitney Young but thought the groups were penetrable since people interacted at various points during the day or throughout their high school experience. "I think that you could tell some of the differences in some of the like really, really snooty people. I don't want to say snooty people, but some of the more well-off people, I think that they kind of clung to each other; but for the most part, because we were all there, it was kind of like . . . at some point you had to interact and you did it OK. I just feel like I knew of everyone there, especially in my class that I graduated with, and at some point, I interacted with and did something with everybody there."

The class status at Whitney Young was quite pronounced among Blacks, as the children of the elite and upper-middle-class Blacks established exclusive cliques and donned expensive items. Most of them came from the South Side, and the material, cultural, and educational differences of their parents exacerbated the South Side–West Side rift, though neither side of the city was exclusively affluent or poor.

Von Steuben's students were also from various socioeconomic classes. White students from the North Side tended to be of a higher socioeconomic class than their Black and Latino peers from the North Side, South Side, and West Side. Most of the Black and Latino participants came from lower-middle, working-class, or poor families, including some on public assistance. Ed remembered what it was like attending Von Steuben while being poor:

> I was not only a Black student but also a poor Black student, which means I came there wearing the same clothes every day. That's not an exaggeration. I literally wore the same clothes every day. So I got along, in terms of getting along with the Black students, I got along with the students from my neighborhood who knew me, and they knew the situation. I don't think I got along with the Black students who were, let's say, middle class or well off, or working class. In terms of White students, I was just ignored. It was no interaction at all unless there was some—it wasn't positive if there was an interaction, or it was just more of a snub-type atmosphere.

For Ed, race was still a divider among the poor, as poor Whites did not hang out with poor Blacks.

David remembered a Latino student who possessed only a few items of clothing. David recognized the limits of his parents' money when he was around wealthy friends in summer camps, but knew he was better off than some students who went to his school.

> I never thought of myself as well off. Because I used to go to summer camp up in Wisconsin with all these rich Jewish kids that were more or less, ethnically speaking, of my background. They had all these things I could never relate to. On the other hand, [there] was a kid who only had one freaking shirt. He'd come in every day with the same freaking shirt. He'd go home, you had to take it off. He lived in an attic with three other people, his sister and his two

> parents. They would hand-wash that shirt out. Just rinse it out, every day. And I'll never forget; [it] blew me away.

Some White students at Von Steuben were around people of even higher economic status than themselves, but for Black and Latino students unfamiliar with wealth, their White peers at the school seemed financially better off. Ralo recalled class in the following way:

> I used to joke a lot, or actually I still do. And I used that as a way to get to know these people and get them not to dislike me. Because even though a lot of them were from different cultures, they were from a different breed as well, meaning that they come from a different socioeconomic background than I came from. I mean, we lived in an apartment building the first eighteen years of my life, and I brought my friends home from Von, and these people lived in, at that time, $200,000 homes. And I'm thinking, "Geez, I'm out of my league here." So I just kept humble, and I joked around a lot and they liked me for that, and we became friends.

Class was somewhat an issue for Ralo. "It was a certain elite . . . what I called elite kids that they obviously came from money and they had their *own* little world that hardly no one could break into. And, I mean, you could just tell that they were cut from a different cloth. So I mean, we hung out with them, we said hello to them, there was never any animosity toward them, but you just never could get into their little world." As students formed cliques based on class, it sometimes overlapped with race and ethnicity. When Ralo invited friends over, they often did not come back: "I grew up in the ghetto, so you see what the difference of two streets does. Because, like I said, my elementary school was mixed, but we all lived in the ghetto. I mean, our income levels were minimal at best across the board. Like I said, we had people from Vietnam that just came over, so I mean . . . they hardly spoke the language, so what kind of a job could they actually have? So I came from a very poor background, and the kids that I went to high school with, *they* have been established for generations." Ralo still made friends across class lines, despite the clear differences in the material status of their families.

Keith assessed class differences based on who participated in the free and reduced lunch program. Since the program was based on income, those who received free and reduced lunches were from lower socioeconomic families. Keith said, "But . . . even in grammar school and high school though, I felt that we were always aware that there was difference. . . . We were very aware that my neighborhood was different from your neighborhood." He remembered his elementary school teacher calling students up to receive their lunch tickets:

> I can't recall any particular event that made me think that the teachers were treating kids differently based on race. But the fact is, especially, more so in grammar school, because it was so clear. I mean, all the kids, all the Black, I would say 95 percent of the Black kids that got bused to my school in grammar school were from the West Side. And, you know, we're not talking Beverly.[16]
>
> I just remember the first time that . . . when you bought your lunch ticket that was one of the first times that I thought that it was not about money. Because if you paid for lunch full price, you paid forty cents, reduced was twenty cents, and then free. And what the teacher would do every morning is, all the kids that paid full price, she would say, "OK, all of the kids that are paying for lunch, come up and give your money." And I forget how she explained it the first day, but the way it worked was she would go, "Paid," and then all the kids paying full price, we would walk up and give her our forty cents. Then she'd say, "Reduced," and all the kids that were paying half of that, which was twenty cents, they'd go up and give her money. And then, "Free," and all those kids would walk up and get the little ticket. And then I remember, when we came home with the form at the beginning of the school year, I said, "Mom," I'm like, "I brought this from school." And my mom looked at it and she said, "Oh, don't even worry about it." And I said, "Why?" And [she] goes, "Because we don't qualify for free lunch." And so I remember that being strange that every morning, and looking back on that, every single kid that paid full price was a neighborhood kid except for me. And then a couple of the neighborhood kids paid that reduced lunch. But almost every single kid on free lunch was a Black kid that took the bus.

Based on Keith's recollections, the Black students on the bus with him to his grammar school were also poorer than the students who attended the school from the neighborhood. Race and class were often intertwined. By high school he was aware of the class differences, particularly between neighborhoods.

Keith's brother, Kenneth, remembered a friend whose father was a pharmacist and whose mother worked at a university. "I knew that there were some families that were better off. And I knew they were a little financially better off than I was. But I never felt that they held it against me. . . . I don't recall there being a problem." Whereas Keith recalled students who had less than his family, Kenneth remembered people who were better off than they were. Marc agreed with Kenneth that socioeconomic class was not divisive. "I don't think it made a difference about economic status. I don't think anyone chose to associate or not associate with anyone around that. There might be other things, like you had the same amount of classes, you had the same gym teacher, I mean, it'd be a myriad of other things besides that, I think." Marc was likewise aware of his family's modest income, and though he agreed that class was not a cause of division, he also refused to let people see how modestly he lived.

Annette noticed the issue of social class because she had reduced lunch. "When I first got to the school, my mom was a single parent. We didn't pay for lunch. It was reduced lunch. I do remember being made to feel uncomfortable about it by the teachers who made a point to say something out loud." Annette's teacher embarrassed her on occasion. "I think I was looking for my change and he said, 'You got reduced lunch as it is already, you should have your money together.' He made it a point to embarrass me. That was the one thing that actually made me cry. That's just horrid. You know, what an asshole."

Like participants from the other high schools, Bogan participants noticed certain accessories and clothing that pointed to class differences, though the divide was not as drastic as it was at Von Steuben and Whitney Young. Both Black and Latino Bogan graduates thought that White students came from families with more money, but Whites recognized that they were less well off than others thought.

Black participants observed some class differences. Angela saw the difference with clothing and accessories. "We didn't wear uniforms back then. You usually knew those that were a different, a higher I should say, economic level—with the clothing and the accessories. . . . But it didn't seem to be a big issue." Stephen's mother refused to buy him fancy clothes, but he made friends with those from different socioeconomic classes. Still, he noticed that some cliques formed along class lines. "I think people got along well 'cause in my freshman year . . . my mom wasn't the one to buy the nice clothes and all that. [Did] the people with the nicer clothes and got their haircuts every week or whatever, hang out? Yeah, they did. Did they look down on people? I would think so, but you know, it kind of balanced out. I mean the saditty [uppity] people all with the saditty people; the cute people all with the cute people; average people all with the average people. So, I mean, I think that's anywhere."

Participants like Kelly and Stanford were poor but were not treated differently. Stanford stated, "Nobody knew we [were] poor." Kelly's family was on public assistance. She said, "I don't know . . . who else's family was on public assistance. And nobody looked down on me because I was. And I don't think they knew it. . . . There were a lot of things that I couldn't afford or that I couldn't participate in or couldn't do or whatever. But I don't recall any problems with anybody saying, 'Oh, that's the poor kid.' Or, 'Oh, we're rich,' and you know, 'We got it going on like that.' I don't recall there being any real segregation according to socioeconomic status."

Diana, a Latina, thought people paid attention to class once there were big school events. People's ability to buy clothes for prom or other events was noticeable. "I don't think anybody really knew anybody else's income. I think the only time . . . people knew anything about it was like when there was a big event coming up like the prom or homecoming or something where a student couldn't afford to go or couldn't afford to buy the latest or the best dress, or something like that. I think that's the only time where, like, 'Oh, you don't have money for that? Oh, OK.' But other than that, it never occurred to anybody else that they had more or less money than you do." As one of the few Latinas in her neighborhood, Oralia noticed class issues beginning in grammar school. She knew her friends had better things than she did. She could not always tell how much money a student came from, but she could identify material markers of financial success.

> You don't know what people make. You don't know what that means. In grammar school, I would go to my friend's house who lived right across the street. And she had things that we didn't have; same thing with my other friend across the street. Both of their dads were cops. . . . They had everything, to me it was a luxury, luxurious homes. But yet, I think about it now, we were living in the same neighborhood. Our parents had to make about the same amount of money or else you would have been in a different neighborhood. But I didn't know that at the time. To me, they just had everything.
>
> In high school, people just automatically assumed if you were coming in from Little Village or Pilsen that you made less money because you're living in an apartment. You didn't own a home. You just assumed. Now was that true? I don't know. They seemed to have nice clothes; they were clean. How do you really know how much people have? I think that's the way, the preppy kids, they dressed nice, or we had little scooters. People started getting scooters in the '80s. If you had a scooter that meant you had money.[17]

Some participants remembered cars as a marker of class. Michelle, a White participant, noted, "The only time I realized it, [that] people had more or less money than what my family had, was when we went to high school. Because, some kids would come to high school with really, really nice, expensive cars. Well I should say expensive, like a Mustang. Whereas somebody else is driving their older brother's beater." Tracy also noticed subtle class differences: "I think high school's the great equalizer. I really don't remember, when you're attending a public high school, I really do think it's the great equalizer. I think if you're in maybe a private school environment, it's a little different. But I recall that there were a couple of students that it was clear that they came from a little more money than maybe the average person because they had a car or because they were doing fancy stuff to their hair or maybe wearing designer jeans." Tracy saved her babysitting money in order to keep up with the Joneses. "I wore designer jeans too, I just had to babysit for a month to get 'em . . . to get the money to buy them. So I don't recall that there were any real divisions monetarily other than whether or not you had a car or designer jeans."

Raul observed the impact of class on different genders. "Usually when it came to like finance, like moneywise, I think girls were the ones that had more of a tough time. You know, "'cause look at the clothes I'm wearing, I've got the Gucci bag." That's when all that stuff came around. But as far as with . . . guy-wise, I think we just probably [look at] who had the best car. But everybody would still talk to everybody. And I didn't see no big deal about that. And there was no really, nobody richie rich anyways going there 'cause it is a public school."

Racial insensitivity, identity issues, and class differences were sources of conflict and division between students at these three schools, just as they are for many American high school students. However, the desegregation policies in Chicago provided school environments that brought together very different types of students. The racial and ethnic differences in desegregated schools were expected. Students often brought their communities' and families' racial beliefs with them into the schools. Harold Washington's death is an excellent example of how the divisions in the city were brought into the schools. School desegregation offered students an opportunity to integrate and perhaps even become friends with students who seem vastly different. Yet school environments alone are not enough to keep out the racial divisions of the outside world, particularly when school staff avoided broaching these issues. Students often found ways to reject racism when it occurred, and school staff stepped in when issues escalated.

The differences between members of the same racial and ethnic groups also played out in these schools. Young people struggled to figure out where they fit in; over twenty years later, they still remembered the pain that caused them. Many Black participants felt like outsiders of their race when they chose to hang out with Whites and appeared to assimilate. Participants of mixed ethnic or racial groups, especially half-Latino, half-White participants who were raised in White communities, were often rejected by both groups because they did not exclusively belong to any. This rejection was traumatizing. Class differences could be evaluated based on material items possessed by students—clothes, cars, accessories, and so on. Whitney Young and Von Steuben had clearer class distinctions; the cliques among students there were more difficult for poorer students to penetrate. These differences led to difficulties for some. As participants came of age, however, they found a way, beyond the pressures and expectations of others, to figure out who they were. Their lives after high school furthered their development.

The level of integration in these schools was hampered by the external segregation, racial incidents within school, internal group sanctions, and class differences. Still, these students experienced isolated, low-level forms of integration. Individuals crossed segregated boundaries, attended desegregated schools, and pursued interracial interactions, no matter how minor. But occurring in isolation, these experiences did little to shift the racial boundaries or power dynamics and White privilege. The intrusions of the external society and internal differences were a reminder that even isolated integration was tenuous. Once they left high school, participants were reminded of the segregated realities of the rest of the society.

7

After High School and Desegregation Benefits

Out of sixty-eight participants, only four reported not attending college after high school. These participants were a small sample of students who graduated from Whitney Young, Von Steuben, and Bogan High Schools, but their college attendance rates were remarkable considering that 40 percent of their Chicago Public Schools classmates dropped out. Although the three schools were far better than participants' neighborhood schools, the college attendance rates differed among Whitney Young, Von Steuben, and Bogan students. This signified the ways in which schools reproduce social inequality. The school one attended could determine one's chances of graduating and attending college. Whitney Young, Von Steuben, and Bogan were among the high-status schools in Chicago Public Schools; yet across the three, students were prepared for life after high school in different ways. Participants from Whitney Young and Von Steuben were more likely to attend four-year colleges and universities than participants from all races and ethnicities at Bogan. Whitney Young's magnet and Von Steuben's science-focused curricula were geared toward college preparation, while students at Bogan were prepared for the working world. As a result, Bogan participants were more likely than Von Steuben or Whitney Young participants to attend community college or no college at all. Participants' socioeconomic backgrounds, decisions about starting a family, and the amount of information they received about college may have altered or delayed their decisions to attend college.

While desegregated schools may have prepared participants academically for college life, some were caught off guard by the lack of diversity and instances of racism at the college they attended. Participants expected that the integration they experienced in high school would also be apparent at the college they chose to attend. Some Black participants faced a rude awakening about the world outside their high schools. Their false sense of security was quickly disrupted in the isolated college towns they moved to, where they encountered students who had never had access to the diversity they took for granted.

Whether or not they attended college, participants of every race recognized the value of their experience in desegregated high schools, as it broadened their outlook on different racial and ethnic groups. It affected their views of the world, even if the world had not changed around them. Their experiences were transformative. Despite desegregation's limited impact on Chicago Public Schools, it broadened the horizons of the students who attended desegregated high schools and increased their capacity to understand people beyond their own race or ethnicity.

College Attendance

Because Von Steuben and Whitney Young were college preparatory schools, and Bogan's curriculum was more focused on career training, Bogan students were less likely to attend four-year colleges and universities. They had access to honors courses and college prep courses, but many were being prepared for technical careers and entry-level business positions. Table 7.1 provides the data about participants' college attendance. Of the twenty-seven Bogan graduates, only eleven went straight to a four-year college, three began at a community college before transferring to a four-year college, nine attended only two-year colleges, and four did not attend college at all. Of the four who never attended college, two were White, one was Black, and one was a Latina. This indicates that race or ethnicity was not a key factor for Bogan students' lack of college attendance. Instead, it demonstrates Bogan's career-focused curriculum.

Von Steuben and Whitney Young students had a better college attendance record than their Bogan peers. Twenty-five of thirty-two Von Steuben participants went to a four-year college or university. Four students attended both two- and four-year institutions, and two only attended community college. Some participants from Von Steuben attended prestigious and state flagship universities. Three attended Northwestern, and three attended the University of Illinois at Urbana-Champaign. All four Whitney Young graduates went to prestigious, flagship, or liberal arts colleges and universities. One student went to Boston College before transferring to Stanford; two attended the University of Illinois, the state's flagship institution; and one attended Bradley, a private liberal arts institution in Illinois.

Table 7.1
College Attendance Rates

School	Number answering question	Four-year college	Two- and four-year college	Community college only	No college
Whitney Young	4	4	0	0	0
Von Steuben	32	25	4	2	0
Bogan	27	11	3	9	4

In chapter 4, participants indicated some counselors' unfavorable college advice. Black and Latino participants in this and other studies were less informed about the process of getting into college, and students often had more access to this information when they were in higher academic tracks.[1] Participants' decisions to attend college were also influenced by their family circumstances. If parents never attended college, they had not set it as an expectation, and their children did not receive appropriate advice in school, students were less likely to see college as a priority and had less information about college affordability.[2] Additionally, participants' choices about starting a family made going to or finishing college a more difficult decision.

Most Von Steuben participants successfully went on to college right away, but Anthony's experience shows how social class and insufficient information about college can affect a student's decision, even if he or she attended a high-quality high school. Anthony graduated from Von Steuben and started working in a low-paying job. He attributed his decision to work after high school to a lack of parental guidance and information, as well as his desire to make money. Growing up poor, Anthony declared that he was "tired of being broke." He began working in high school and, like any student without major expenses, thought his Popeye's Chicken job, where he made around $3.35 an hour, was a big deal. He said, "I thought the heavens had opened up! And God ordained *me* . . . to be rich! [*Laughter.*]" When he graduated high school, he only thought of making money. He worked at Amoco gas station on Warren and Western, where he made $4.15 to $4.30 an hour and received a nickel raise after six months, bringing home around $600 a month with no bills.

The gas station was near the Rockwell Gardens housing projects and he often had to warn patrons that they were about to be robbed. Anthony recounted, "I mean this was a high-crime area 'cause Rockwell Gardens was about half a mile literally down the street. And people were getting robbed at my station while I'm looking at 'em. 'Cause I couldn't do nothing about it 'cause it was one of those booth stations. And I'm [on the microphone] like, 'Hey, you need to hang up that pump. They coming!' [*Laughter.*] Ain't that something. You getting your gas and somebody's like 'You need to quit. Bring me the money back later.'" Anthony became manager after previous managers were either fired or quit. He managed to turn a profit at the store at nineteen years old, crediting the fact that he never stole money. When his employers asked what he was doing, he simply stated that he was doing what they had taught him. The store ended up being one of the top-ranked stores in the city under Anthony's leadership.

Anthony thought he was in "heaven" until one day a Pepsi vendor who came into Amoco to make a delivery while Anthony was doing inventory told him that he had the ability to move beyond his current station in life.

> He was a real nice guy, had to be in his . . . early twenties. . . . And me and him had just a regular average conversation. He said, "Dude, you sound very smart. Why are you here?" I said, "What do you mean why I'm here?" He said, "Why are you here at this gas station? You sound like you can do better than this." I said, "I'm making money, dude." To me I was. I was making like $700 [to $800] . . . a month now. . . . My rent wasn't nothing but $400, I was renting my own place. He said, "But where you gonna go with this? How far you gonna go?" I said, "I don't know." He said, "You ain't got no college degree, you're not gonna go that far. You can only go so far. . . . You ever thought about getting in the air force?" "What, the military? Are you kidding me? No."
>
> Something happened later on that day when I thought about it more and more. He gave me a card to a recruiter. I called the recruiter maybe that Wednesday. By that Friday I was having a meeting with him. I ended up going into the air force as a pararescue. And one thing about the military for me, I didn't know what I wanted to do in life. But it gave me a steady check until I figured out what I wanted to do. It was better than being on the street, trying to figure out what I wanted to do. I was doing something with a skill that taught me how to be a medic. It taught me how to do things. I jumped out of planes, did things like that until I figured out what I wanted to do. I said, "OK, I want to go to college," even though I had a skill that would transcend into the civilian world to make decent money. I wanted to go to college. . . . I was in Louisiana. I went to LSU [Louisiana State University] for three years and then ultimately UIC [University of Illinois at Chicago].

Anthony was tired of being poor and instead focused on working to meet immediate needs without thinking about long-term career plans. If he was informed about college, perhaps he was not ready to hear the advice. Whatever the case, it took a vendor and not a teacher, a counselor, or his parents to show him the possible long-term consequences of his choices. While Anthony admitted that he joked around too much in high school and ended up on a general academic track, perhaps no one from high school provided the direction he needed to get to college. When parents are uninformed about college, schools take on a greater role in providing that information.

Raul, from Bogan, made his college decision based on what his family had done before him. He knew he wanted to work with his hands, so even though teachers tried to push him to take honors classes, he resisted because those classes were unnecessary for his future career plans. Raul observed his cousins attend the University of Illinois on scholarship their first year, and without funding the remaining years. He acknowledged that he lacked the book smarts of his cousins and thought the cost of college would be exorbitant. Consequently, he stated, "I ended up going to a technical school. I paid it on my own." Raul made his decision based on the reality of his career aspirations and the financial position of his family. Although Raul lacked adequate information about college, his family's experiences with both college and work led him to a decision he felt was good for him. Teachers pushed him to take honors classes, but no one told him about the financial aid options at colleges and universities. As a result, he decided that he could not afford college and chose instead to develop his skills at a technical school.

For some Bogan graduates, unexpected life changes kept them from attending or graduating from college. One White graduate became pregnant before she finished high school, and though she graduated, she never attended college. Another's father passed away her senior year, and she decided to work to help her family rather than attend college. Sirena and Gina, also Bogan graduates, attended community college with the intention of later matriculating to four-year universities. However, family obligations kept them from their goals. Sirena married her high school sweetheart, had children, and found it difficult to try to go back to school. After community college, she acquired administrative skills from a job-training organization. She said, "Later I got married, had kids. So it wasn't even a thought at that point. I thought I'm probably going to stay home and be a mom. But later I decided to go back because my kids were getting a little bigger. I went out on the job world." Likewise, when Gina was ready to go to a four-year college, she found out she was pregnant. At that point, with obligations to her children and a sixty-to-eighty-hour workweek, she was unable to return. Diana, another Bogan graduate, married young, and it took six years before she attended a community college. She lacked the finances for college and it "was the last thing on [her] mind" when she graduated high school.

For these participants, life choices and circumstances made going to or finishing college difficult. In part, their choices were determined by socioeconomic status. Anthony and Raul made choices based on their observations of the world around them. For Anthony, growing up in poverty meant that any money he made seemed to make him better off than his parents. Raul knew he lacked the finances and probably believed he was not college material, which is why he turned down opportunities to be in honors classes. Gender also played an important factor. The women who started families did not have the luxury to attend school, work, and raise children at the same time. They deferred their dreams to take care of their families. Their decisions to marry and have children at a young age were likely influenced by socioeconomic class, as the children of middle-class families are more likely to delay having a family until after college.

Racial Experiences in College

Participants who attended colleges and universities became aware of the difference between racial interactions in a desegregated high school and those at a predominantly White college. Most acknowledged the lack of diversity in small university towns and predominantly White institutions, though a few believed that high school prepared them to interact with different people in college. Black participants experienced overt racism for the first time in their lives and were shocked by it. A few Black participants had long desired to attend historically Black colleges and universities (HBCUs) and did so despite the diversity they enjoyed in high school. It became clear that despite whatever differences they faced at their individual high schools and whatever boundaries they crossed, the larger society still held firm racial boundaries.

Some White students were caught off guard by segregation and the lack of diversity at their universities. Both David and Craig had gotten used to the diversity of their desegregated public schooling in Chicago. David, a Von Steuben graduate, discussed the adjustment he had to make: "When I went to the University of Illinois a couple years later for my undergrad, I was disoriented. With all these kids from corn country and you just didn't know how to relate to them." David's brother, Craig, a graduate of Whitney Young, also had to adjust to the lack of diversity at Bradley University in Peoria, Illinois. "Outside of . . . kindergarten and first grade, I'd always been surrounded by people from all over the city. I mean . . . it was my perception of a normal school. It struck me as the strangest thing when I went to Bradley for undergrad . . . that suddenly there wasn't that usual mix of people. It was kind of strange."

Other participants saw their desegregated high school experiences as a natural precursor to their diverse colleges and universities. Marc, a Black Von Steuben graduate, thought his experience in high school prepared him for the diversity at the University of Illinois (U of I). While David considered U of I segregated, Marc thought it was diverse. Marc observed, "It was a very good time in my life because I interacted with people from all around the world and literally I know I was going to the U of I where there would be literally people from all over the world who grew up in different parts of the world." Marc's experience with diversity at Von Steuben equipped him to embrace students from around the world.

Similarly, the time Erin spent at Von Steuben enhanced her ability to comfortably interact with her Black roommate at Illinois State University. Others witnessing their interactions were uncomfortable because they had never seen Blacks and Whites teasing each other. Erin stated,

> One of my college roommates was African American. We stayed together during the summer; so we worked together at the local bookstore in Normal, Illinois—you know, little White farm town—and terrified the kids that were there because we would tease each other. She would tell me about fish fries with spaghetti? And I'm going, "Those two foods don't go together! Who are your family? . . . Those foods don't *go* together!" She was from the South Side of Chicago . . . so we would tease each other in class. And she would tease me about Passover. I made her eat matzo, and this stuff will bind you up for your life. So we would tease each other, and everyone would get very nervous, *very* nervous.

Erin had relaxed exchanges with her roommate because she attended high school with Black girls from the South Side. The other students who witnessed them had come from White segregated environments where such interactions were uncommon. For them, boundary crossing seemed abnormal.

Erin and Marc comfortably enjoyed their interactions with people from different races in college. Yet some Black participants faced racism at their colleges. Melissa recalled her experience at Southern Illinois University Carbondale:

> When you go to college everything is not all Black unless you go to Tuskegee or Morehouse. I went down to the hick town of Illinois. One of the most prejudice places in the state! . . . I was just outside with some of my friends minding my own business and we were called a nigger. And of course, my friends, they went up there, I was just like, whatever. And the police was like, "Well you all gotta leave." And I was like, "I live here, I don't have to leave." . . . I was like, "Look, this is what it is. They should not be yelling racial slurs out the window. And they called you because that's what they did and they know we know where they live. . . . I could have gone up to their room but I didn't. I'm standing here and I'm not bothering anybody and I live here and I'm not moving. That's that." So . . . he was like, "Well OK . . . but we don't want any problems." I was like, "Well then you need to tell them to stop calling people out their names. They don't know us, we don't know them. We're not bothering them."

Black students attending college in Carbondale well into the 2000s were still called niggers.

Sylvia also remembered experiencing racism: "I went to Luther College, a private school in Decorah, Iowa. . . . That was truly segregation. Believe me, it was the worst experience of my life!" When asked whether she remained at the school for four years, she responded,

> No, no! Two was too many. I had a basketball scholarship. Actually, Von Steuben's coach had connected me with a . . . full ride to Dubuque [College]. Me being stupid, trying to follow a boy, I turned it down. My mother never knew why. But I turned it down and that's how I ended up in Iowa. I ended up there two years. They were very racist. Believe me, very racist. But . . . I must say, by the grace of God, one Black girl and a couple White families and that's how I made it through. I made it all four semesters. But I transferred to Valparaiso, another racist school—made a mistake. I ended up at Western Illinois University. But my experience in Iowa, I had never seen White people treat Black like that until I got there. I truly did not know serious racism until I got there.

Tracy, from Von Steuben, also recalled racism in college and its impact on her ability to easily relate to others. She had the opposite experience of Erin.

> I remember we were doing an orientation exercise and this one girl was just like, she was not gonna be my partner. And I was just like, "Oh!" But that wasn't in high school. So to be honest with you, I didn't encounter racism or being treated differently because of my ethnic background until I went away from Von. And I was kind of embarrassed when I went to my reunion. Because I found myself, because we become conditioned to the exposures we've had or the environments that we're in. I found myself extending my hand to one of my White classmates because in corporate America you limit your interaction and personal space with people. And she was like, "Move your hand out the way and give me a hug!" And I was like, "Oh hey! I'm so sorry!" Then I had to apologize. But I felt like . . . I've become reconditioned. And that was a wakeup call.

Since these participants had enjoyed positive integrative experiences in high school, the racism in college astonished them. They were prepared for diversity in college, not for the reality check that their desegregated high schools were unique places, atypical of the larger society. Desegregated schools and the military were the two places in American society responsible for extensive racial interaction.[3] Attending predominantly White colleges and universities certainly exposed students to people from around the world. However, the location of the schools, particularly those in isolated, rural communities and small towns, often meant diversity was unwelcome. Students also came in contact with White students, staff, and faculty members who had grown up or lived in segregated communities and held stereotypical or racist assumptions about the ability of Black students.

Three Black graduates attended HBCUs, most of which were founded before and during the Jim Crow era in the South. Their previous knowledge of these institutions made them viable options. Rayshawn, a graduate of Bogan, had always wanted to attend an HBCU, though her experience at Bogan made that decision difficult. In the end, she decided she wanted to be in the environment of an HBCU. "Since I was nine, ten, I said I'm going to Black college. . . . I had attended a couple of graduations at Black colleges as a child, loved the idea and the atmosphere. When it was time for me to start looking at colleges, I looked at Illinois State, but I really looked at the Black colleges. And in the end . . . I attended a Black college." Even if Rayshawn had not received a scholarship to attend a Black college, she still would have chosen one. In making her decision, she said,

> I was torn because, the experience was really great at Bogan, with the multiculturalism involved and so I said, "Well, I could go to U of I. I could go here. I could go there." But then I said, "Well, I also miss that camaraderie. I miss some of that camaraderie of being . . . in an all-Black school." And I had heard all of these great stories about the cultural oneness and the family-oriented aspect of attending a Black college. Yes, you could still get the same academic caliber, but you could also get this cultural end of things. You go to the White schools, and you . . . might be the only one.

Rayshawn's choice was between the cultural richness of an HBCU and the isolation of a White institution. Her decision meant that she avoided the racism and prejudice that existed on predominantly White campuses.

Angela, from Von Steuben, and Kelly, from Bogan, also chose to attend Black colleges. As with Rayshawn, their exposure to these institutions made them viable options. Angela wanted to attend a Black college to be near family. "My family's from Louisiana. I love Louisiana. I also wanted to attend an all-Black, predominantly Black college so that I could see what it's like. A good portion of my family have attended many of the major African American colleges and done very well." Kelly enjoyed the variety of schools she attended. She said, "I went to a Black elementary school here in Chicago. I went to a White high school here in Chicago. I went to a Black university, a HBCU . . . on the East Coast." She felt enriched by the variety of educational experiences she had.

Participants who attended predominantly White colleges and universities either enjoyed the diversity or hated the isolation or racism of the schools. Those who attended Black colleges did so largely because they were exposed to them. Their attendance at desegregated schools did not alter their decisions to attend an HBCU. In the end, college was unlike high school, though their experiences at desegregated schools influenced their expectations of the former. They anticipated diversity in the larger world, but most of their experiences in college were racially segregated.

Benefits of Desegregation

The overall fight for school desegregation was to provide Black students with access to resources customarily given only to White schools. Desegregation brought students together, enabling isolated integration as students interacted with and learned from each other. W.E.B. Du Bois argued that the benefits of "mixed" schools include "wider contacts," self-confidence, and suppression of an inferiority complex that comes from being in schools and competing with Whites. Such schools provide broader education for all students. But he also understood the drawbacks students face in places where their culture is unappreciated and unacknowledged and where they are mistreated by White teachers; and he acknowledged the value of segregated schools despite their poor conditions.[4] In the end, Du Bois called for education, regardless of whether it came in mixed or separate schools.

Broader education and contacts were certainly attained in the three desegregated schools examined here. Most participants identified the values of desegregated schools, including tolerance for people of different races and ethnicities and a greater understanding and appreciation of other cultures, as the benefits of desegregation. Going to school and being in classes with others helped participants break down stereotypes and understand other groups better. The oral history interviews were conducted with graduates, most of whom had just attended their class reunions. They had time to fondly reminisce about their experiences. While they were asked about both the benefits and the downsides of desegregation, most easily proclaimed that they benefited greatly from their experiences. Based on their experiences, some outlined their perceptions about the limitations of segregated environments, how much they learned about different racial and ethnic groups, and how class, gender identity, and religious stereotypes were shattered at their desegregated schools.

Black and Latino participants recognized that growing up in segregated neighborhoods limited the way people saw the world. Teresa found her experience liberating: "I grew up in . . . an all-Black neighborhood and that was my experience. . . . And to actually go to Von Steuben and experience all these different cultures was, I think, life changing. 'Cause you grow up a certain way, you have certain thoughts, and then when those mind-sets get totally reversed, it's liberating actually. It really is." She also thought desegregation "gives you tools to find out about a person before you make snap judgments. All one race isn't like whatever you think they're like." Camille also saw the advantages since she grew up in a Black community. "I feel that at a young age . . . especially growing up in the neighborhood I grew up in, and on the West Side most people were just used to dealing with their own culture. It was good for me to have knowledge of different cultures already before going into the work world. Most people, once they get into the work world, they're just now dealing with different cultures. But since I went to high school with a lot of different cultures, I was already prepared." Melissa acknowledged that growing up in a segregated environment limited one's perspective. "It kind of lets you know that the world is just not all Black. It's really sad that some of us never get out of our community. We never get out of the neighborhood, so we never get to see what's out there. For me, Von was the world. 'Cause I got to leave my community and I traveled through other communities to get to Von. And then when I got to Von I saw all of the communities. To me that was the best experience ever."

Nora saw what she believed could be the limitations of growing up in a segregated Mexican American neighborhood. "I think that it's changed a lot of my ideas about people because we were segregated in those communities, in Pilsen, in Little Village. The people stay in those communities because it's safe. You don't have to learn the language, you don't have to go far to do anything. You don't have to learn to drive. So it benefited me. . . . It gives you what I think college is supposed to do which is open your mind to different ways of thinking. Everything isn't, pardon the pun, black and white."

Black and Latino participants remembered how desegregation opened their understanding of different cultural groups. Tracy, from Von Steuben, viewed the benefits in this way: "Being African American, and coming to a different community, getting into an element where you have so many different ethnic groups, and coming together on one accord, just for the sake of learning, was positive for me. Yeah, naturally you kind of gravitate towards your own groups. But at the end of the day you have to do so much with each other that you build a level of tolerance for each other." For Tracy, attending a desegregated school helped open up the world for individuals who were not used to being around different groups.

Edgar, a Latino from Von Steuben, said of desegregation, "Well, there's an incredible appreciation that you have for different backgrounds. Things that you never knew that are common with the different backgrounds." Rayshawn, from Bogan, saw the value in attending a desegregated school. "It taught me to appreciate others better. It taught me to understand the differences in the cultures and to understand, even if a person said something mean or biased, it taught me to understand why he or she may do that (because it's a learned behavior), and therefore I wouldn't take it so personally or wouldn't be so offended by it." Terrace, a Black participant from Von Steuben, thought the experienced shattered stereotypes. "I think a lot of those racial stereotypes, they just don't ring true. I think that when you are surrounded by all those different races, you don't have time to really think about that because you're interacting with them yourself that it's OK. You kind of think of them as people. . . . Just because there's different races doesn't mean a whole lot. So when you interact with them you just treat people the way you want to be treated. So I think it helped."

Melissa believed that being around people from different nationalities enriched her experiences. She recalled getting to know Filipinos, Koreans, Mexicans, Puerto Ricans, Cubans, and people from the Middle East. When people talked negatively about the different groups, she insisted, "You don't have to listen to all that negative talk about, oh Mexicans are this and Puerto Ricans are this. . . . You actually have friends who are all these different nationalities. So, I mean, you know for yourself personally that everyone is not like that." Raul, from Bogan, was still surprised by people who had never intermingled with other races. He said, "Sometimes I get amazed when I get to meet people that never seen a Hispanic, Black, the way they act and the questions they ask me. And to me that's one big benefit that . . . desegregation did for a lot of kids to know different races. Because sometimes I feel sorry for these people . . . living with blinds."

White participants from Bogan also recognized the benefits of school desegregation, as it helped them see past their assumptions, fears, and parental beliefs. Tracy thought, "Desegregation is humanizing. When you are with different people of different races all the time, you have to be blind not to see that a human is a human is a human." Michelle stated, "I honestly look at it more as . . . tolerance. . . . It's . . . no longer an unknown . . . the other groups of people, these other types of people. Therefore, you're not fearful of them. . . . I think that it makes everybody kind of better people when you're around people and you can understand them." Michelle thought she benefited from "being able to look . . . past people's skin color or their ethnicity." She observed, "I want to say that you don't see it, you see the person." Melanie felt desegregation gave her a chance to know people beyond the limited views her family members had: "I think I had a good experience. I think I was exposed to things that I normally wouldn't have been exposed to. One, my parents . . . was very anti anything that's not White. So it's not like I'd have a lot of exposure unless I was somewhere in school or whatever that I wasn't able to be exposed to some of these other cultures and behaviors."

Two Whitney Young students, Josephine and Eve, acknowledged the benefits beyond race alone. They recognized class, culture, religion, and gender diversities and learned not to judge a book by its cover. Josephine noted,

> Going into high school, it was really powerful for me to see how other people live. I think that really appeals to the anthropologist in me and the border crosser in me, if you will. It's just, I've been curious about how other people live

> and how that compares to how I grew up and what my family and what my cultural values are. So it just really opened me up to different ways of doing things and thinking about things. I feel like it also helped me see how people from different classes, how they can conceive of themselves in the world—their self-concept and their sense of what's possible is very different. I think, sometimes, in us working-class people, while we work hard, we sometimes don't feel like we deserve much or that our purview of possibility is a lot smaller, or limited. And so it was really cool to kind of hang out with kids who had parents or grandparents who had gone to medical school or who were professional.

Eve had interesting interactions with people who shattered the stereotypes of race, religion, and gender expectations:

> I hung out with folks who were quote-unquote "skinheads." And they probably weren't real technical skinhead, because they wouldn't have been hanging out with me. [*Laughter.*] There was a [White] guy in our class who . . . was . . . an atheist or something. . . . Our teacher . . . brought up the Bible. And the teacher was like, "Wow I wish I had my Bible here to pull out for the class," and so the guy is like, "Oh I have mine." He's like, "What are you doing with one?" You know, so little stereotypes like that. We hung out with a guy who was like a little punk rocker, and *he* ran for prom queen. [*Laughter.*] And I actually was on his little committee.

These experiences helped Eve understand that people from various backgrounds, with different ideas about the world, could get along and learn from each other.

Anthony summed up the experience of attending a desegregated school with a story of the outpouring of support for a Von Steuben student who passed away.

> We had a guy, one of our classmates, he was an underclassman our senior year. Right after we graduated, he died. He went into the military and he got shot. . . . But it was a year after we graduated. He was from the '89 class. That funeral was in the inner city of Chicago. It was tons of non–African Americans there. Von Steuben was close. Not only just our class. . . . We were close with a lot of classes. It was a lot of people at that funeral that were not Black. And it wasn't just for show. It was an authentic touch, an authentic feeling. That's what I remember about Von and that aspect. And that's what I think will be different, or what was different about being in a predominantly, be it African American or White school. . . . You don't develop that level of intimacy for another culture 'cause you're not exposed to it on a regular basis.

Graduates of Bogan, Von Steuben, and Whitney Young High Schools clearly benefited from Chicago's school desegregation in terms of both academics and interracial interactions. The college preparatory curriculum, particularly at Von Steuben and Whitney Young, provided important opportunities for these graduates. Most pursued at least some college, while many of their peers in neighborhood schools failed to graduate high school. Study participants were academically prepared, but some were surprised by college environments that were far less integrated than their high schools.

The experiment in school desegregation failed to transform the wider community, although seeds were planted for increased understanding and tolerance of difference.[5] Even with school desegregation, study participants had to make sacrifices by enduring long commutes to schools, stigmatism from their neighborhood peers, microaggressions from school staff, normalized White curriculum, and some tense interactions with peers. Most navigated these obstacles to make integration work at their schools. Many benefited from school desegregation. At the very least, they gained tolerance and understanding of different cultures and racial groups. Those who fully immersed themselves in the integrated experience acquired valuable friendships and transformed worldviews while crossing multiple borders in the process. All of this occurred despite the various external and internal obstacles that made integration difficult.

Participants in this study were personally transformed, experienced integration at a basic level, and individually crossed segregated boundaries. Sharon Stanley recognizes the contested definitions of integration and argues that "a mutually transformative integration, rather than mere desegregation or assimilation, promises to contest White supremacy itself."[6] A deeper level of integration has to include institutions outside of schools. If not, segregation and racial stratification remain enduring aspects of society, and even as individuals have interracial interactions, boundaries remain in place that protect White privilege and undermine deeper forms of integration and social change.

During Chicago's greatest efforts to desegregate, desegregation was severely limited and segregation persisted. In contemporary Chicago, desegregation has ended, access to top schools is limited, and students and their families are increasingly abandoning the schools and city in search of better educational and housing opportunities elsewhere. The benefits students experienced were short lived and unsustainable in a society that values White supremacy and continuing segregation, making boundary crossing a different experience for the current generation.

Conclusion

Continuing Inequality

At its height in the 1980s, Chicago's school desegregation was severely limited in its reach. The Supreme Court's *Parents Involved v. Seattle* decision (2007) overturned voluntary desegregation in Seattle and Jefferson County, Kentucky. In 2009, Judge Charles P. Kocoras ended Chicago's desegregation consent decree.[1] Many insisted that desegregation either was a failure or had run its course, and after President Barack Obama's election, some even claimed we were in a postracial America. The *Parents Involved* case severely restricted school desegregation, and with the end of the consent decree, it further decreased the integrative opportunities for successive generations of Chicago Public Schools students. Once the Supreme Court decision and the end of the consent decree terminated the use of race in school admissions, Chicago Public Schools focused its equity efforts on socioeconomic-based assignments instead of race-based assignments.[2] These changes benefited Whites.

With shifting policy changes and shifting demographics, the percentage of Black students declined at two of the schools studied here. Von Steuben became a majority-Latino school. In 1988, when most of the participants graduated, Von Steuben was 33.3 percent White, 32.2 percent Black, 18.2 percent Latino, and 16.4 other (mostly Asian). By 2018, it was 57.2 percent Latino, 16.3 percent White, 11 percent Black, and 12.8 percent Asian. Bogan, once the stronghold of desegregation resistance, had been all but abandoned by Whites. In 1988, it was 42.1 percent White, 28.7 percent Black, 19 percent Latino, and 10.1 percent Asian or other. In 2018, it was 50.3 percent Black, 48.6 percent Latino, and only 0.5 percent White. Whitney Young had the most dramatic decline for Black students. In 1990, after most participants graduated, the school was 65.1 percent Black, 13.8 percent Latino, 12.9 percent White, and 8.1 percent Asian. In 2018, it was 29 percent White, 28 percent Latino, 23 percent Black, and 16 percent Asian.[3] All of the racial and ethnic subgroups had increased while Blacks declined.

After desegregation ended, the media paid attention to the decreasing spots available at the city's top schools for Black and Latino students.[4] In 2018, though Whites were only 10 percent of the Chicago Public Schools population, they had acquired 23 percent of the premium spots at the top city schools, and Asians were only 4 percent but had 10 percent of the spots at the top schools. Blacks and Latinos were disproportionately disadvantaged. According to *Education Week*, Chicago's eleven elite schools had only 34 percent Latino and 29 percent Black students, despite their overwhelming populations in the Chicago Public Schools.[5] Latinos became the largest demographic group (46.7 percent, with Blacks at 36.6 percent, Whites at 10.5 percent, and Asians at 4 percent).[6] The concerns that Black Chicago Board of Education members had in the 1980s were confirmed, as Black students had less access to the best schools. The new focus on socioeconomics led to a decreased focus on Black students. Black Chicagoans remained highly segregated, and they increasingly abandoned the public schools and the city of Chicago for northwest Indiana, Iowa's quad cities, and, in a return migration, the South.[7] Latinos' segregation increased as they became a larger proportion of the city's population and the largest group in the school system. Whites disproportionately benefited from the end of desegregation.

Since the participants graduated from their high schools in the late 1980s and early 1990s, school reform efforts have focused on corporate-style reform favoring punishment over development, accountability initiatives that included high-stakes testing, and neoliberal reforms that led to the privatization of schools. Chicago made national headlines as teachers held a strike in 2012 and forty-nine mostly Black schools were closed in 2013, the largest mass closure of school in U.S. history. In the areas where the traditional public schools closed, 71 percent of the 108 charter schools that opened between 2000 and 2015 were within 1.5 miles of the closed schools, demonstrating the focus on privatization.[8]

Contemporary school choice plans have taken a very different meaning from what school desegregation advocates had in mind. Under desegregation-style school choice initiatives, integration occurred. The goal was to bring students of different racial groups into the same schools as a way to alleviate the inequalities segregated schooling produced. School desegregation plans like those in Chicago and interdistrict plans that occurred around the country "were created to provide families that have historically had the fewest school choices with high-quality educational options." The contemporary school choice initiatives have increased segregation by race and class, what Noliwe Rooks calls "segrenomics, or the business of profiting specifically from high levels of racial and economic segregation."[9]

Scholars have continued to debunk the "superman" status of charter schools and school choice and have identified how these schools have failed to provide the improvements they promised and, with bipartisan political support, philanthropic groups, hedge funds, venture capitalists, and entrepreneurs, have effectively siphoned off public money for private interests.[10] David Stovall argues that "missing from the prevailing perceptions of charter schools and school choice are the realities of White supremacy, neoliberalism, disinvestment, mass displacement, hypersegregation, and the politics of disposability."[11]

Contemporary school choice in Chicago has drawn increasing interest from scholars, including those who closely follow how choice affects students. Carla Shedd examined how students traverse school, neighborhood, and interactions with the law. She found that students' school choice options were tempered by safety concerns, as crossing borders within the city meant crossing between gang territories and thereby losing the protection of neighborhood friends and gangs. Kate Phillippo's study illustrates how competitive school choice creates a contest in which students compete for access to limited resources in eighth grade. Their decisions have significant consequences for their economic futures. Mary Pattillo, in her study of contemporary school choice, also in Chicago, argues that school choice is more about schools choosing students rather than the other way around. Schools hold more power in the choice dynamics.[12] Like the graduates' observations in the present study, each of these important studies illuminates the ongoing struggles students have in negotiating choice, being chosen, and crossing geographic and racial boundaries to gain a better education.

Scholars and advocates of school integration rightfully argue that the contemporary school choice initiatives are devoid of the effective school desegregation reform efforts that were initiated in the past. School desegregation was imperfect, yet it helped close the racial achievement gaps, broadened the academic opportunities and life chances for numerous students, and led to important interracial interaction between students. As this study has shown, students made integration happen in their schools as they crossed racial boundaries, negotiated long commutes, faced ostracism from neighborhood peers and microaggressions from school staff, and dealt with the politics and racism brought into the schools from outside. Their boundary crossing came with both significant sacrifice and significant gain. Graduates, even those who recounted stories of racial disturbances within their schools, proudly described the benefits they gained as a result of their sacrifice. Rayshawn, from Bogan, best expressed the sentiment: "We had White friends and Black friends and Hispanic friends, and everybody was laughing and joking and there [were] some tense moments. Now I won't say it was perfect. We did experience some racial tension throughout the years at different points that I do remember. But for the most part, I would say the good outweighed the bad."

The complicated history of school desegregation, from policy creation, to implementation, and then to dismantlement, provides a bird's-eye view of American society. So much time was spent resisting the policy and studying the resistance that few paid attention to the quiet accomplishments of the students who attended these schools, circumvented racial norms, and experienced isolated integration. Their stories remind us that broader possibilities exist beyond the internal and external boundaries placed on individuals and groups and that we share a common humanity, even as others exploit our differences for political gain. The ultimate work needed to transform American society is to disassemble the boundaries and to create an integrated society where assimilation is not the end goal, but diversity, equity, and inclusion are truly valued.

Acknowledgments

I am enormously grateful to the graduates of Von Steuben, Bogan, and Whitney Young for sharing their stories with me and my research team. I had a vision for this book, but the participants brought it to life and broadened my understanding of their experiences. Special thanks to the four reunion organizers who gave my research team access to Bogan's and Von Steuben's class reunions. I also want to thank my former graduate students who helped me interview the participants in 2008: Mahauganee Shaw Bonds, Lindsey Cowles, Jacob Hardesty, and Juan Berumen. Their curiosity pushed me to explore unanticipated topics and to see the value in subjects I might have bypassed. I could not have done this work without the graduates and my research team. I would also like to thank other students—Alexis Saba (who greatly assisted me with transcribing interviews), Hyesun An, Quinton Stroud, Morgan Rae Whitaker, and Tanya Garnica for additional research and editing, and Megan Covington, Josclynn Brandon, Dajanae Palmer, Kristen Hengtgen, and Jasmine Hawkins for reading chapters of the final draft.

Several colleagues read chapters for me or provided feedback at conferences. This list includes Kate Phillippo, David Garcia, David Stovall, Mirelsie Velázquez, Fithawee Tzeggai, Lilia Fernandez, Ann Marie Ryan, Derrick Aldridge, V. P. Franklin, Jeanne M. Powers, Eileen Tamura, John Rury, Elizabeth Todd-Breland, and Benjamin Justice. Special thanks to the two anonymous reviewers, whose critical feedback made this a better book. Thanks to my accountability partners in Indiana University's faculty writing groups, the National Center for Faculty Development and Diversity's Faculty Success Program, Eddie Cole Jr., Katrina Overby, and Abi Gundlach Graham. Eddie and I walked through this process together as we both worked to complete our books. Gizelle Fletcher provided editing for an earlier version of my work, Gina Gail Fletcher and I wrote together numerous times, and Daisy Lovelace provided the place for a much-needed summer writing retreat. Thanks to Raquel Hill, Dionne Cross Francis, Brenda Williams, Yvette McDonald, Joy Williamson Lott, Katrina Sanders, Eboni Zamani Gallaher, Christopher M. Span, Michelle Purdy, Kim Phillips, and Kim Livingston Smith for their continued support. Special thanks to Jordan Blekking for the maps, and Lisa Banning for providing her continued support and shepherding me through this process. Thanks to my Indiana University colleagues in the Department of Educational Leadership and Policy Studies, the School of Education, and the Office of the Vice Provost for Diversity and Inclusion for bearing with me as I juggled multiple responsibilities, including two administrative positions.

My family was, without a doubt, an essential part of this book project. My daughter, Najerie, helped me organize early portions of the manuscript and encouraged me through multiple revisions. My father, George K. Danns, took time out of his own busy research schedule to read my manuscript more than once and helped me find the forest among the trees. Well after an intense two-day discussion of my book, he continued to push me to be more explicit about the meaning and importance of my work. My mother, Ann, and sister Tam provided the support, encouragement, and love I needed to finish this book.

This project was partially supported by Indiana University's New Frontiers Program, funded by Lilly Endowment and administered by the Office of the Vice Provost for Research. Portions of this book were previously published in articles including "'Other Minority': Multi-ethnic School Desegregation Experiences in Two Chicago Communities," *Race Ethnicity and Education*, published online, April 30, 2019; and "Policy Implications for School Desegregation and School Choice in Chicago," *Urban Review* 50, no. 4 (2018): 584–603.

Notes

Introduction

1 Henry J. Perkinson, *The Imperfect Panacea: American Faith in Education*, 4th ed. (Boston: McGraw Hill, 1995).
2 For more on opportunity hoarding, see John L. Rury and Aaron Tyler Rife, "Race, Schools and Opportunity Hoarding: Evidence from a Post-war American Metropolis," *History of Education* 47 (2018): 87–107.
3 Dionne Danns, *Desegregating Chicago's Public Schools: Policy Implementation, Politics, and Protest, 1965–1985* (New York: Palgrave Macmillan, 2014).
4 Erica Frankenberg and Elizabeth DeBray, *Integrating Schools in a Changing Society: New Policies and Legal Options for a Multiracial Generation* (Chapel Hill: University of North Carolina Press, 2011), 7.
5 Sharon A. Stanley, *An Impossible Dream? Racial Integration in the United States* (New York: Oxford University Press, 2017), 3; Elizabeth Anderson, *Imperative of Integration* (Princeton, NJ: Princeton University Press, 2010), 2.
6 I use the term *racialized* to refer to racial and ethnic groups considered minorities, particularly since Latinos are not considered to belong to a race. Natalie Molina, *How Race Is Made in America: Immigration, Citizenship, and the Historical Power of Racial Scripts* (Berkeley: University of California Press, 2014).
7 Joane Nagel, "Constructing Ethnicity: Creating and Recreating Ethnic Identity and Culture," *Social Problems* 41 (February 1994): 152–176.
8 Michèle Lamont and Virág Molnár, "The Study of Boundaries in the Social Sciences," *Annual Review of Sociology* 28 (2002): 168.
9 Fredrik Barth, *Ethnic Groups and Boundaries* (Boston: Little, Brown, 1969), 9–10; Richard Alba, "Bright vs. Blurred Boundaries: Second-Generation Assimilation and Exclusion in France, Germany, and the United States," *Ethnic and Racial Studies* 28 (January 2005): 20–49.
10 Alba, "Bright vs. Blurred Boundaries," 23; Aristide R. Zolberg and Long Litt Woon, "Why Islam Is like Spanish: Cultural Incorporation in Europe and the United States," *Politics and Society* 27 (March 1999): 5–38.
11 Richard Kluger, *Simple Justice* (New York: Vintage Books, 1975); James T. Patterson, Brown v. Board of Education: *A Civil Rights Milestone and Its Troubled*

Legacy (Oxford: Oxford University Press, 2001); Derrick Bell, *Silent Covenants:* Brown v. Board of Education *and the Unfulfilled Hopes for Racial Reform* (Oxford: Oxford University Press, 2004); Rachel Devlin, *A Girl Stands at the Door: The Generation of Young Women Who Desegregated America's Schools* (New York: Basic Books, 2018).

12 Jeffrey L. Littlejohn and Charles H. Ford, *Elusive Equality: Desegregation and Resegregation in Norfolk's Public Schools* (Charlottesville: University of Virginia Press, 2012); Davidson M. Douglas, *Reading, Writing, and Race: The Desegregation of the Charlotte Schools* (Chapel Hill: University of North Carolina Press, 1995); Liva Baker, *The Second Battle of New Orleans: The Hundred-Year Struggle to Integrate the Schools* (New York: HarperCollins, 1996); Frye Gaillard, *The Dream Long Deferred: The Landmark Struggle for Desegregation in Charlotte, North Carolina* (Chapel Hill: University of North Carolina Press, 1988); Constance Curry, *Silver Rights* (Chapel Hill: Algonquin Books of Chapel Hill, 1995); David S. Cecelski, *Along Freedom Road: Hyde County, North Carolina, and the Fate of Black Schools in the South* (Chapel Hill: University of North Carolina Press, 1994); R. Scott Baker, *Paradoxes of Desegregation: African American Struggle for Educational Equity in Charleston, South Carolina, 1926–1972* (Columbia: University of South Carolina Press, 2006); Sarah Caroline Thuesen, *Greater Than Equal: African American Struggles for Schools and Citizenship in North Carolina, 1919–1965* (Chapel Hill: University of North Carolina Press, 2013). See also Charles C. Bolton, *The Hardest Deal of All: The Battle over School Integration in Mississippi, 1870–1980* (Jackson: University of Mississippi Press, 2005); Karen Anderson, *Little Rock: Race and Resistance at Central High School* (Princeton, NJ: Princeton University Press, 2010); and Jill Ogline Titus, *Brown's Battleground: Students, Segregationists, and the Struggle for Justice in Prince Edward County, Virginia* (Chapel Hill: University of North Carolina Press, 2011).

13 Davidson M. Douglas, *Jim Crow Moves North: The Battle over Northern School Desegregation, 1865–1954* (Cambridge: Cambridge University Press, 2005); Gregory S. Jacobs, *Getting around* Brown*: Desegregation, Development, and the Columbus Public Schools* (Columbus: Ohio State University Press, 1998); Jack Dougherty, *More Than One Struggle: The Evolution of Black School Reform in Milwaukee* (Chapel Hill: University of North Carolina Press, 2004); Danns, *Desegregating Chicago's Public Schools*; Ronald P. Formisano, *Boston against Busing: Race, Class, and Ethnicity in the 1960s and 1970s* (Chapel Hill: University of North Carolina Press, 2004); Joyce A. Baugh, *The Detroit School Busing Case:* Milliken v. Bradley *and the Controversy over Desegregation* (Lawrence: University of Kansas Press, 2011); Steven J. L. Taylor, *Desegregation in Boston and Buffalo: The Influence of Local Leaders* (Albany: State University of New York Press, 1998); Alan B. Anderson and George W. Pickering, *Confronting the Color Line: The Broken Promise of the Civil Rights Movement in Chicago* (Athens: University of Georgia Press, 1986); Stephen Kendrick and Paul Kendrick, *Sarah's Long Walk: Free Blacks of Boston and How Their Struggle for Equality Changed America* (Boston: Beacon, 2006).

14 Amy Stuart Wells and Robert L. Crain, *Stepping over the Color Line: African-American Students in White Suburban Schools* (Hartford, CT: Yale University Press, 1997); Howell S. Baum, Brown *in Baltimore: School Desegregation and the Limits of Liberalism* (Ithaca, NY: Cornell University Press, 2010); Brett Gadsden,

Between North and South: Delaware, Desegregation, and the Myth of American Sectionalism (Philadelphia: University of Pennsylvania Press, 2012); Sarah Garland, *Divided We Fail: The Story of an African American Community That Ended the Era of School Desegregation* (Boston: Beacon, 2013); Tracy E. K'Meyer, *From* Brown *to* Meredith: *The Long Struggle for School Desegregation in Louisville, Kentucky, 1954–2007* (Chapel Hill: University of North Carolina Press, 2013).

15 Rubén Donato, *The Other Struggle of Equal Schools: Mexican Americans during the Civil Rights Era* (New York: State University of New York Press, 1997); David G. García, *Strategies of Segregation: Race, Residence, and the Struggle for Educational Equality* (Oakland: University of California Press, 2018); Richard R. Valencia, *Chicano Students and the Courts: The Mexican American Legal Struggle for Educational Equality* (New York: New York University Press, 2008); Guadalupe San Miguel Jr., *Brown, Not White: School Integration and the Chicano Movement in Houston* (College Station: Texas A&M University Press, 2001); Carlos Kevin Blanton, *George I. Sanchez: The Long Fight for Mexican American Integration* (New Haven, CT: Yale University Press, 2014); Rubén Donato and Jarrod S. Hanson, "Legally White, Socially 'Mexican': The Politics of De Jure and De Facto School Segregation in the American Southwest," *Harvard Educational Review* 82 (Summer 2012): 202–225.

16 Barbara W. Sommer and Mary Kay Quinlan, *The Oral History Manual*, 2nd ed. (Lanham, MD: AltaMira, 2009), 1.

17 Ken Howarth, *Oral History: A Handbook* (Phoenix Mill, UK: Sutton, 1998), 4.

18 Jack Dougherty, "From Anecdote to Analysis: Oral Interviews and New Scholarship in Educational History," *Journal of American History* 86 (September 1999): 722.

19 Paul Thompson, *The Voice of the Past: Oral History* (Oxford: Oxford University Press, 1988), 2; William W. Cutler III, "Oral History: Its Nature and Uses for Educational History," *History of Education Quarterly* 11 (Summer 1971): 184–194.

20 Vanessa Siddle Walker, *The Lost Education of Horace Tate: Uncovering the Hidden Heroes Who Fought for Justice in Schools* (New York: New Press, 2018).

21 Richard White, *Remembering Ahanagran: Story Telling in a Family's Past* (New York: Hill and Wang, 1998), 4.

22 Jesús Salvador Treviño, dir., *Star Trek: Voyager*, season 4, episode 17, "Retrospect," aired February 25, 1998, on CBS.

23 Jan Vansina, *Oral Tradition as History* (Madison: University of Wisconsin Press, 1985), 4–5; Donald A. Ritchie, *Doing Oral History: A Practical Guide*, 2nd ed. (Oxford: Oxford University Press, 2003), 27.

24 Barbara Shircliffe, "'We Got the Best of That World': A Case for the Study of Nostalgia in the Oral History of School Desegregation," *Oral History Review* 28 (Summer/Fall 2001): 60.

25 Hilton Kelly, *Race, Remembering, and Jim Crow's Teachers* (New York: Routledge, 2010), 12.

26 Caroline Eick, *Race-Class Relations and Integration in Secondary Education: The Case of Miller High* (New York: Palgrave Macmillan, 2010), 2.

27 Faustine Jones, *A Traditional Model of Educational Excellence: Dunbar High School of Little Rock, Arkansas* (Washington, DC: Howard University Press, 1981); Cecelski, *Along Freedom Road*; Vanessa Siddle Walker, *Their Highest Potential: An African American School Community in the Segregated South* (Chapel Hill: University of North Carolina Press, 1996); Vivian Gunn and Curtis L. Morris,

Creating Caring and Nurturing Educational Environments for African American Children (Westport, CT: Bergin and Garvey, 2000); Vivian Gunn Morris and Curtis L. Morris, *The Price They Paid: Desegregation in an African American Community* (New York: Teachers College Press, 2002); Sonya Ramsey, *Reading, Writing, and Segregation: A Century of Black Women Teachers in Nashville* (Urbana: University of Illinois Press, 2008); Kelly, *Race, Remembering*, 12; Vanessa Siddle Walker, *Hello Professor: A Black Principal and Professional Leadership in the Segregated South* (Chapel Hill: University of North Carolina Press, 2009); Alison Stewart, *First Class: The Legacy of Dunbar, America's First Black Public High School* (Chicago: Lawrence Hill Books, 2013); Sharon Gay Pierson, *Laboratory of Learning: HBCU Laboratory Schools and Alabama State College Lab High in the Era of Jim Crow* (New York: Peter Lang, 2014); John L. Rury and Shirley A. Hill, *The African American Struggle for Secondary Schooling, 1940–1980* (New York: Teachers College Press, 2012).

28 Pierson, *Laboratory of Learning.*

29 Walker, *Hello Professor*; Walker, *Lost Education of Horace Tate.*

30 Michelle Purdy, *Transforming the Elite: Black Students and the Desegregation of Private Schools* (Chapel Hill: University of North Carolina Press, 2018); Elizabeth Todd-Breland, *A Political Education: Black Politics and Educational Reform in Chicago since the 1960s* (Chapel Hill: University of North Carolina Press, 2018); Worth Kamili Hayes, *Schools of Our Own: Chicago's Golden Age of Black Private Education* (Evanston, IL: Northwestern University Press, 2020).

31 Donato, *Other Struggle of Equal Schools*; Rubén Donato, *Mexican and Hispanos in Colorado Schools and Communities, 1920–1960* (Albany: State University of New York Press, 2007).

32 García, *Strategies of Segregation*, 9–10.

33 Mirelsie Velázquez, *Puerto Rican Chicago: Schooling the City, 1940–1977* (Champaign: University of Illinois Press, forthcoming).

34 Kluger, *Simple Justice*; Cecelski, *Along Freedom Road*; R. Scott Baker, *Paradoxes of Desegregation*; Dougherty, *More Than One Struggle*; George Noblit, ed., *School Desegregation: Oral Histories towards Understanding the Effects of White Domination* (Rotterdam: Sense, 2015); Pamela Grundy, *Color and Character: West Charlotte High and the American Struggle over Educational Equality* (Chapel Hill: University of North Carolina Press, 2017); Barbara J. Shircliffe, *Desegregating Teachers: Contesting the Meaning of Equality of Education Opportunity in the South post* Brown (New York: Peter Lang, 2012).

35 K'Meyer, *From* Brown *to* Meredith; Garland, *Divided We Fail.*

36 Eick, *Race-Class Relations*; Amy Stuart Wells et al., *Both Sides Now: The Story of School Desegregation's Graduates* (Berkeley: University of California Press, 2009), 5–7, 44.

37 Amy Stuart Wells et al., "How Desegregation Changed Us: The Effects of Racially Mixed School on Students and Society," Teachers College, Columbia University, accessed January 2008, 5, https://www.tc.columbia.edu/articles/2004/march/how-desegregation-changed-us-the-effects-of-racially-mixed-/.

38 Dionne Danns, "'Why Are You Going All the Way Up There to That White School?' Oral History, Desegregation, and Chicago Experiences," in *Using Past as Prologue: Contemporary Perspectives on African American Educational History*, ed. Dionne Danns, Michelle A. Purdy, and Christopher M. Span (Charlotte, NC: Information Age, 2015).

Chapter 1 Segregation, Politics, and School Desegregation Policy

1 "Theodore Parker and the 'Moral Universe,'" NPR, September 2, 2010, https://www.npr.org/templates/story/story.php?storyId=129609461.
2 Richard Rothstein, *The Color of Law: A Forgotten History of How Our Government Segregated America* (New York: Liveright, 2017), 39.
3 Mary Pattilo, *Black Picket Fences* (Chicago: University of Chicago Press, 1999).
4 Douglas S. Massey, *Categorically Unequal: The American Stratification System* (New York: Russell Sage Foundation, 2007), 59; Douglas S. Massey and Nancy A. Denton, *American Apartheid: Segregation and the Making of the Underclass* (Cambridge, MA: Harvard University Press, 1993).
5 Rothstein, *Color of Law.*
6 Beryl Satter, *Family Properties: Race Real Estate, and the Exploitation of Black Urban America* (New York: Metropolitan Books, 2009), 5.
7 Kevin Kruse, *White Flight: The Making of Modern Conservatism* (Princeton, NJ: Princeton University Press, 2005), 60.
8 Leon F. Litwack, *North of Slavery: The Negro in the Free States, 1790–1860* (Chicago: University of Chicago Press, 1961); Hilary J. Moss, *Schooling Citizens: The Struggle for African American Education in Antebellum America* (Chicago: University of Chicago Press, 2009).
9 Isabel Wilkerson, *The Warmth of Other Suns: The Epic Story of America's Great Migration* (New York: Random House, 2010); Nicholas Lemann, *The Promised Land: The Great Migration and How It Changed America* (New York: Vintage Books, 1991); James R. Grossman, *Land of Hope: Chicago, Black Southerners and the Great Migration* (Chicago: University of Chicago Press, 1989); Pattilo, *Black Picket Fences.*
10 US Census, 1960–1990.
11 Gabriela F. Arredondo, *Mexican Chicago: Race, Identity, and Nation, 1916–39* (Urbana: University of Illinois Press, 2008); Lilia Fernandez, *Brown in the Windy City: Mexicans and Puerto Ricans in Postwar Chicago* (Chicago: University of Chicago Press, 2012); Felix M. Padilla, *Puerto Rican Chicago* (Notre Dame, IN: University of Notre Dame Press, 1987).
12 Fernandez, *Brown in the Windy City*; US Census, 1960–1990; Chicago Public Schools, "Racial/Ethnic Survey: Students, as of October 31, 1968"; Chicago Public Schools, "Racial/Ethnic Survey: Students, as of October 31, 1990," both in Box Dept. of Research, Evaluation and Planning, Racial Ethnic Survey: Students, 1969–1995, Chicago Board of Education Archives.
13 The Supreme Court outlawed restrictive covenants in 1948, and Congress passed the Fair Housing Act prohibiting blockbusting and racial steering in 1968.
14 While Marquette Park is discussed, these were citywide tactics. Gregory Gordon and Albert Swanson, "Chicago: Evolution of a Ghetto," United Press International, 1977, 13, 19–20, 22, Chicago Urban League Papers, Series III, Box 169-1831, Special Collections, University of Illinois at Chicago.
15 Amanda I. Seligman, *Block by Block: Neighborhoods and Public Policy on Chicago's West Side* (Chicago: University of Chicago Press, 2005).
16 Roberto Suro, "Busing Worth the Fuss? Exaggerated Rhetoric Blamed for Fears of Violence," *Chicago Sun-Times*, September 4, 1977, 48.
17 James R. Ralph Jr., *Northern Protest: Martin Luther King, Jr., Chicago, and the Civil Rights Movement* (Cambridge, MA: Harvard University Press, 1993),

120–123; Orlando Bagwell and W. Noland Walker, dirs., *Citizen King* (ROJA Productions film for American Experience with BBC, 2004).

18 Gordon and Swanson, "Chicago," 5.

19 Chicago Urban League, "Marquette Park: A Descriptive History of Efforts to Peacefully Resolve Racial Conflict," 1977, 15–19, Chicago Urban League Papers, Series III, Box 169-1832, Special Collections, University of Illinois at Chicago.

20 Suro, "Busing Worth the Fuss?," 48.

21 Suro, 15, 20; Gordon and Swanson, "Chicago."

22 Maria Kefalas, *Working-Class Heroes: Protecting Home, Community, and Nation in a Chicago Neighborhood* (Berkeley: University of Chicago Press, 2003), 8.

23 Kefalas.

24 Kefalas, 43.

25 Fernandez, *Brown in the Windy City*, 10.

26 Padilla, *Puerto Rican Chicago*, 117.

27 Fernandez, *Brown in the Windy City*, 11.

28 William Julius Wilson, *When Work Disappears: The World of the New Urban Poor* (New York: Vintage Books, 1996), 29–30.

29 Michelle Alexander, *The New Jim Crow: Mass Incarceration in the Age of Colorblindness* (New York: New Press, 2010).

30 Wilson, *When Work Disappears*, 59, 111–146.

31 Massey, *Categorically Unequal*, 19.

32 Robert J. Sampson, *Great American City: Chicago and the Enduring Neighborhood Effect* (Chicago: University of Chicago Press, 2012).

33 Clive Webb, *Massive Resistance: Southern Opposition to the Second Reconstruction* (New York: Oxford University Press, 2005).

34 Ronald P. Formisano, *Boston against Busing: Race, Class, and Ethnicity in the 1960s and 1970s* (Chapel Hill: University of North Carolina Press, 2004); Dionne Danns, *Desegregating Chicago's Public Schools: Policy Implementation, Politics, and Protest, 1965–1985* (New York: Palgrave Macmillan, 2014).

35 Danns, *Desegregating Chicago's Public Schools*; Lawrence J. McAndrews, *The Era of Education: The Presidents and the Schools, 1965–2001* (Urbana: University of Illinois Press, 2004).

36 Raymond Wolters, *Right Turn: William Bradford Remolds, the Reagan Administration, and Black Civil Rights* (New Brunswick, NJ: Transaction, 1996); Robert R. Detlefsen, *Civil Rights under Reagan* (San Francisco: Institute for Contemporary Studies Press, 1991).

37 Paul Kleppner, *Chicago Divided: The Making of a Black Mayor* (DeKalb: Northern Illinois University Press, 1985); Teresa Cordova, "Harold Washington and the Rise of Latino Electoral Politics in Chicago, 1982–1987," in *Chicano Politics and Society in the Late Twentieth Century*, ed. David Montejana (Austin: University of Texas Press, 1999).

38 Kleppner, *Chicago Divided*, 136–139.

39 Kleppner, 177–184, 241–143.

40 Kleppner, 208–209, 216–218.

41 Cordova, "Harold Washington."

42 Ibram X. Kendi, *Stamped from the Beginning: The Definitive History of Racist Ideas in America* (New York: Nation Books, 2016).

43 Goodwin Liu and William L. Taylor, "School Choice to Achieve Desegregation," *Fordham Law Review* 74 (2005): 791–823.

44 See James T. Patterson, Brown v. Board of Education: *A Civil Rights Milestone and Its Troubled Legacy* (Oxford: Oxford University Press, 2001); Jill Ogline Titus, *Brown's Battleground: Students, Segregationists, and the Struggle for Justice in Prince Edward County, Virginia* (Chapel Hill: University of North Carolina Press, 2011); Rachel Devlin, *A Girl Stands at the Door: The Generation of Young Women Who Desegregated America's Schools* (New York: Basic Books, 2018); and Guadalupe San Miguel Jr., *Brown, Not White: School Integration and the Chicano Movement in Houston* (College Station: Texas A&M University Press, 2001).

45 Michael Fultz, "The Displacement of Black Educators Post-*Brown*: An Overview and Analysis," *History of Education Quarterly* 44 (Spring 2004): 11–45; David J. Connor and Beth A. Ferri, "Integration and Inclusion: A Troubling Nexus: Race, Disability, and Special Education," *Journal of African American History* 90 (Winter 2005): 107–127; Kathy-Anne Jordan, "Discourses of Difference and the Overrepresentation of Black Students in Special Education," *Journal of African American History* 90 (Winter 2005): 128–149; Benjamin Kearl, "'Through a Thoroughly Individualized Process': A Genealogical Policy Study of Special Education" (PhD diss., Indiana University Bloomington, 2018).

46 R. Scott Baker, *Paradoxes of Desegregation: African American Struggles for Educational Equity in Charleston, South Carolina, 1926–1972* (Columbia: University of South Carolina Press, 2006).

47 Rubén Donato and Jarrod S. Hanson, "Legally White, Socially 'Mexican': The Politics of De Jure and De Facto School Segregation in the American Southwest," *Harvard Educational Review* 82 (Summer 2012): 202–227; Richard R. Valencia, *Chicano Students and the Courts: The Mexican American Legal Struggle for Educational Equality* (New York: New York University Press, 2008).

48 Dionne Danns, *Something Better for Our Children: Black Organizing in Chicago Public Schools, 1963–1971* (New York: Routledge, 2003); Elizabeth Todd-Breland, *A Political Education: Black Politics and Education Reform in Chicago since the 1960s* (Chapel Hill: University of North Carolina Press, 2018); David A. Badillo, "Litigating Bilingual Education: A History of the Gomez Decision in Illinois," in *Latinos in the Midwest*, ed. Rubén O. Martinez (East Lansing: Michigan State University Press, 2011); Mirelsie Velázquez, *Puerto Rican Chicago: Schooling the City, 1940–1977* (Champaign: University of Illinois Press, forthcoming).

49 Danns, *Desegregating Chicago's Public Schools.*

50 Alan B. Anderson and George W. Pickering, *Confronting the Color Line: The Broken Promise of the Civil Rights Movement in Chicago* (Athens: University of Georgia Press, 1986); Ralph, *Northern Protest*; John L. Rury, "Race, Space, and the Politics of Chicago's Public Schools: Benjamin Willis and the Tragedy of Urban Education," *History of Education Quarterly* 39 (Summer 1999): 117–142; Danns, *Something Better for Our Children.*

51 Gary Orfield, *The Reconstruction of Southern Education: The Schools and the 1964 Civil Rights Act* (New York: Wiley-Interscience, 1969), 151–207; Coordinating Council of Community Organizations, "The Chicago Title VI Complaint to H.E.W.," *Integrated Education* 3 (December 1965–January 1966): 10.

52 James Redmond et al., *Increasing Desegregation of Faculties, Students and Vocational Education Programs* (Chicago: Board of Education, August 1967).

53 Danns, *Desegregating Chicago's Public Schools*; Tracey L. Steffes, "Managing School Integration and White Flight: The Debate over Chicago's Future in the 1960s," *Journal of Urban History* 42 (2016): 709–732.

54 See Michael W. Homel, *Down from Equality: Black Chicagoans and the Public Schools, 1920–1941* (Urbana: University of Illinois Press, 1984), 133–178; Danns, *Something Better for Our Children*; Danns, *Desegregating Chicago's Public Schools*; Fernandez, *Brown in the Windy City*; and Velázquez, *Puerto Rican Chicago*.
55 Todd-Breland, *Political Education*, 60–78; Jerald E. Podair, *The Strike That Changed New York: Blacks, Whites, and the Ocean Hill-Brownsville Crisis* (New Haven, CT: Yale University Press, 2002).
56 Joseph P. Hannon, "Access to Excellence: Recommendations for Equalizing Educational Opportunities," April 12, 1978, ix, Box Desegregation 1976–1980, Chicago Board of Education Archives; Danns, *Desegregating Chicago's Public Schools*.
57 Chicago Urban League, *Access to Excellence: An Analysis and Commentary on the 1978–79 Program Proposals* (Chicago: Urban League, 1979), retrieved from ERIC database (ERIC ED 187 780), 1.
58 *United States of America v. Board of Education of the City of Chicago*, 80 C 5124 (Ill, April 1980).
59 Chicago Board of Education, *Comprehensive Student Assignment Plan,* vol. 1 (Chicago: Board of Education, 1982), 134.
60 Claire Smrekar and Ellen Goldring, *School Choice in Urban America: Magnet Schools and the Pursuit of Equity* (New York: Teachers College Press, 1999).
61 Steffes, "Managing School Integration."
62 Steffes; Nicholas Kryczka, "Building a Constituency for Racial Integration: Chicago's Magnet Schools and the Prehistory of School Choice," *History of Education Quarterly* 59 (February 2019): 1–34; Fithawee Tzeggai, "Defining Racial Equity in Chicago's Segregated Schools: The Complicated Legacy of Desegregation Reform for Urban Education Policy" (Institute for the Study of Societal Issues Working Papers, University of California, Berkeley, 2016), https://escholarship.org/uc/item/8204p4f8; Robert Havighurst, *The Public Schools of Chicago* (Chicago: Board of Education, 1964); Phillip Hauser et al., *Integration of the Public School—Chicago: A Report to the Board of Education, City of Chicago* (Chicago: Advisory Panel on Integration of the Public Schools, 1964).
63 Chicago Board of Education, *Comprehensive Student Assignment Plan*; Kryczka, "Building a Constituency"; Ruth Love, "September '82: The School of Your Choice," *Chicago Sun-Times*, April 23, 1982, special supplement.
64 Chicago Board of Education, *Comprehensive Student Assignment Plan*, 194–198.
65 Apart from Von Steuben, which was more selective, the metropolitan high schools were predominantly minority schools. There were twenty-three specialty programs that had an in-depth study of a subject. Educational teaming brought two or more schools together for desegregation and to share academic offerings. Community academies provided academic programs like magnet schools but were at predominantly Black schools. Chicago Board of Education, *Comprehensive Student Assignment Plan*, 138, 165, 169, 247–249.
66 G. Alfred Hess Jr. et al., *Who Benefits from Desegregation? A Review of the Chicago Desegregation Program, 1980 to 1986* (Chicago: Panel on Public School Policy and Finance, December 1987), iii.

Chapter 2 Busing, Boycotts, and Elementary School Experiences

1 This chapter is derived in part from Dionne Danns, "'Other Minority': Multiethnic School Desegregation Experiences in Two Chicago Communities," *Race*

Ethnicity and Education, published online, April 30, 2019, https://doi.org/10.1080/13613324.2019.1604504. Chicago Urban League, "Marquette Park: A Descriptive History of Efforts to Peacefully Resolve Racial Conflict," 1977, 45–46, Chicago Urban League Papers, Series III, Box 169-1832, Special Collections, University of Illinois at Chicago.

2 Dionne Danns, *Desegregating Chicago's Public Schools: Policy Implementation, Politics, and Protest, 1965–1985* (New York: Palgrave Macmillan, 2014); Matthew F. Delmont, *Why Busing Failed: Race, Media, the National Resistance to School Desegregation* (Oakland: University of California Press, 2016); Dionne Danns, *Something Better for Our Children: Black Organizing in Chicago Public Schools, 1963–1971* (New York: Routledge, 2003).

3 Chicago Urban League, "Marquette Park," 45–46.

4 Gregory S. Jacobs, *Getting around* Brown*: Desegregation, Development and the Columbus Public Schools* (Columbus: Ohio State University Press, 1998), 30; Delmont, *Why Busing Failed*, 3.

5 Educational teaming brought two or more schools together for desegregation and to share academic offerings. Chicago Board of Education, *Comprehensive Student Assignment Plan: School by School Analysis*, vol. 2 (Chicago: Board of Education, 1982).

6 Linda Wertsch and Don Wycliff, "8 Schools on S.W. Side Affected by White Boycott," *Chicago Sun-Times*, January 14, 1982, 20; Casey Banas, "Boycott by White Pupils Hits Desegregation Plan," *Chicago Tribune*, January 14, 1982, A16.

7 See Gilbert G. Gonzalez, *Chicano Education in the Era of Segregation* (Cranbury, NJ: Associated University Presses, 1990); Rubén Donato, *The Other Struggle for Equal Schools* (Albany: State University of New York Press, 1997).

8 Roberto Suro, "City, U.S. Settle Schools Dispute," *Chicago Sun-Times*, October 13, 1977, 4; Casey Banas and James Coates, "U.S. Approves Teacher Integration Plan," *Chicago Tribune*, October 13, 1977, 1; Roberto Suro, "HEW Ends Teacher-Shift Demand," *Chicago Sun-Times*, October 9, 1977, 3.

9 Guadalupe San Miguel Jr., *Contested Policy: The Rise and Fall of Federal Bilingual Education in the United States 1960–2001* (Denton: University of North Texas, 2004), 1.

10 The Emergency School Aid Act provided funding for school desegregation. Danns, *Desegregating Chicago's Public Schools*, 81, 183. For more information on bilingual education in Illinois, see David A. Badillo, "Litigating Bilingual Education: A History of the Gomez Decision in Illinois," in *Latinos in the Midwest*, ed. Rubén O. Martinez (East Lansing: Michigan State University Press, 2011).

11 Wertsch and Wycliff, "8 Schools," 20; Banas, "Boycott by White Pupils," A16.

12 Kevin Kruse, *White Flight: The Making of Modern Conservatism* (Princeton, NJ: Princeton University Press, 2005).

13 Quoted in Jeff Lyon, "Fearful Women Fight to 'Save' Bogan Schools," *Chicago Tribune*, August 10, 1977, 1.

14 Robert Suro, "Busing Worth the Fuss? Exaggerated Rhetoric Blamed for Fears of Violence," *Chicago Sun-Times*, September 4, 1977, 4, 48.

15 Kruse, *White Flight*; Jacobs, *Getting around* Brown, 30.

16 Office of Civil Rights, *Proceedings under Title VI of the Civil Rights Act of 1964: Initial Decision in the Matter of Chicago Public School District #299 and Illinois Office of Education and City of Chicago, Illinois* (Washington, D.C.: Office of Civil

Rights, Department of Health, Education and Welfare, February 15, 1977), retrieved from ERIC database (ERIC ED 135 931).

17 Danns, *Something Better for Our Children.*

18 Gary Orfield, Susan E. Eaton, and the Harvard Project on School Desegregation, *Dismantling Desegregation: The Quiet Reversal of* Brown v. Board of Education (New York: New Press, 1996).

19 Chicago Fact Book Consortium, *Local Community Fact Book: Chicago Metropolitan Areas, 1980* (Chicago: Chicago Review Press, 1984), 179, 168.

20 Chicago Fact Book Consortium, *Local Community Fact Book*, 137.

21 Chicago Board of Education, *Comprehensive Student Assignment Plan*, vol. 1 (Chicago: Board of Education, 1982), 252, 260.

22 Ibid., 165.

23 Chicago Fact Book Consortium, *Local Community Fact Book*, 149–150.

24 Chicago Board of Education, *Comprehensive Student Assignment Plan*, 267–268; Chicago Board of Education, *Comprehensive Student Assignment Plan: School by School Analysis*.

25 Chicago Board of Education, *Comprehensive Student Assignment Plan*, 166.

26 Maria Saucedo was an additional predominantly Latino magnet school added after 1978.

27 These totals were arrived at from the data in the G. Alfred Hess Jr. et al., *Who Benefits from Desegregation? A Review of the Chicago Desegregation Program, 1980 to 1986* (Chicago: Panel on Public School Policy and Finance, December 1987), ii–viii.

Chapter 3 "The World Is Bigger Than Just My Local Community"

1 Michelle Obama, *Becoming* (New York: Crown, 2018), 54, 57, 59.

2 James F. Redmond, "Whitney M. Young Magnet High School," n.d., no box, Folder—Whitney Young High School, Chicago Board of Education Archives.

3 "30 Years of Academic Excellence at Whitney M. Young Magnet High School, 1975–2005," 2005, no box, Folder 48—Whitney Young Magnet High School, Chicago Board of Education Archives.

4 Andy Shaw, "Young School Admission Battle Tuesday," *Chicago Sun-Times*, April 7, 1975; Connie Moore and Daniel U. Levine, "Whitney Young Magnet High School of Chicago and Urban Renewal," *Planning and Changing* 7 (Winter 1977): 148–154.

5 "Whitney Young Magnet High School," n.d., no box, Folder 48—Whitney Young Magnet High School, Chicago Board of Education Archives.

6 "History," Von Steuben Metropolitan Science Center, accessed April 24, 2012, http://www.vonsteuben.org/history.jsp (page no longer available).

7 Von Steuben Metropolitan Science Center, "A Handbook of Information for the North Central Visitation Committee," 1990, 9–10, in the author's possession; Carl F. Kaestle and Marshall S. Smith, "The Federal Role in Elementary and Secondary Education, 1940–1980," *Harvard Educational Review* 52, no. 4 (1982): 384–418.

8 Von Steuben Metropolitan Science Center, "Handbook of Information," 10–11.

9 "William J. Bogan Technical High School: Profile 2003–04," n.d., Box—Bogan High School, Folder 1, Chicago Board of Education Archives; Dionne Danns, *Desegregating Chicago's Public Schools: Policy Implementation, Politics, and Protest, 1965–1985* (New York: Palgrave Macmillan, 2014); Bill Grady, "Bogan Area Pupils Boycott over Busing," *Chicago Tribune*, June 8, 1977.

10 *Medallion Yearbook* (Chicago: Bogan High School, 1986), Chicago Board of Education Archives.

11 The dropout rates refer to the percentage of students who entered a school freshman year but did not graduate from the same school within four years. Chicago Public Schools, "Chicago Public High School Dropout Profile: A Report on the Class of 1988," 1990, Box Dept. of Research, Evaluation and Planning, School Dropouts, Chicago Board of Education Archives; Chicago Public Schools, "Dropouts: A Descriptive Review of the Class of 1986 and Trend Analysis of 1982–1986 Classes," 1988, Box Dept. of Research, Evaluation and Planning, School Dropouts, Chicago Board of Education Archives; Robert Balfanz and Nettie Legters, *Locating the Dropout Crisis: Which High Schools Produce the Nation's Dropouts? Where Are They Located? Who Attends Them?* (Baltimore: Center for Research on the Education of Students Placed at Risk, 2004), http://files.eric.ed.gov/fulltext/ED484525.pdf.

12 See Michael W. Homel, *Down from Equality: Black Chicagoans and the Public Schools, 1920–1941* (Urbana: University of Illinois Press, 1984); and Dionne Danns, *Something Better for Our Children: Black Organizing in Chicago Public Schools, 1963–1971* (New York: Routledge, 2003).

13 In some instances, Black schools were reshaped to make them more attractive to White students by removing memorabilia that identified the schools as Black. Derrick Bell, *Silent Covenants:* Brown v. Board of Education *and the Unfulfilled Hopes for Racial Reform* (New York: Oxford University Press, 2004); Amy Stuart Wells et al., *Both Sides Now: The Story of School Desegregation's Graduates* (Berkeley: University of California Press, 2009); David S. Cecelski, *Along Freedom Road: Hyde County, North Carolina, and the Fate of Black Schools in the South* (Chapel Hill: University of North Carolina Press, 1994); Sarah Garland, *Divided We Fail: The Story of an African American Community That Ended the Era of School Desegregation* (Boston: Beacon, 2013).

14 Joyce A. Hughes, "Statement of Joyce A. Hughes on Final Desegregation Plan," December 31, 1981, 3, Chicago Board of Education Archives; Joyce A. Hughes, "Statement of Joyce A. Hughes: Revised Final Desegregation Plan," January 23, 1982, Chicago Board of Education Archives.

15 Chicago Urban League, *Access to Excellence: An Analysis and Commentary on the 1978–79 Program Proposals* (Chicago: Urban League, 1979), retrieved from ERIC database (ERIC ED 187 780), 6–9.

16 Mary Pattillo, in her study of contemporary school choice, also in Chicago, argues that school choice is more about schools choosing students than the other way around. Mary Pattillo, "Everyday Politics of School Choice in the Black Community," *Du Bois Review* 12, no. 1 (2015): 41–71.

17 The test results were divided into five categories (stanine 1, stanine 2 and 3, stanine 4, stanine 5, stanine 6+). Stanines 1–3 were below average, 4–6 were average, and 7–9 were above average. Stanine 6 represented the 60th–76th percentiles. Chicago Public Schools, "Chicago Public High School Dropout Profile"; Kary S. Kublin, "Understanding Your Child's ITBS Test Scores," accessed March 7, 2016, http://www.slideshare.net/jasonflom/decoding-your-childs-itbs-scores (page no longer available).

18 CPS determined the dropout rates based on cohorts. For the cohort entering high school in 1984 and graduating in 1988, there were a total of 28,439 students. Of those students, 2,442 transferred out of CPS and another 2,106 were still attending but had not completed their studies in 1988. This left a remaining 23,891

students, of whom 9,584 dropped out, leaving the cohort with a 40.1 percent dropout rate (Blacks, 41.2 percent; Whites, 36.7 percent; Hispanics, 43.5 percent; and Asians, 15.3 percent).

19 Chicago Public Schools, "Chicago Public High School Dropout Profile."

20 Chicago Fact Book Consortium, *Local Community Fact Book: Chicago Metropolitan Areas, 1980* (Chicago: Chicago Review Press, 1984).

21 Danns, *Something Better for Our Children*, 99–106; Dionne Danns, "Chicago Teacher Reform Efforts and the Politics of Educational Change," in *Black Protest Thought and Education*, ed. William Watkins (New York: Peter Lang, 2005).

22 Amanda I. Seligman, *Block by Block: Neighborhoods and Public Policy on Chicago's West Side* (Chicago: University of Chicago Press, 2005); Danns, *Desegregating Chicago's Public Schools*.

23 Marshall was another school that student activists protested in the 1960s, largely because of its overcrowding. Danns, *Something Better for Our Children*.

24 Gage Park was her neighborhood high school, and she thought Bogan "was a much better school." Gage Park was an experimental desegregated school for years, and it had quotas to maintain racial balance. The school remained stably desegregated in 1985.

25 Robert J. Sampson, *Great American City: Chicago and the Enduring Neighborhood Effect* (Chicago: University of Chicago Press, 2012); Kate L. Phillippo and Briellen Griffin, "The Social Geography of Choice: Neighborhoods' Role in Students' Navigation of School Choice Policy in Chicago," *Urban Review* 48 (October 2016): 668–695.

26 Danns, *Something Better for Our Children*.

27 Chicago Board of Education, *Comprehensive Student Assignment Plan*, vol. 1 (Chicago: Board of Education, 1982).

28 See Lois André-Bechely, *Could It Be Otherwise? Parents and the Inequalities of Public School Choice* (New York: Routledge, 2005), 89–128.

29 Danns, *Desegregating Chicago's Public Schools*.

30 Richard Alba, "Bright vs. Blurred Boundaries: Second-Generation Assimilation and Exclusion in France, Germany, and the United States," *Ethnic and Racial Studies* 28 (January 2010): 24.

31 Signithia Fordham and John Ogbu, "Black Students' School Success: Coping with the Burden of 'Acting White,'" *Urban Review* 18 (Fall 1986): 176–206.

32 Roslyn Arlin Mickelson and Anne E. Velasco, "Bring It On! Diverse Responses to 'Acting White' among Academically Able Black Students," in *Beyond Acting White: Reframing the Debate on Black Student Achievement*, ed. Erin McNamara Horvat and Carla O'Connor (Lanham, MD: Rowman and Littlefield, 2006).

33 Prudence L. Carter, "Intersecting Identities: 'Acting White,' Gender, and Academic Achievement," in Horvat and O'Connor, *Beyond Acting White*; Prudence L. Carter, *Keepin' It Real: School Success beyond Black and White* (New York: Oxford University Press, 2005).

34 Obama, *Becoming*, 40.

35 Gary Orfield, "Voluntary Desegregation in Chicago: A Report to Joseph Cronin, State Superintendent of Education," February 26, 1979, retrieved from ERIC database (ERIC ED 171 832).

36 James Sanders, *Education of an Urban Minority: Catholics in Chicago, 1833–1965* (New York: Oxford University Press, 1977); Worth Kamili Hayes, "The Rise and Fall of a Black Private School: Holy Name of Mary and the Golden Age of Black

Private Education in Chicago, 1940–1990," in *Using Past as Prologue: Contemporary Perspectives on African American Educational History*, ed. Dionne Danns, Michelle A. Purdy, and Christopher M. Span (Charlotte, NC: Information Age, 2015), 203.

37 Hayes, "Rise and Fall," 213.

38 Chicago Board of Education, *Comprehensive Student Assignment Plan*, 29–31. The public school and city demographics come from Chicago Public Schools, "Racial/Ethnic Survey—Students as of October 31, 1970"; Chicago Public Schools, "Racial/Ethnic Survey—Students as of October 31, 1980," Box Dept. of Research, Evaluation and Planning, Racial Ethnic Survey: Students, 1969–1995, Chicago Board of Education Archives.

39 Carter, "Intersecting Identities," 117.

40 G. Alfred Hess Jr. et al., *Who Benefits from Desegregation? A Review of the Chicago Desegregation Program, 1980 to 1986* (Chicago: Panel on Public School Policy and Finance, December 1987).

Chapter 4 "I Don't Know If It Was a Racial Thing or Not"

1 Derald Wing Sue, "Microaggressions: More Than Just Race," Psychology Today, November 17, 2010, https://www.psychologytoday.com/us/blog/microaggressions-in-everyday-life/201011/microaggressions-more-just-race.

2 Robert L. Green, "Student Desegregation Plan for the Chicago Public Schools: Recommendations on Educational Components," approved April 19, 1981, Chicago Board of Education Archives; Chicago Public Schools Monitoring Commission for Desegregation Implementation, *Monitoring Commission Report on the Status of Implementation of Desegregation Staff Development Components of the Student Desegregation for Chicago Public Schools* (Chicago: Monitoring Commission for Desegregation Implementation, April 1985), retrieved from ERIC database (ERIC ED 336 463), 1–3.

3 Chicago Public Schools Monitoring Commission for Desegregation Implementation, *Monitoring Commission Report*, 1–3, 53, 66–71; Chicago Board of Education, *Man's Inhumanity to Man: Teacher Resource Unit* (Chicago: Board of Education, 1980).

4 Dionne Danns, *Desegregating Chicago's Public Schools: Policy Implementation, Politics, and Protest, 1965–1985* (New York: Palgrave Macmillan, 2014).

5 Data from Chicago Public Schools, "Racial/Ethnic Survey: Staff as of October 31, 1980"; Chicago Public Schools, "Racial/Ethnic Survey: Staff as of October 31, 1983"; Chicago Public Schools, "Racial/Ethnic Survey: Staff as of October 31, 1984"; and Chicago Public Schools, "Racial/Ethnic Survey: Staff as of October 31, 1985," all in Box 1, Office of Accountability, Department of Research, Evaluation, and Planning: Racial/Ethnic Survey of Staff, 1969–1990, Chicago Board of Education Archives.

6 Paul Wong, Chienping Faith Lai, and Richard Nagasawa Tieming Lin, "Asian Americans as a Model Minority: Self-Perceptions and Perceptions by Other Racial Groups," *Sociological Perspectives* 41 (March 1998): 95–118.

7 Jeanie Oakes, *Keeping Track: How Schools Structure Inequality* (New Haven, CT: Yale University Press, 1985).

8 James E. Rosenbaum, *Making Inequality: The Hidden Curriculum of High School Tracking* (New York: John Wiley and Sons, 1976), 111–118.

9 Ibid., 111.

10 Charles T. Clotfelter, *After* Brown*: The Rise and Retreat of School Desegregation* (Princeton, NJ: Princeton University Press, 2004), 137.

11 Oakes, *Keeping Track*, 3.
12 Rosenbaum, *Making Inequality*, 109; Clotfelter, *After* Brown, 137; Oakes, *Keeping Track*.
13 Amy Stuart Wells et al., *Both Sides Now: The Story of School Desegregation's Graduates* (Berkeley: University of California Press, 2009), 96.
14 Ibid., 28.
15 Mwalimu J. Shujaa, *Too Much Schooling, Too Little Education: A Paradox of Black Life in White Societies* (Trenton, NJ: Africa World, 1994), 11.
16 Martha Biondi, *The Black Revolution on Campus* (Berkeley: University of California Press, 2012); Ibram H. Rogers, *The Black Campus Movement: Black Students and the Racial Reconstitution of Higher Education, 1965–1972* (New York: Palgrave Macmillan, 2012); Gael Graham, *Young Activists: American High School Students in the Age of Protest* (DeKalb: Northern Illinois University Press, 2006); Dionne Danns, *Something Better for Our Children: Black Organizing in Chicago Public Schools, 1963–1971* (New York: Routledge, 2003); Dionne Danns, "Chicago High School Students' Movement for Quality Public Education, 1966–1971," *Journal of African American Education* 88 (Spring 2003): 138–150; Dwayne C. Wright, "Black Pride Day, 1968: High School Student Activism in York Pennsylvania," *Journal of African American Education* 88 (Spring 2003): 151–162; Peniel E. Joseph, "Dashikis and Democracy: Black Studies, Student Activism, and the Black Power Movement," *Journal of African American Education* 88 (Spring 2003): 182–203; John L. Rury and Shirley Hill, "An End of Innocence: African-American High School Protest in the 1960s and 1970s," *History of Education* 42 (August 2013): 486–508.
17 Danns, *Something Better for Our Children*.
18 Noreen S. Ahmed-Ullah, "CPS Unveils Curriculum for African-American Studies," *Chicago Tribune*, December 12, 2013, http://articles.chicagotribune.com/2013-12-12/news/ct-curriculum-african-american-met-20131212_1_ceo-barbara-byrd-bennett-cps-curriculum.
19 David S. Cecelski, *Along Freedom Road: Hyde County, North Carolina, and the Fate of Black Schools in the South* (Chapel Hill: University of North Carolina Press, 1994); Vanessa Siddle Walker, *Their Highest Potential: An African American School Community in the Segregated South* (Chapel Hill: University of North Carolina Press, 1996); Wells et al., *Both Sides Now*.
20 William F. Tate, Gloria Ladson-Billings, and Carl A. Grant, "The *Brown* Decision Revisited: Mathematizing a Social Problem," in *Beyond Desegregation: The Politics of Quality in African American Schooling*, ed. Mwalimu J. Shujaa (Thousand Oaks, CA: Corwin, 1996), 42.
21 Carter G. Woodson, *The Mis-education of the Negro* (1933; Trenton, NJ: African World, 1993), xiii.
22 Shujaa, *Too Much Schooling*.
23 Von Steuben Metropolitan Science Center, "A Handbook of Information for the North Central Visitation Committee," 1990, 71–72, 94, in the author's possession.

Chapter 5 "We Were from All Over Town"

1 Jakobi Williams, *From the Bullet to the Ballot: The Illinois Chapter of the Black Panther Party and Racial Coalition Politics in Chicago* (Chapel Hill: University of North Carolina Press, 2013).

2 Beverly Daniel Tatum, *"Why Are All the Black Kids Sitting Together in the Cafeteria?" and Other Conversations about Race* (New York: Basic Books, 1997), 52–54.
3 An "Oreo," as in the cookie, is someone who is Black on the outside and White on the inside.
4 Karolyn Tyson, *Integration Interrupted: Tracking, Black Students, and Acting White after* Brown (New York: Oxford University Press, 2011), 51–52; Tatum, *"Why Are All?,"* 62–63.
5 Joane Nagel, "Constructing Ethnicity: Creating and Recreating Ethnic Identity and Culture," *Social Problems* 41 (February 1994): 152–176.
6 Roberta English, "'Oreo' Stereotyping Creates Black Identity Crisis," *New Expressions*, June 1988, 8–9.
7 Signithia Fordham and John Ogbu, "Black Students' School Success: Coping with the Burden of 'Acting White,'" *Urban Review* 18 (Fall 1986): 176–206.
8 Tyson, *Integration Interrupted*, 77.
9 English, "'Oreo' Stereotyping," 8–9.
10 Charles V. Willie, *Oreo: A Perspective on Race and Marginal Men and Women* (Wakefield, MA: Parameter, 1975), 11–12.
11 Caroline Eick, *Race-Class Relations and Integration in Secondary Education: The Case of Miller High* (New York: Palgrave Macmillan, 2010).
12 Charles T. Clotfelter, *After* Brown*: The Rise and Retreat of School Desegregation* (Princeton, NJ: Princeton University Press, 2004), 140–142.
13 *Visions Yearbook* (Chicago: Von Steuben High School, 1986), Chicago Board of Education Archives; *Medallion Yearbook* (Chicago: Bogan High School, 1986), Chicago Board of Education Archives.
14 *Medallion Yearbook*.
15 Amy Stuart Wells et al., *Both Sides Now: The Story of School Desegregation's Graduates* (Berkeley: University of California Press, 2009), 188.
16 Clotfelter, *After* Brown, 144.
17 Frank F. Furstenberg Jr., "How Families Manage Risk and Opportunity in Dangerous Neighborhoods," in *Sociology and the Public Agenda*, ed. William Julius Wilson (Newbury Park, CA: Sage, 1993), 238–239.
18 Robert J. Sampson, *Great American City: Chicago and the Enduring Neighborhood Effect* (Chicago, University of Chicago Press, 2012).
19 Mary Pattillo-McCoy, *Black Picket Fences: Privilege and Peril among the Black Middle Class* (Chicago: University of Chicago Press, 1999).
20 Lilia Fernandez, *Brown in the Windy City: Mexicans and Puerto Ricans in Postwar Chicago* (Chicago, University of Chicago Press, 2012).
21 Quoted in James T. Patterson, Brown v. Board of Education: *A Civil Rights Milestone and Its Troubled Legacy* (Oxford: Oxford University Press, 2001), 87.
22 Wells et al., *Both Sides Now*, 105–106.

Chapter 6 "We All Got Along"

1 Dempsey J. Travis, *"Harold," the People's Mayor: An Authorized Biography of Mayor Harold Washington* (Chicago: Urban Research, 1980), 287–288.
2 Paul Kleppner, *Chicago Divided: The Making of a Black Mayor* (DeKalb: Northern Illinois University Press, 1985).

3 Ed Vrdolyak was a rival of Harold Washington. Gary Rivlin, *Fire on the Prairie: Harold Washington, Chicago Politics, and the Roots of the Obama Presidency* (Philadelphia: Temple University Press, 2013), 253–254.
4 Charles T. Clotfelter, *After* Brown*: The Rise and Retreat of School Desegregation* (Princeton, NJ: Princeton University Press, 2004), 1, 39.
5 Amy Stuart Wells et al., *Both Sides Now: The Story of School Desegregation's Graduates* (Berkeley: University of California Press, 2009), 95.
6 Linda Wertsch and Don Wycliff, "8 Schools on S.W. Side Affected by White Boycott," *Chicago Sun-Times*, January 14, 1982, 20; Casey Banas, "Boycott by White Pupils Hits Desegregation Plan," *Chicago Tribune*, January 14, 1982, A16.
7 Chicago Public Schools, "Racial/Ethnic Survey: Students as of October 31, 1980"; Chicago Public Schools, "Racial/Ethnic Survey: Students as of October 31, 1981"; Chicago Public Schools, "Racial/Ethnic Survey: Students as of October 31, 1982"; Chicago Public Schools, "Racial/Ethnic Survey: Students as of October 31, 1983"; Chicago Public Schools, "Racial/Ethnic Survey: Students as of October 31, 1984; all in Box Dept. of Research, Evaluation and Planning, Racial Ethnic Survey: Students, 1969–1995, Chicago Board of Education Archives.
8 Sharon A. Stanley, *An Impossible Dream? Racial Integration in the United States* (New York: Oxford University Press, 2017), 3.
9 Karolyn Tyson, *Integration Interrupted: Tracking, Black Students, and Acting White after* Brown (New York: Oxford University Press, 2011); Prudence L. Carter, "Intersecting Identities: 'Acting White,' Gender, and Academic Achievement," in *Beyond Acting White: Reframing the Debate on Black Student Achievement*, ed. Erin McNamara Horvat and Carla O'Connor (Lanham, MD: Rowman and Littlefield, 2006).
10 Kerry Ann Rockquemore, David L. Brunsma, and Daniel J. Delgado, "Racing to Theory or Retheorizing Race? Understanding the Struggle to Build a Multiracial Identity Theory," *Journal of Social Issues* 65, no. 1 (2009): 13–34.
11 Chi-Ying Cheng and Fiona Lee, "Multiracial Identity Integration: Perceptions of Conflict and Distance among Multiracial Individuals," *Journal of Social Issues* 65, no. 1 (2009): 51–68.
12 Pancho Villa was a Mexican revolutionary in the early 1900s.
13 Cheng and Lee, "Multiracial Identity Integration," 64.
14 *Baldwin Hills* was a reality show about Black youths who grew up in affluent families in California.
15 Willard B. Gatewood, *Aristocrats of Color: The Black Elite, 1880–1920* (Bloomington: Indiana University Press, 1990).
16 Beverly is an affluent neighborhood on Chicago's South Side.
17 Little Village and Pilsen both had less than 25 percent homeownership compared with Ashburn, which had 90 percent homeownership in 1980. Chicago Fact Book Consortium, *Local Community Fact Book: Chicago Metropolitan Areas, 1980* (Chicago: Chicago Review Press, 1984), 83–88, 167–168, 178–179.

Chapter 7 After High School and Desegregation Benefits

1 James E. Rosenbaum, *Making Inequality: The Hidden Curriculum of High School Tracking* (New York: John Wiley and Sons, 1976), 116; Amy Stuart Wells et al., *Both Sides Now: The Story of School Desegregation's Graduates* (Berkeley: University of California Press, 2009), 101.

2 Sylvia Hurtado et al., "Differences in College Access and Choice among Racial/Ethnic Groups: Identifying Continuing Barriers," *Research in Higher Education* 38 (February 1997): 43–75.
3 Wells et al., *Both Sides Now*, 7.
4 W. E. Burghardt Du Bois, "Does the Negro Need Separate Schools?," *Journal of Negro Education* 4 (July 1935): 328–335.
5 Wells et al., *Both Sides Now*.
6 Sharon A. Stanley, *An Impossible Dream? Racial Integration in the United States* (New York: Oxford University Press, 2017), 3.

Conclusion

1 "More Than 20-Year-Old School Integration Case Now Closed," Chicago Public Schools, September 25, 2009, http://www.cps.edu/News/Press_releases/2009/Pages/09_25_2009_PR1.aspx (page no longer available).
2 "Socio-economic Data Will Be Used Instead of Race-Based Criteria," Chicago Public Schools, November 10, 2009, http://www.cps.edu/News/Press_releases/2009/Pages/11_10_2009_PR1.aspx (page no longer available).
3 Illinois School Report Card, accessed June 26, 2019, https://www.illinoisreportcard.com/School.aspx?source=studentcharacteristics&source2=studentdemographics&Schoolid=150162990250003.
4 Steve Bogira, "Chicago's Entire School Desegregation Strategy Needs a Turnaround," *Chicago Reader*, June 23, 2014, https://www.chicagoreader.com/Bleader/archives/2014/06/23/chicagos-entire-school-desegregation-strategy-needs-a-turnaround.
5 Catherine Gewertz, "The Battle over Who Gets into Elite Public High Schools," *Education Week*, May 7, 2019, https://www.edweek.org/ew/articles/2019/05/08/the-battle-over-who-gets-into-elite.html; Juan Perez Jr. "CPS Analysis Shows 150,000 Seats Unfilled; Black and Latino Students Have Less Access to Top Programs," *Chicago Tribune*, September 17, 2018, https://www.chicagotribune.com/news/breaking/ct-met-chicago-public-school-analysis-closing-20180914-story.html.
6 "CPS Stats and Facts," Chicago Public Schools, accessed June 26, 2019, https://cps.edu/About_CPS/At-a-glance/Pages/Stats_and_facts.aspx.
7 David Mendell, "The Real Problem with Chicago's Shrinking Population," *Chicago Magazine*, May 8, 2017, https://www.chicagomag.com/Chicago-Magazine/June-2017/Chicagos-Population-Problem/.
8 Elizabeth Todd-Breland, *A Political Education: Black Politics and Education Reform in Chicago since the 1960s* (Chapel Hill: University of North Carolina Press, 2018), 221–222; Eve L. Ewing, *Ghosts in the Schoolyard: Racism and School Closings on Chicago's South Side* (Chicago: University of Chicago Press, 2018).
9 Amy Stuart Wells, Miya Warner, and Courtney Grzesikowski, "The Story of Meaningful School Choice: Lessons from Interdistrict Transfer Plans," in *Educational Delusions? Why Choice Can Deepen Inequality and How to Make Schools Fair*, ed. Gary Orfield and Erica Frankenberg and associates (Berkeley: University of California Press, 2013), 188–189; Noliwe Rooks, *Cutting School: Privatization, Segregation and the End of Public Education* (New York: New Press, 2017), 2.
10 Diane Ravitch, *Reign of Error: The Hoax of the Privatization Movement and the Danger to America's Public Schools* (New York: Random House, 2013); Pauline

Lipman, *The New Political Economy of Urban Education* (New York: Routledge, 2011); Kristen L. Buras, *Charter Schools, Race, and Urban Space: Where the Market Meets Grassroots Resistance* (New York: Routledge, 2015).

11 David Stovall, "Charter Schools and the Event of Educational Sharecropping: An Alternative Take on the Chicago Phenomenon," in *Twenty-First-Century Jim Crow Schools: The Impact of Charters on Public Education*, by Raynard Sanders, David Stovall, and Terrenda White (Boston: Beacon, 2018), 42.

12 Carla Shedd, *Unequal City: Race, Schools, and Perceptions of Injustice* (New York: Russell Sage Foundation, 2015); Kate Phillippo, *A Contest without Winner: How Students Experience Competitive School Choice* (Minneapolis: University of Minnesota Press, 2019); Mary Pattillo, "Everyday Politics of School Choice in the Black Community," *Du Bois Review* 12, no. 1 (2015): 41–71.

Index

About the Author

DIONNE DANNS is a professor at Indiana University Bloomington. She has authored two books, *Something Better for Our Children: Black Organizing in Chicago Public Schools, 1963–1971* and *Desegregating Chicago's Public Schools: Policy Implementation, Politics, and Protest, 1965–1985*, and coedited *Using Past as Prologue: Contemporary Perspectives on African American Educational History*.